Keystroke	Action
Ctrl+Shift+F6	Previous Open Doc
F7	Indent
Shift+F7	Indent
Shift+F7	Center Line
Ctrl+F7	Hanging Indent
Alt+F7	Flush Right
Alt+Shift+F7	Decimal Tab
F8	Select
Shift+F8	Select Cell
Ctrl+F8	Margins
Alt+F8	Styles
F9	Font
Shift+F10	Repeat
Ctrl+F10	Macro Record
Alt+F10	Macro Play
Alt+Shift+F10	Activate Feature Bar Help
F11	Insert Image
Shift+F11	Edit Box
Ctrl+F11	Horizontal Line
Ctrl+Shift+F11	Vertical Line
Alt+F11	Text Box Create
Ctrl+A	Abbreviations Expand
Ctrl+B	Attribute Bold
Ctrl+Shift+B	Insert Bullet
Ctrl+C	Copy
Ctrl+Shift+C	Drop Cap
Ctrl+D	Date Text
Ctrl+Shift+D	Date Code
Ctrl+E	Justify Center
Ctrl+F	Font
Ctrl+G	Go To
Ctrl+I	Attribute Italic
Ctrl+J	Justify Full
Ctrl+K	Case Toggle
Ctrl+L	Justify Left
Ctrl+N	New Document
Ctrl+O	Open
Ctrl+Shift+O	Outline Define
Ctrl+P	Print
Ctrl+Shift+P	Print Document
Ctrl+R	Justify Right
Ctrl+Shift+R	Redo
Ctrl+S	Save
Ctrl+Shift+S	Save All
Ctrl+T	Template/New Document
Ctrl+U	Attribute Underline
Ctrl+V	Paste
Ctrl+W	WordPerfect Characters
Ctrl+X	Cut
Ctrl+Z	Undo
Ctrl+Shift+Z	Undelete

Keystroke	Action
	Editing Keystrokes
←	One character left
→	One character right
Ctrl+←	One word left
Ctrl+→	One word right
↑	One Line Up
↓	One Line Down
Ctrl+↑	Beginning of the preceding paragraph
Ctrl+↓	Beginning of the next paragraph
Home	Beginning of the current line (after codes)
Home, Home	Beginning of the current line (before codes)
End	End of the current line
PgUp	Top of the editing screen
PgDn	Bottom of the editing screen
Alt+PgUp	First line of preceding page
Alt+PgDn	First line of following page
Ctrl+Home	Top of the document
Ctrl+End	Bottom of the document
Insert	Toggle Inset/Typeover mode
Delete	Delete character/code to the right of the insertion point
Backspace	Delete character/code to the left of the insertion point
Ctrl+Backspace	Delete current word
Ctrl+Delete	Delete from the insertion point to the end of the current line
Ctrl+Enter	Insert Hard Page (page break)
Ctrl+-	Insert Hard Hyphen
Ctrl+Shift+-	Insert Soft Hyphen
Shift+Tab	Insert Hard Back Tab (margin release)
	Shortcut Keys
F1	Help
Shift+F1	Help What Is
Ctrl+F1	Speller
Ctrl+Shift+F1	QuickCorrect
Alt+F1	Thesaurus
Alt+Shift+F1	Grammatik
F2	Find and Replace
Shift+F2	Find Next
F3	Save As
Shift+F3	Save
Alt+F3	Reveal Codes
Alt+Shift+F3	Ruler Bar
F4	Open File
Shift+F4	New Document Window
Ctrl+F4	Close
Ctrl+Shift+F4	Close without Saving
Alt+F4	Exit
Ctrl+P (or F5)	Print
Shift+F5	Zoom Full Page
Ctrl+F5	Draft View
Alt+F5	Page View
Alt+Shift+F5	Hide Bars
Ctrl+F6	Next Open Document

Using

WordPerfect® 6.1 for Windows

Joshua C. Nossiter

que

Using WordPerfect 6.1 for Windows

Library of Congress No.: 95-69236

ISBN: 0-7897-0293-2

97 96 95   4 3 2

Interpretation of the printing code: the rightmost double-digit number is the year of the book's printing; the rightmost single-digit number, the number of the book's printing. For example, a printing code of 95-1 shows that the first printing of the book occurred in 1995.

Publisher: *Roland Elgey*

Vice President and Publisher: *Marie Butler-Knight*

Associate Publisher: *Don Roche, Jr.*

Editorial Services Director: *Elizabeth Keaffaber*

Director of Marketing: *Lynn E. Zingraf*

Credits

Managing Editor
Michael Cunningham

Acquisitions Editor
Deborah F. Abshier

Product Director
Lisa D. Wagner

Technical Editor
Robert Hartley

Production Editor
Nancy E. Sixsmith

Editor
Lynn Northrup

Novice Reviewer
Beth Lucas

**Assistant Product
Marketing Manager**
Kim Margolius

Technical Specialist
Cari Skaggs

Acquisitions Assistant
Tracy M. Williams

Operations Coordinator
Patricia J. Brooks

Editorial Assistant
Jill Pursell

Book Designer
Sandra Schroeder

Cover Designer
Dan Armstrong

Production Team
Steve Adams
Chad Dressler
DiMonique Ford
Aren Howell
Barry Jorden
Kaylene Riemen
Kris Simmons
Brenda Sims

Indexer
Carol Sheehan

Composed in *ITC Century, ITC Highlander,* and *MCPdigital* by Que Corporation.

Dedication

For Jason and Madeline, who never let me forget about life beyond the computer screen.

About the Author

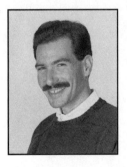

Joshua C. Nossiter received a B.A. in English from Dartmouth College and an M.B.A. in Finance from Columbia University. He has worked in broadcasting in California and in public finance on Wall Street. His interest in computers dates back to the 1970s, when he first began using the Dartmouth mainframe system. Josh now lives in San Francisco with his two children, where he writes about software, among other things.

Acknowledgments

Many highly skilled people at Que helped to turn a pile of manuscript into the useful tool I hope you'll find *Using WordPerfect 6.1 for Windows* to be. My thanks to all the Que team for transforming a lot of intense work into something pretty close to fun.

Partly as a result of the author's chronic inability to meet deadlines, certain members of the team were tested more than others. Remarkably, all came through the ordeal smiling.

Debbie Abshier, Acquisitions Editor, never wavered. She proved once again that unfailing cheerfulness and a flexible approach to due dates is a sure-fire formula for success.

Lisa Wagner, Product Development Specialist, is as responsible as anyone for what you hold in your hands. The way she turns a mess of words and images into a book is miraculous. Her encouragement kept the project going through not a few late nights.

Nancy Sixsmith, Production Editor, skillfully juggled the pieces. She's one editor who handles a red pen with equal measures of judgment and tolerance.

Lynn Northrup, Editor, cast her peerless eagle-eyes over the manuscript. Even the muddiest patches of prose couldn't shake her good humor.

Thanks to my fellow Que authors of *Using WordPerfect 6.1 for Windows, Special Edition*, an excellent reference which I highly recommend for further study. One of those authors, Read Gilgen, had the thankless job of weeding the manuscript.

The world's most courteous Technical Editor, Robert Hartley, made many valuable contributions to the text.

Thanks also to Don Roche, Associate Publisher, for once again turning me loose on a great piece of software. I hope readers will have as much fun with WordPerfect as I did.

Trademarks

We'd like to hear from you!

As part of our continuing effort to produce books of the highest quality, Que would like to hear your comments. To stay competitive, we *really* want you, as a computer book reader and user, to let us know what you like and dislike about this book or other Que products.

You can mail comments, ideas, or suggestions for improving future editions to the address below, or send us a fax at (317)581-4663. For the on-line inclined, Macmillan Computer Publishing now has a forum on CompuServe (**GO QUEBOOKS** at any prompt), through which our staff and authors are available for questions and comments. The address of our Internet site is **http://www.mcp.com** (World Wide Web).

In addition to exploring our forum, please feel free to contact me personally to discuss your opinions of this book. On CompuServe, I'm at 74404,3307; on the Internet, I'm **lwagner@que.mcp.com**.

Thanks in advance—your comments will help us to continue publishing the best books available on computer topics in today's market.

Lisa D. Wagner
Product Development Specialist
Que Corporation
201 West 103rd Street
Indianapolis, IN 46290
USA

Contents at a Glance

{Table of Contents}

The WordPerfect window
see page 12

*How do I
enter text?*

see page 24

Chapter 3: WordPerfect Help Is All Around You

Searching for Help

see page 48

Part II: Editing and Formatting, for Perfect Documents

Chapter 4: Good Writing Means Rewriting: Editing Text

How do I get the insertion point where I want it?

see page 55

Reveal codes take you behind the scenes

see page 63

How do I change fonts?

see page 79

How do I set the margins?

see page 88

Chapter 7: Setting Up the Page

Headers
and
Footers

see page 112

Part III: Getting the Words Right, On Screen and Page

Chapter 8: Choose Your Words...Easily! (Spell Them, Too.)

Chapter 9: The Printer's Craft

Part IV: Let WordPerfect Do Some of the Work for You

Chapter 10: Templates for Fancy Documents, Fast

I can't think of the right word!

see page 132

How do I print more than one copy?

see page 150

What's a template?

see page 161

Chapter 11: Documents with Style(s)

What can I do
with styles?

see page 181

I want this
style in
another
document

see page 187

Chapter 12: WordPerfect's Labor-Saving Devices

What's a
macro?

see page 195

Chapter 13: Merges, for Letters by the Bushel

Mail
merges are
great for
form letters

see page 205

Envelopes,
too?

see page 215

Part V: How to be a Desktop Publisher

Columns are easy in WordPerfect

see page 226

Chapter 14: When Only Columns Will Do

Chapter 15: Dressing Up Your Text

Do-it-yourself watermarks

see page 254

see page 259

Chapter 16: Jazz Up a Document with Graphics

Add a picture

see page 269

Add a caption

see page 277

Tables

see page 284

Chapter 17: Tables Turn Documents into Spreadsheets

Formulas and calculations

see page 295

I need a table of contents

see page 321

see page 338

Chapter 21: Import, Export, Convert: Sharing Files between Programs

Converting old WordPerfect for DOS files

see page 366

"oh-lay"

Part VIII: Indexes

Action Index

Show me where... quick!

Help Index

Help!
I'm stuck!

Introduction

I pick up the phone, and the receiver starts squawking right away: "I want to print a few pages of my latest chapter. Not the whole chapter, just a few pages. How do I do it?"

My phone rings all the time with variations on that theme. There are a lot of WordPerfect users among my family and friends, and they all have "How do I do it?" questions for me. This book was written to answer their questions, and yours, too.

WordPerfect is easy to use. Really! Once you know what button to press and where to find it, even complicated word processing jobs like creating a newsletter become simple point-and-click affairs. Quick jobs like short letters or memos are quicker still when you use WordPerfect.

But there's a lot here. WordPerfect does almost anything imaginable with text and graphics, and you usually get several different ways to do it. There are loads of features you'll use all the time, and some that you'll use rarely, if ever. Until you get to know the program, figuring out how to do a specific chore is not always obvious. *Using WordPerfect 6.1 for Windows* is designed to cut through the clutter to give you just the information you need.

What makes this book different?

If you phone a pal with questions about WordPerfect, you want straight answers, not a lot of jargon. Otherwise, you'd probably hang up. I tried to write *Using WordPerfect 6.1 for Windows* just as I'd answer telephone queries from my WordPerfect-using friends, with plain English that gets right to the point.

You don't have to spend a lot of time with *Using WordPerfect 6.1 for Windows*. It's designed so that a quick look shows you the fastest and easiest ways to create and edit documents.

What's more, you'll find plenty of Tips to speed up your work, Cautions to help you avoid trouble, Q&As to solve mysteries, and Notes with useful tidbits of information.

If you're new to WordPerfect, you'll discover that learning the program can really be fun. You experienced WordPerfect users will find easier ways to do things, and you'll learn about useful features you might not have come across before.

It's no accident that WordPerfect is a best-seller. There's enough word processing power here to satisfy a publishing tycoon.

How do I use this book?

Most of the time you'll want fast help with doing a specific chore. The Action Index at the back of the book is a good place to start. It lists common word processing tasks, and directs you right to the page where you'll find the task explained. If you can't find what you want in the Action Index, check the Table of Contents next. It's very detailed, and chances are your job will be listed there.

When you have some spare time, try browsing. Each chapter of *Using WordPerfect 6.1 for Windows* is divided into sections. Looking through the section headings is a good way to discover WordPerfect features you didn't know about. You might also get ideas about using WordPerfect to tackle your work in new ways.

Of course, there's nothing to stop you from sitting down and reading a chapter through from beginning to end. To really master WordPerfect features, that's the way to go. I can't promise you a thriller, but I've tried to keep things lively.

How this book is put together

When you have a big project to do, you probably break it up into smaller parts and tackle them one at a time. WordPerfect is a big program, so that's how this book is set up, too. There are eight parts:

Part I: Everything I Need to Get Started

Whether you plan on occasional visits or extended daily sessions, here's the place to find out what you're getting into. You'll learn how WordPerfect works, the basics of creating a document, and how to get help fast, whenever you need it.

Part II: Editing and Formatting, for Perfect Documents

These are the things you'll do when you fire up WordPerfect every day. From short memos to epics, WordPerfect can handle whatever you throw at it. If you make a mistake, or need to make changes of any kind, you'll see that editing is easy and quick. And with a few basic formatting tools, you can turn out handsome pages in no time.

Part III: Getting the Words Right, On Screen and Page

Writing is all about words. You'll discover that finding and spelling the right words is painless with WordPerfect's spell checker and thesaurus. Grammatik, WordPerfect's grammar checker, even helps you arrange your words correctly in sentences. A wealth of formatting features is a click or two away, to help you create documents that are as attractive to look at as they are easy to read. And when it's time to print, the chapter on printing will help you produce good-looking print jobs.

Part IV: Let WordPerfect Do Some of the Work for You

When you want a professional-looking document, without spending a lot of time tinkering with formatting, WordPerfect's templates are the answer. A template gives you perfect, ready-made formatting—just type the text, and you're done! Features like macros and Abbreviations even do some of your typing for you. If you want to design your own document formatting, WordPerfect's Styles save and apply your formatting creations.

Part V: How to be a Desktop Publisher

Columns organize pages neatly and readably, and WordPerfect makes working with columns a straightforward chore. Tables go columns one better; a table is not only a great organizing tool, but WordPerfect tables can even turn your documents into spreadsheets. Pop up a table, enter your data, and use WordPerfect's built-in calculator for everything from addition and subtraction to financial calculations.

How do you produce fifty letters, each one personalized with the recipient's name and address? You could spend a few days on the project and type fifty different letters, or you could use WordPerfect's Merge feature and do the job in minutes. When you want to mass-produce documents that look custom-made, Merge takes care of the job effortlessly.

Part VI: Getting the Most Out of WordPerfect

Build a kid's playhouse, and you can get by with a hammer and saw. Build an office building, and you need more powerful equipment. Big documents need special tools, too, and WordPerfect has them. There are automated outlines, instant tables of contents, and other useful features to help you cope with big writing jobs. And as your writing jobs pile up, WordPerfect has a handy file manager to keep you on top of your work.

Even the best writing benefits from attractive fonts and eye-grabbing graphic effects. From fancy borders to colorful pictures, WordPerfect puts a collection of decorative graphics at your fingertips. Adding graphics to text is as easy as clicking and dragging. You'll also find everything you need to dress up the text. And with WordPerfect's amazing TextArt, you can even turn text *into* graphics.

Part VII: Expert WordPerfect Features for Non-Experts

Graphics can be as informative as they are decorative. That's exactly what a chart is—a picture that tells a story. There's no great trick to creating a spectacular chart in WordPerfect; just type your data, point, and click. With WP Draw, WordPerfect's drawing program, even non-artists can whip up attention-getting artwork in minutes. And because everything in WordPerfect works together, you can easily pop charts and drawings into your documents.

Setting up perfect pages used to be the province of skilled layout artists. With WordPerfect, you get a battery of tools that help you produce pages of near-typeset quality. That's what desktop publishing is all about, and WordPerfect takes all the mystery out of it.

You'll come to think of WordPerfect as an electronic desk, with all your writing and drawing tools ready for use. Just like your desktop, you can customize WordPerfect to set up your tools the way you want them. And when you need a file from another application, copy it right into WordPerfect and work on it there. Exchanging files between WordPerfect and other programs is as easy as working on someone else's file at your own desk.

Part VIII: Indexes

To top it all off, instead of just one index, we finish up with a couple of special indexes to help you find what you need quickly. Turn to the Action Index for tricks to help you get things done fast, and the Help Index for troubleshooting tips to help you out of sticky situations. (You'll also find a normal index for looking up words and traditional stuff like that.)

Special book elements

This book has a number of special elements and conventions to help you find information quickly—or to skip stuff you don't want to read right away.

!(Tip)

Tips either point out information often overlooked in the documentation or help you use your software more efficiently, such as through a shortcut. Some tips help you solve or avoid problems.

*{Note}

Notes contain additional information or "reminders" of important information you should know.

X<Caution>

Cautions alert you to potentially dangerous consequences of a procedure or practice, especially if there could be serious or even disastrous results, such as loss or corruption of data.

?Q&A

What are Q&A notes?

Cast in the form of questions and answers, these notes provide you with advice on ways to avoid or solve common problems.

 Plain English, please!

These notes explain the meanings of technical **terms** or computer **jargon.** 🙾

Sidebars are interesting nuggets of information

Sidebars provide interesting, nonessential reading, side-alley trips you can take when you just want some relief from "doing stuff." You might find technical details, anecdotes, or interesting background information.

Throughout the book, we'll use a comma to separate the parts of a pull-down menu command. For example, to start a new document, you'll choose File, New. That means "Pull down the File menu and choose New from the list."

If you see two keys separated by a plus sign, such as Ctrl+B, that means to press and hold the first key, press the second key, then release both keys.

Right-click means clicking the right mouse button.

And when we talk about dragging, we mean holding down the left mouse button and moving the mouse pointer.

This Is No Ordinary Blank Page!

*Driving a car is easy
once you learn what all
the buttons and levers do.
With WordPerfect, you'll
be just as comfortable
behind the wheel.*

In this chapter:

- How do I start WordPerfect?
- What am I looking at in the WordPerfect window?
- Menus? Toolbar? Power Bar? Explain, please!
- I need to see more of my document

B efore the car, people walked. A pre-automobile Englishman named Allerdyce went hunting and walked thirty miles. After a bite to eat, he walked another sixty miles to get home. He did the chores, walked sixteen miles to a ball, danced, walked home in the morning, then spent the day partridge shooting. All told he covered one hundred and thirty miles in three days and two nights.

Great exercise, but if he'd had a car, he would have used it.

Writing with pen and paper is like walking. You get where you're going, but slowly. If you take a wrong turn, retracing your steps means a lot of crossing out. Writing with WordPerfect is more like driving a car. Spend a few minutes learning which buttons to push, and you get to where you're going quickly and effortlessly. Make a mistake, and a click or two of the mouse sets you back on the right road again. And this model of WordPerfect comes fully equipped; every imaginable option and accessory is at your fingertips.

What can WordPerfect do for me?

From a quick memo, to a lengthy report, to a newsletter complete with headlines and graphics, WordPerfect gives you everything you need to get the job done quickly. WordPerfect checks your spelling, finds you the right word, and even checks your grammar. And WordPerfect makes it easy to add color and graphics to give your writing jobs extra pizzazz.

WordPerfect helps make your good work even better.

Where do I start? Running WordPerfect

When you installed WordPerfect, the installation program added the WordPerfect program group to the Windows Program Manager.

If you're not already in Windows, type **win** at the C: prompt to go straight to Program Manager. Once you're in Program Manager, double-click the WPWin 6.1 icon, which looks like this:

 The WordPerfect (WPWin 6.1) program group displays, as shown in figure 1.1.

Double-click the WordPerfect icon to start WordPerfect.

Fig. 1.1
The WPWin 6.1 program group offers different icons for some of WordPerfect's main features.

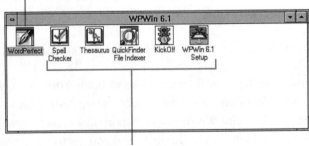

Double-clicking the other icons runs them as stand-alone programs.

 Those other icons in the WPWin 6.1 program group represent program features—the Spell Checker for example. They can be run outside of WordPerfect, even when WordPerfect is shut down. Suppose you're writing a memo in the Windows Notepad. Double-click the Spell Checker icon to display the Spell Checker dialog box. Then type in a word to check the spelling. That works for the Thesaurus, too.

 Now double-click the WordPerfect icon in the WPWin 6.1 program group to run WordPerfect.

How do I get out of here?

 To exit WordPerfect, select File, Exit, or double-click the program Control menu box at the upper left of the window.

What's in the WordPerfect window?

Writers liked older versions of WordPerfect because the program displayed a (nearly) blank screen. Like the blank sheets of paper we used to roll into typewriters, the view was uncluttered, hence not distracting. On the other hand, you had to refer to a little slip of cardboard to remember the commands.

The not-distracting look has gone the way of the typewriter. When you run WordPerfect now, that blank page is framed by a host of useful gadgets (see graphics page).

The WordPerfect window

The **title bar** shows the document name and descriptions of buttons and menu commands.

Click any of the items on the **menu bar** for a drop-down menu of commands and options.

The **Toolbar** holds buttons, or icons that represent tools. One click executes the most frequently used commands.

The **Power Bar** holds buttons that control formatting and display options.

The **Previous Page** and **Next Page** buttons jump the display through a document one page at a time.

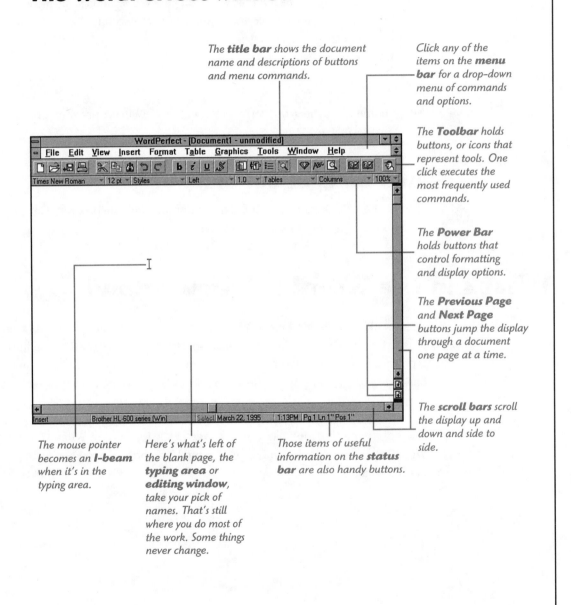

The **scroll bars** scroll the display up and down and side to side.

The mouse pointer becomes an **I-beam** when it's in the typing area.

Here's what's left of the blank page, the **typing area** or **editing window**, take your pick of names. That's still where you do most of the work. Some things never change.

Those items of useful information on the **status bar** are also handy buttons.

Why does my mouse pointer keep changing shape?

If you move the mouse pointer around the window, you'll notice that it mutates from white arrow to I-beam as it travels from the Tool, Power, scroll, and status bars to the typing area. As the white arrow, the pointer selects menu options or executes commands when clicked. As the I-beam, click it to move the insertion point or drag it to select text.

Position the pointer at the upper or lower border of the Toolbar, and it undergoes another transformation. When the pointer turns into that grabby-looking hand, you can click and drag the Toolbar to a different location. For example, you could drag the Toolbar to the left side of the screen so it displays vertically at the left.

What do the buttons do?

You've probably noticed something else as you move the mouse pointer around the window. When you point at a button, a little label appears with the button's name. That's called a **QuickTip**. At the same time, a description appears in the title bar, offering a little more information about what the button does. Figure 1.2 shows a QuickTip and the title bar's corresponding description.

Fig. 1.2

Point at any button to get a QuickTip and title bar description, along with its keyboard shortcut if there is one.

Plain English, please!

Those items on the Toolbar that we've been calling **buttons** (because they look like buttons) represent **tools**, hence the term "Toolbar." You might also see them referred to as **icons** because they're little pictures. The items on the Power Bar are also buttons. Click them to display drop-down lists, then choose items from the lists. The bars are there to help you work faster by putting important commands within easy reach.

The status bar is not just for show

WordPerfect has some pleasant surprises in store for you. One is the **status bar** down at the bottom of the window. Not only does it display useful information, you can plug that information right into your document! Double-click the date, for example, and the current date is inserted (at the insertion point), right in your document!

Same thing for the time. Figure 1.3 shows you what happens when you double-click the date and time on the status bar.

Fig. 1.3
Double-click the status bar items to display dialog boxes or execute commands, like inserting the date and time.

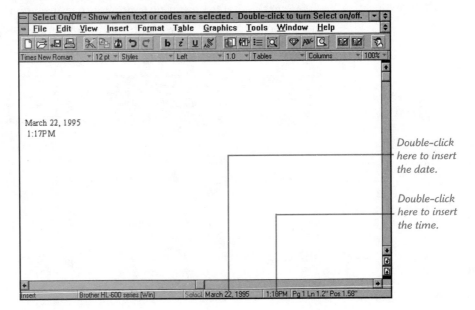

Double-click here to insert the date.

Double-click here to insert the time.

Double-click the printer display on the status bar; you'll see the Select Printer dialog box. Each of the displays on the status bar is actually a button; just point at it to see a description of what it does in the title bar.

Menus and QuickMenus, for all WordPerfect's features

Restaurant menus group choices by type: appetizers, main courses, and so on. WordPerfect menus do the same thing, which makes it a lot easier to find what you're looking for among the program's many features.

Click any item on the menu bar to get a menu of related features. You'll find file commands under the File menu, for example. A description of what the command does appears in the title bar, as shown in figure 1.4.

Fig. 1.4

The title bar shows a description of the highlighted command in any menu, along with its keyboard shortcut—the key-strokes required to use the feature directly from the keyboard.

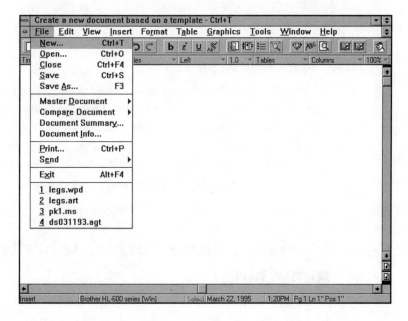

Q&A

I clicked a menu command to see the description, but instead I executed the command! How do I get the description without the command?

When you click a menu command, you do indeed execute the command. To see the description before you commit yourself, use the up and down arrow keys to scroll through the pull-down menu. The highlight bar moves from command to command as you scroll, and the corresponding description appears in the title bar.

Why are some menu items dimmed or gray? Why doesn't anything happen when I select them?

Dimmed or grayed menu items simply mean that you can't use that particular feature right now. For example, before you type any text, the Cut and Copy items are dimmed in the <u>E</u>dit menu, since you don't have any text to cut or copy. At least you can see where the feature is so you'll know where to find it when you really need it.

 Plain English, please!

Whew! Lots of technical terms flying around. If you haven't figured these out yet, you'll probably want to know that a **keyboard shortcut** is how you use the keyboard to get to a WordPerfect feature without using the menus. A **pull-down menu** is just a menu you see when you click an item on the menu bar. Also, you don't really have to pull it down—it drops down by itself. When you do click a menu item, you **execute**, or activate, a feature. **"**

My right mouse button actually *does* something?

Here's another of WordPerfect's nice surprises: the right mouse button becomes a handy tool. Try pointing at the Toolbar, then click the right mouse button. A QuickMenu pops up with a list of all the WordPerfect Toolbars. Each Toolbar contains the tools needed for different tasks, such as working with tables, preparing legal documents, or designing publication-quality documents.

If there's text in the editing window, point at the left margin (directly to the left of your text) and right-click for a QuickMenu with a choice of selection options and the Margins command. Point anywhere else in the editing window, right-click, and you get the QuickMenu shown in figure 1.5.

Fig. 1.5
QuickMenus pop up with a right click of the mouse.

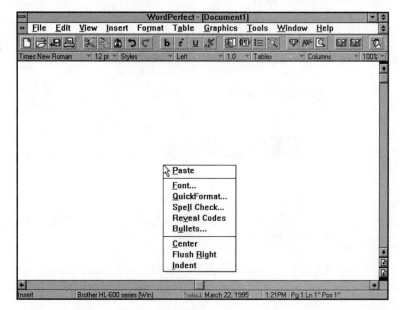

There are QuickMenus for the Power Bar and status bar, too. Point at either one, and right-click for QuickMenus that allow you to add or remove items on the bars.

Dialog boxes do a bunch of commands at once

A lot of WordPerfect commands require more information from you before the program can execute them. Whenever that happens, a dialog box pops up. Click Format, Font, for example, and you'll get the dialog box shown in figure 1.6.

Fig. 1.6

The Font dialog box holds a host of options to control the size and appearance of the characters in your document.

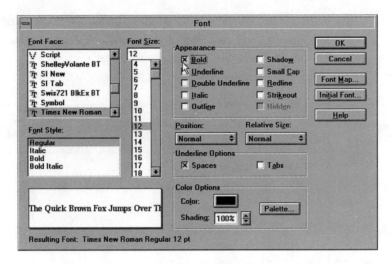

Dialog boxes often have **check boxes**, like the ones under Appearance in figure 1.6. Click a box to select or deselect an item. The × in the check box next to Bold shows that Bold is selected.

Click an item under Font Face to select it, and your selection is highlighted. The preview box, at the lower-left corner, shows you what you selected.

Some dialog boxes contain edit boxes, such as the Point Size box, which require you to type in text. Most dialog boxes also have special push buttons, such as OK, Cancel, or Help.

The easiest way of getting around in a dialog box is to use the mouse. Click a button, check box, or list item to select it. If you need to type in text, click the edit box where the text goes. That puts the insertion point in the edit box, and you can just start typing.

When you're finished with a dialog box, click the OK button. To back out without making any changes to the document, click the Cancel button, or simply press the Escape (Esc) key. And if you have any questions about any of the dialog box items, click the Help button.

I want to see more (or less) of this document

Change your point of view, and you see things differently. WordPerfect gives you several ways of looking at your documents. Click View on the menu bar, and take your choice of three display options:

- Draft shows you your text, but it doesn't display the margins, which means you won't be able to see headers, footers, or footnotes.

- Page displays all your text, including everything in the margins. When you start up WordPerfect, the display is in Page mode until you change it.

- Two Page displays two pages of a document at once, as shown in figure 1.7. You can make editing changes in Two Page mode, but it's next to impossible to see body text. Two Page mode is a quick way of previewing how your pages will look in print.

Fig. 1.7

Two Page mode gives you the big picture of your document.

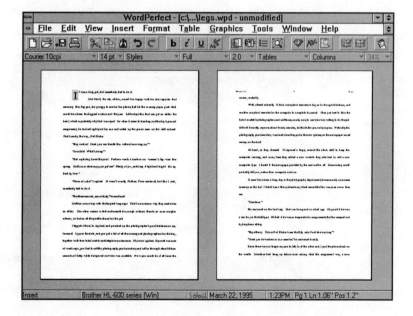

To flip quickly between Page and Draft modes, press Ctrl+F5 for Draft mode or Alt+F5 for Page mode.

Telescope the screen with Zoom

Ever try looking at the same thing from either end of a telescope? It'll look tiny or huge, and that's just what you get with WordPerfect's Zoom control.

 The Page/Zoom Full button on the Toolbar helps you quickly zoom out for the big picture. Click it again to zoom back in for a normal view of your document.

You can change the normal view by using the Zoom button at the right end of the Power Bar. Click the button, and take your choice of zoom levels from the pull-down menu shown in figure 1.8.

The **zoom percentage** is the ratio of the screen display to the printed page. Lower the ratio to see more of the page; increase the ratio to see a smaller area in magnified detail. Figure 1.8 shows you what Zoom control is all about.

Fig. 1.8
A document zoomed to 150%. Use the Power Bar Zoom button to see document detail or the big picture.

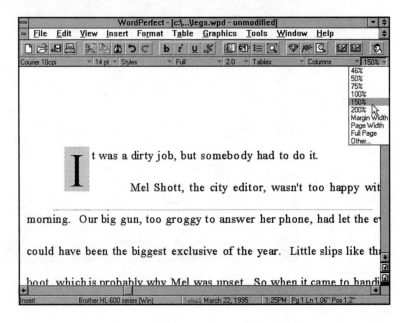

If you want to adjust the zoom ratio to some value other than the choices on offer from the Power Bar button, click <u>V</u>iew, <u>Z</u>oom. That pops up the Zoom dialog box, in which you can set the magnification level to anything you want.

Scrolling turns the on-screen page

Getting from page one to page two in a book is pretty straightforward; you just turn the page. Turning pages in a WordPerfect document is just as straightforward. Click the Previous Page or Next Page buttons on the scroll bar to get from page to page in a document.

The problem is, you normally won't see an entire page of a document on the screen. The Previous Page and Next Page buttons take you from the top of one page to the top of the next page, but you see only one window's worth of the page, about a third of it, at a time.

That's okay though, because WordPerfect gives you plenty of ways to scroll through a document:

- Click the scroll bar up and down arrows to scroll through the document one line at a time.

- Click the scroll bar between the up and down arrows to advance or retreat one window at a time. Click above the scroll button to move back through the document; click below the scroll button to advance forward.

- Drag the scroll button up or down to advance or retreat through the document by variable amounts.

 Q&A

How come WordPerfect seems to jump around when I scroll from page to page?

You're in Page mode. Click <u>V</u>iew, <u>D</u>raft to switch to draft mode. With no margins to display, scrolling through WordPerfect will seem a lot smoother.

Moving the insertion point as you scroll

As you press the arrow keys, or press Page Up or Page Down on the keyboard, the insertion point also moves through the document. If you move the insertion point past the window-full of document you happen to be looking at, the document scrolls to the new position automatically.

There are some other ways to move the insertion point through a document, which we'll look at in Chapter 2.

2

Creating a New Document

In this chapter

- How do I enter text?

- I need to create a new document

- Template? What's that?

- I want to save the document with a name I'll remember

- I want my document back, but I can't remember its name!

WordPerfect can't come up with the ideas for your new document, but it does make translating those ideas into words a lot easier.

From cave paintings on, people have always set their thoughts down on something permanent. Getting a thought down, in pictures or writing, makes the thought clearer. Dr. Samuel Johnson, who wrote the first modern dictionary of the English language, once said, "No man but a blockhead ever wrote except for money."

Great man though he was, even Dr. Johnson was wrong sometimes. We write for a lot of reasons, not the least of which is that writing helps us think. Written words capture our thoughts.

As you see in this chapter, WordPerfect makes writing easier. WordPerfect's polished documents make captured thoughts clearer, for ourselves and for our readers.

How do I enter text in a WordPerfect document?

The best way to start writing is to start writing. If you don't like what you've written, you can always go back and change it. Two hundred years ago, editing with a quill pen must have been a bit of a chore. (That might explain Dr. Johnson's attitude.)

Changing things around in WordPerfect is a breeze. Setting your words down in a clear and attractive way is just as easy.

Just start typing?

One way to tackle a new document in WordPerfect is to wing it. Just type, and the words appear in the editing window. When you finish typing, you can edit your work, save it, and print it, all with a few clicks of the mouse.

You'll want to keep these two things in mind when you type in WordPerfect:

- WordPerfect is smarter than a typewriter. Just keep typing, even when you get to the end of a line. The typed text "wraps" automatically to the next line. When you get to the end of a paragraph, press Enter. That forces the insertion point to move to a new line so that you can start the next paragraph.

- To indent paragraphs, or to align text vertically, press the Tab key, not the spacebar.

 **{Note}**

Do use the spacebar to add a space after commas or two spaces after periods as you'd do normally. Just don't use the spacebar to set off the first line of a paragraph or to align other text. It may look correct on your screen, but if you change fonts or when you print, the alignment may be off.

Word wrap, the gift that comes wrapped

Word wrap has nothing to do with gift wrap, but it's a gift nevertheless. Typewriters require you to slap a lever or (for electric typewriters) press a button at the end of every line. WordPerfect saves you the trouble. By wrapping text at the end of every line, WordPerfect automatically moves the insertion point to a new line when you type past the right margin.

Hard or soft, every line has a return

When you type past the right margin, WordPerfect inserts what's called a **soft return** to move the insertion point to the next line. If you add text or make changes in the paragraph, those soft returns move automatically to accommodate the changes, jumping words up or down to the next line as needed.

Pressing Enter at the end of a paragraph inserts a **hard return**. Hard returns stay where you put them until they're deleted. Because hard returns don't move, you can make changes in a paragraph but still keep the paragraph together.

Think of the sentences in a paragraph as a continuous line, like a long strand of cooked spaghetti. Soft returns bend the strand at the end of each line without breaking it. Hard returns snap the strand wherever you press Enter.

Take a letter

If we wrote a letter by the wing-it method, here's a little exercise to show what we'd do. Feel free to follow these steps and type what's in boldface for the exercise. If you make a typing mistake, press Backspace to correct it.

1 Double-click the date display on the status bar to stick the date in the document at the insertion point. Then press Enter twice to move down two lines.

2 Type the salutation: **Dear Dr. Johnson,** then press Enter twice to move down two lines.

3 Press Tab and type the first paragraph. Don't press Enter at the end of the lines; just keep typing to the end of the paragraph. Type: **We have**

nothing but admiration for the poems, essays, and brilliant epigrams you have left us. Your pioneering dictionary was truly heroic. The changes it made to the English language are still with us, two hundred and forty years later.

4 Press Enter to end the first paragraph, then press Enter again to move down one more line.

5 Press Tab and type the second paragraph: **We cannot agree with you, however, when you say that any writer who doesn't write for money is a blockhead. Writing of some kind has always been a natural expression of the human spirit. Simply by clarifying thought, writing is priceless—even if you don't get paid for it.**

6 Press Enter twice to move down two lines and type **Respectfully yours,**. Our letter looks like figure 2.1.

Fig. 2.1
No chance of getting a reply to this one. Dr. Johnson died in 1784.

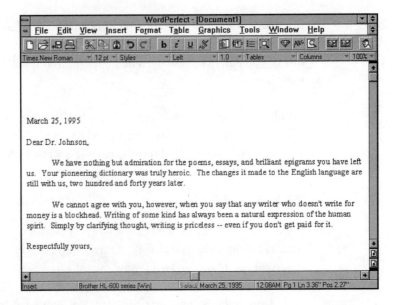

Of course, a letter written this way leaves us with a few questions. How about the recipient's address? We'll want the return address in there somewhere, too. WordPerfect gives us one-inch margins without being asked. But do we really want the letter scrunched up at the top of the page, which is what we'd get with our letter?

View the letter in two-page mode as shown in figure 2.2 by selecting View, Two Page. You can see that our letter's layout could use some work.

Fig. 2.2
This is how the letter would look on the printed page.

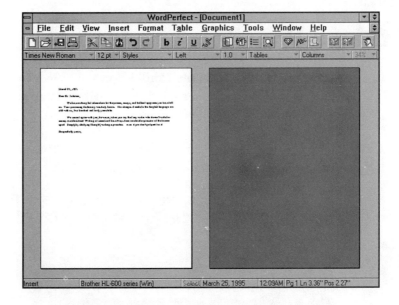

Templates are documents by the numbers

WordPerfect has a second way of tackling new documents that settles all such questions without our having to bother about them. We can use a letter **template** to handle all the layout issues for us. With a template, all we have to do is compose the body of the letter; WordPerfect does the rest of the job.

 Plain English, please!

> A template is any tool used to fit a piece of work to a desired shape. A template is usually an outline or model of the finished product; when the outline is filled in, the result resembles the model.

Ever see a road crew painting STOP on the road? They take a big stencil with cutouts of the letters s, t, o, and p on it. They lay the stencil on the road and paint inside the cutouts, producing perfectly formed letters. That's exactly how WordPerfect templates work. They're just like stencils for documents.

Select a template, enter your text, and a perfectly formatted document results.

Now take a WordPerfect letter!

Let's try that same letter the WordPerfect way. The result will be a professional-looking document, created with no more effort than the wing-it version we've already churned out.

 Click the New Document button on the Toolbar. That pops up the New Document dialog box shown in figure 2.3.

Fig. 2.3
The New Document dialog box gives you a choice of templates.

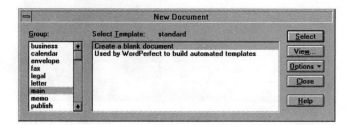

You can take your pick of templates for a new document in the New Document dialog box, including Create a Blank Document. That option gives you the WordPerfect default template, which is what you see whenever you first run the program.

The **default**, or Standard, template contains things like margin and font settings. It's called the default template because WordPerfect uses it until you pick something else.

The first button on the Toolbar is the New Blank Document button, not to be confused with the New Document button we've just clicked. Clicking the New Blank Document button does the same thing as selecting the Create a Blank Document option from the New Document dialog box—it opens a new document with the default template.

The letter template, for a professional-looking letter

Here's how to put a letter template to good use:

1 Under <u>G</u>roup in the New Document dialog box, choose Letter for the choices shown in figure 2.4.

Fig. 2.4
Each group contains a choice of templates.

2 Double-click Traditional Letterhead. If this is the first time you've tried a template, you get the Enter Your Personal Information dialog box, as shown in figure 2.5. If you've used the template before, you go straight to the Letter dialog box (see fig. 2.6). This time, if you see the Letter dialog box, click the <u>P</u>ersonal Info button to display the Personal Information dialog box, as shown in figure 2.5.

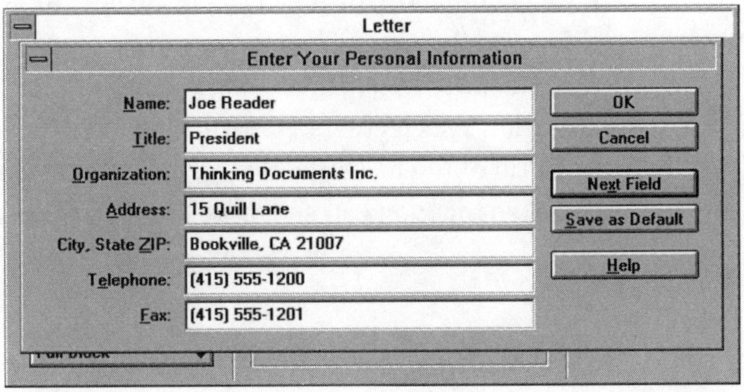

Fig. 2.5
The Personal Information dialog box lets you store information about yourself.

3 In the Personal Information dialog box, enter your name, title, company, address, phone; whatever information you want on the letterhead. Click the <u>S</u>ave as Default button, and WordPerfect will store the information for use with this and other templates. Unless it changes, you'll never have to type this information again.

4 You now find yourself in the Letter dialog box (see fig. 2.6). Enter the Recipient's Name and Address and the Salutation, as shown.

The Letter Format pop-up menu gives you a choice of text alignments. If you feel like experimenting, click the button, hold down the mouse button, and slide the pointer to highlight a different choice. The different alignment effects are shown in the Letter Format window as you make your choices.

Fig. 2.6
Click inside the edit boxes to put the insertion point wherever you want to type.

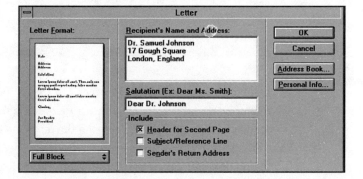

5 Click OK, and WordPerfect's gears spin for a moment as the program formats the letter. Then you get a message from WordPerfect announcing that the letter formatting is complete, and that you can add a letter closing by selecting Letter Closing from the Insert menu. Click OK to get rid of the message. So far, the letter looks like figure 2.7, zoomed to 75% so that you can see more of it.

These buttons appear on the Toolbar when you create a letter using the letter templates.

Fig. 2.7
Notice how we get a new crop of letter-related Toolbar buttons.

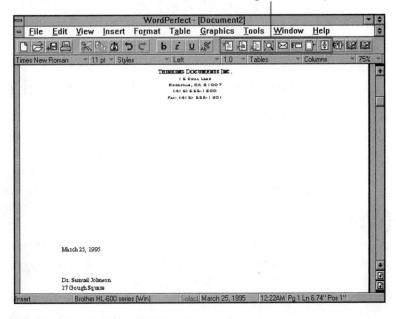

6 Instead of using the Insert menu for the closing, let's use one of the handy letter buttons that appears on the Toolbar (refer to fig. 2.7). Click the Letter Closing button to get the dialog box shown in figure 2.8.

Fig. 2.8
Add the letter closing, initials, and courtesy copies information from this dialog box.

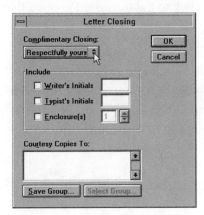

7 Click the Complimentary Closing button and hold down the mouse button. Move the pointer to your choice of closings and release to select it. Click OK, and the closing, with the name and title entered in Personal Information, is inserted in the proper place in the letter.

Save typing with copy and paste

We have a perfect letter layout. Now we just add the body text for a perfect letter. We want those two paragraphs we've already typed to appear between the salutation and the closing of the letter. We could retype them, but why bother? Instead, we'll save time and effort by copying the paragraphs from Document 1 and pasting them into our template letter in Document 2.

 You can keep as many as nine documents open at a time in WordPerfect. When you start WordPerfect, you're automatically in Document 1. Each new document you open is numbered 2, 3, and so on.

To copy text from Document 1 to Document 2, first go to Document 1.

1 Click Window, 1 Document 1 to display our first letter.

2 Move the mouse pointer I-beam to the left margin of the first paragraph of text and click to put the insertion point there. The flashing cursor should be immediately to the left of the tab preceding the first word in the first paragraph, "We."

3 Hold down the Shift key and press the down-arrow key to highlight both paragraphs of text (see fig. 2.9).

Fig. 2.9

Shift+arrow key is the easiest way to highlight text. Or you can drag with the mouse.

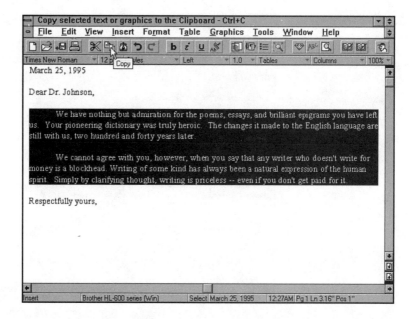

{Note} To drag with the mouse, click, hold down the button, and move the pointer to the end of the text.

4 Now click the Copy button on the Toolbar.

5 Click <u>W</u>indow, <u>2</u> Document 2 to switch to our template letter.

(Tip) To quickly switch from document to document, press Ctrl+F6.

6 Put the mouse pointer I-beam between the salutation and the closing and click to place the insertion point.

7 Click the Paste button on the Toolbar. The copied text is pasted into the letter, as shown in figure 2.10.

Fig. 2.10
Copying and pasting text is easy to do, and it saves a lot of time and typing.

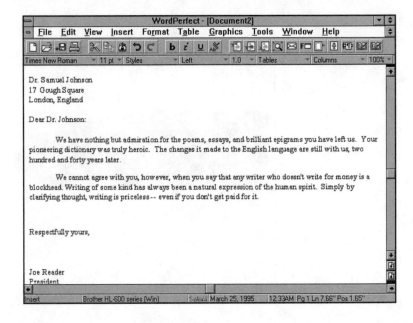

The difference between our template letter on the left and our wing-it effort on the right is shown in figure 2.11.

Fig. 2.11
Same letter, different layouts. The template version looks much more professional.

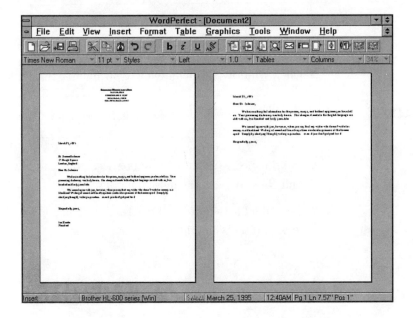

{Note}

In Figure 2.11, I copied the entire first letter in Document 1 and put it on page 2 of Document 2 so that you can see a side-by-side comparison of our two letters.

Q&A

How come when I try this, my copied body text looks bigger than the template text?

The font in the default or Standard template, which is what you get in a new blank document, is Times New Roman in 12-point size. Text inserted by the traditional letter template is Times New Roman in 11-point size. To switch all the 12-point text to 11-point size, put the insertion point to the left of the first occurrence of 12-point text. Click the font size button on the Power Bar and select 11. All the 12-point text will change to 11-point size (which is what I did for figure 2.10).

Document finished? Save it

It's convenient to have WordPerfect number successive documents 1, 2, 3, and so on. That makes it easy to switch back and forth between them. On the other hand, the name Document 1 doesn't tell us much. We need to save our letter with a new name.

Click File, Save As for the dialog box shown in figure 2.12.

Fig. 2.12

The Save As dialog box lets you name a new document. It also tells you a lot about the document you're getting ready to save.

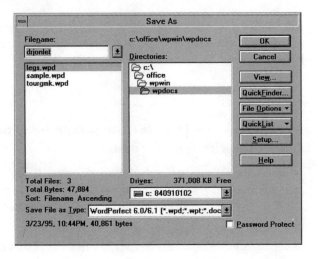

Here's where we name our new document, assign it to a directory, and save it. The default directory for WordPerfect documents is highlighted in the Directories box in figure 2.12. It's called—no prizes for this one—wpdocs.

When you start to accumulate lots of different documents of different types, you'll want to create new directories for them. That makes it easier to keep everything organized. For now, the wpdocs directory is fine, so we don't need to do anything in the Directories box.

What do I use for a name?

Click the Filename box shown in figure 2.12 to put the insertion point in the box.

Now type in a name. You can use up to eight characters, including numbers. WordPerfect supplies the extension .wpd for you, so don't bother typing it yourself.

We'll call our letter DRJONLET (lowercase is okay, too). When you're finished typing the name, click OK. You'll notice that the title bar no longer displays Document 1, but shows our new name instead, to which Word-Perfect has automatically attached the .wpd extension, as shown in figure 2.13.

Fig. 2.13
The "unmodified" in
the title bar disappears
as soon as you make
changes in the
document.

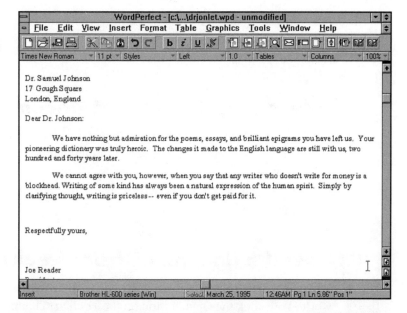

How do I get out of this document?

The document is finished and saved, and you're ready to go home for the day. All you need is the exit. WordPerfect gives you several ways out:

- To exit the program, double-click the Control Menu box in the upper left-hand corner of the title bar. (But don't exit the program right now!)

- You can also click File, Exit, or press Alt+F4 to leave the program. (Again, don't do this yet!)

- Maybe you're through with the document but you've got more work to do. To exit the active document but stay in WordPerfect, click File, Close or press Ctrl+F4. (Okay, you can do this!)

WordPerfect has a built-in file manager

A lot of Windows applications make you go outside the program to the Windows File Manager to take care of file chores. Not WordPerfect. You can delete, move, rename, or print files, even rename and create directories, right from within WordPerfect. If you can't remember a file name, WordPerfect has a powerful search feature that'll find your file for you. And if you want to retrieve the documents you've been working on most recently, you can get them back with two clicks of the mouse.

How do I get my latest documents back?

You named and saved your document and shut down WordPerfect. Now you're back from lunch and you need to open that document again. Click File. The bottom of the File menu lists the last four documents you've worked on, even if you closed WordPerfect. Just click the one you want and get back to work.

I need a document from weeks ago

When you want a file that doesn't happen to be among the last four you've worked on, click the Open button on the Toolbar. That pops up the Open File dialog box shown in figure 2.14.

Fig. 2.14
Does this look familiar? The Open File dialog box bears a striking resemblance to the Save As dialog box.

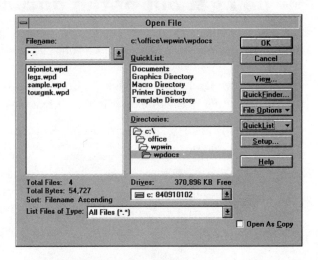

No, you're not having a spell of déjà vu. The Open File dialog box looks just like the Save As dialog box and their triplet sibling, the Insert File dialog box. In each case, you're getting what WordPerfect calls the Directory dialog boxes, the program's file manager.

In the Directory dialog boxes, click the QuickList button and select Show Both to display both pathnames and descriptive names for the WordPerfect subdirectories.

The File Options button gives you a pull-down menu from which you can move, delete, print, or rename files.

View pops up a window with a preview of the selected file for you to inspect. And if you can't remember your file name, click the QuickFinder button. That gives you the QuickFinder dialog box shown in figure 2.15.

Fig. 2.15

Use QuickFinder to track down documents whose names or locations you can't remember.

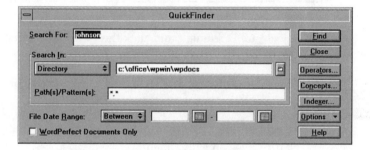

If you can remember a key word or two from your file, type the word or words in the Search For box and click Find. QuickFinder will find the file for you and display the file name, the date it was created, and other useful information.

When you are through locating your file, assuming you really don't want to do anything with it, just press Esc until you return to your document.

I'm ready to print my document

Want to print the whole document, one page, or a range of pages? Click the Print button on the Toolbar. That gets you the Print dialog box (see fig. 2.16). From the Print dialog box, take your choice of what to print:

Fig. 2.16
The Print button on
the Toolbar doesn't
print your document
right away; you get the
Print dialog box first.

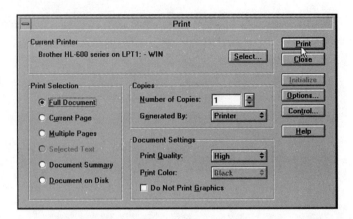

- Select <u>F</u>ull Document and click the <u>P</u>rint button to print the whole document.

- Select C<u>u</u>rrent Page and click the <u>P</u>rint button to print only the page where you last left the insertion point.

- Select <u>M</u>ultiple Pages if you want to print more than one page, but not all the pages, in a document.

  Once you select <u>M</u>ultiple Pages, click the <u>P</u>rint button to pop up the Multiple Pages dialog box. In the P<u>a</u>ge(s)/Label(s) edit box, type in **2,3,5** to print pages 2, 3, and 5, for example. Or type in **2-5** to print pages 2, 3, 4, and 5. Then click the <u>P</u>rint button in the Multiple Pages dialog box.

3

WordPerfect Help Is All Around You

You're bound to run into a few problems from time to time. But no matter where you are, you're never far from the best help in the business.

A veteran newspaper reporter was walking through a San Francisco park one spring afternoon. He joined a handful of spectators watching a kid's baseball team take batting practice. One kid after another stepped up to the plate, missed pitch after pitch, and returned dejected to the bench.

An elegant, silver-haired man detached himself from the onlookers. He picked up a bat, and with a few beautiful swings showed the kids what they were doing wrong. Every journalistic instinct aroused, the reporter approached the silver-haired gent. From long practice, the man with the beautiful swing shook his head, put his finger to his lips, and said, "Just helping out." Some things are more important than a good story. The reporter nodded and walked away.

The quiet batting expert was Joe DiMaggio. It was all in a day's work for the Yankee Clipper, but the reporter, my father, never forgot that moment. Unlike those kids, none of us are likely to get Hall of Fame-caliber help just when we most need it. Unless, that is, we're using WordPerfect—if there was a Hall of Fame for computer help, WordPerfect's would be elected on the first ballot.

On-screen help for what you see on the screen

When you first start using WordPerfect, your most frequent question is likely to be, "What does *that* do, and how do I use it?"

Point at a button on the Toolbar—you see a little label (or **QuickTip**) with the button's name. A description of what the button does appears in the title bar at the same time. If that just raises more questions, WordPerfect supplies a nifty tool to get the answers.

Press Shift+F1, and the mouse pointer grows a little question mark, as shown in figure 3.1.

Fig. 3.1
Press Shift+F1, and click a button when the QuickTip and title bar description don't provide enough information.

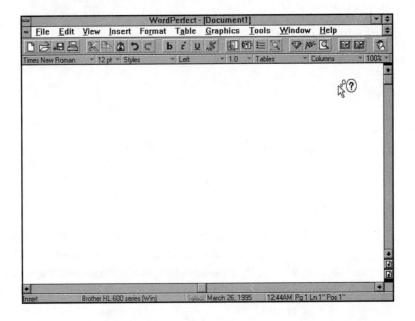

Now click a Toolbar, Power Bar, or status bar button—or anywhere else, for that matter—and a Help window pops up with complete details on how to use that WordPerfect feature. Clicking the Coach button with the pointer question mark got us the help explanation shown in figure 3.2.

Fig. 3.2
These handy help windows describe WordPerfect features and provide step-by-step instructions.

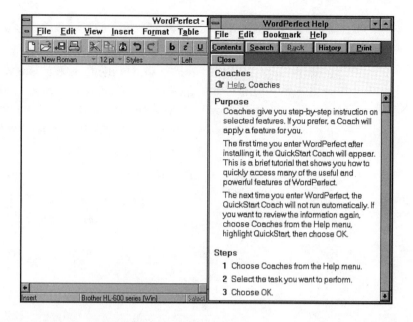

This Coach is a winner

Suppose the WordPerfect manual is nowhere handy, and good old Uncle Fred palmed your copy of *Using WordPerfect* on his last visit. Meanwhile, you have a pile of labels to print up, and no idea of how to do it. No problem. Just click the Coach button.

WordPerfect Coaches can't do anything for your batting average, but they do guide you, step-by-step, through over two dozen WordPerfect features, some of which you see listed in the Coaches dialog box in figure 3.3.

Fig. 3.3
WordPerfect Coaches show you exactly what to do, and they don't ever get annoyed, no matter how many times you ask them for help!

Hey Coach, how do I do labels?

Scroll down the list of features and double-click Labels in the Coaches dialog box, then click the Continue button in the Creating Labels box that pops up next. You get the Coach's instruction to choose Labels from the Format menu. Click the Show Me button in the Coach's box, and watch your mouse pointer travel across the screen and select the Format menu for you, as shown in figure 3.4.

Fig. 3.4

You'll think your mouse has come to life as you watch the pointer skitter across the screen on its own.

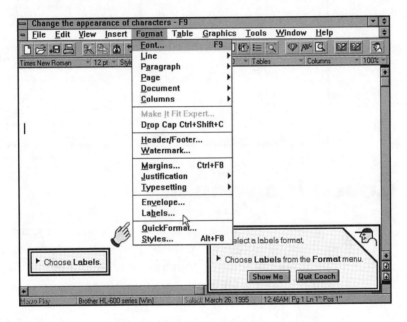

Click Labels on the Format menu for the Labels dialog box, and the Coach will guide you through each step of label creation. You can continue or you can exit at any time. Click Quit Coach to send him back to the locker room.

Press F1 for all the help

Helpful as they are, Coaches only cover a relative handful of WordPerfect features. For comprehensive help, press F1 (or select Contents from the Help menu) for the WordPerfect Help Contents window, shown in figure 3.5.

Fig. 3.5
Just about anything
you can do in
WordPerfect is covered
by the help system.

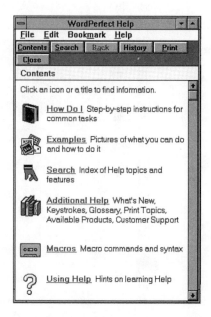

How do I...

Click How Do I in the Help Contents window for the Indexes window. Like a shelf of instruction manuals, the Indexes window holds a complete set of step-by-step instructions on WordPerfect tasks.

Click any topic—for example, Print Documents—and the corresponding book icon springs open to show all the subtopics, like chapters in a book. Click any of those chapters, for example—Print Document—and you get a list of all the subjects covered in the chapter, as shown in figure 3.6.

Fig. 3.6
Working your way
through help can be
like peeling away an
onion layer by layer.
No tears, though.

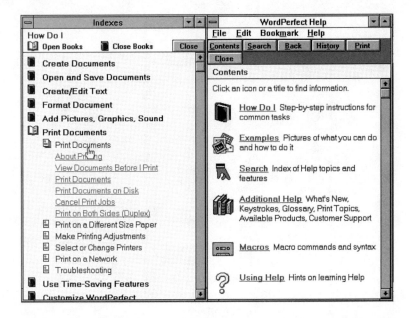

Click any of those subjects for a help window with instructions, general information, and a list of related topics. Those related topics, called **jump terms,** have a solid underline. Click any of them—for example, View Documents Before I Print—to "jump" directly to that topic.

You'll also see **glossary terms,** such as directory dialog box, shown with a broken underline. Click a glossary term and a definition pops up, as shown in figure 3.7.

Fig. 3.7

If Help uses an
unfamiliar term,
chances are it'll have
a broken underline.
Click for a definition.

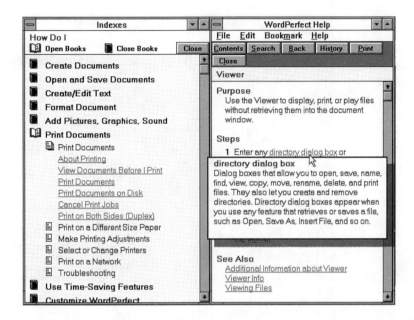

When you're through with Help, press Esc to close Help and return to your document.

(Tip)

> You'll also see little light bulbs scattered throughout the text in the help windows. Click the light bulb for a useful **Hint** relating to the topic you're looking up.

Help by example

Click Examples in the Help Contents window for seven examples of common types of documents. They're shown as pictures in the Examples window. Click any of the pictures, and a blow-up appears to the right of the original pictures, with arrows pointing to each of the specialized elements in the document.

Click an arrow for instructions on how to create that element for yourself, as shown in figure 3.8.

Fig. 3.8

When you have a specialized document to create, check the examples in Help first.

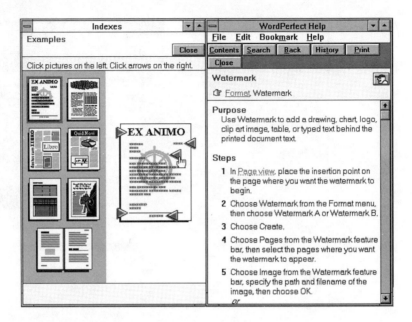

Searching for Help

How Do I and Examples are great for browsing, but if you have a specific topic you want help with, click Search in the Help Contents window. That pops up the Search dialog box, which is the express route to useful help. Type in the first few letters of your topic in the Word edit box. The Show Topics box scrolls to your chosen topic.

Double-click the highlighted topic or click Show Topics, and the subtopics appear in the Go To box. Double-click the one you want, and you get (finally) the specific help you're after. This really is the quickest way to specific help, although it's probably easier done than said. Figure 3.9 shows you the Search dialog box in action.

Fig. 3.9

Click any of the topics in the Go To box for the corresponding help window.

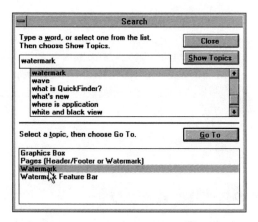

Help! I'm lost in Help!

There's a lot of help in WordPerfect Help, and once you start flipping from topic to sub-topic, it's easy to lose sight of the subject you were after in the first place.

Click <u>B</u>ack in the Help dialog box to work your way back through all the help topics you've looked at, one by one. Or click His<u>t</u>ory to see a list of every help topic you've visited on this trip to Help.

If you know you want to revisit a topic, but you want to go on to related subtopics first, click Book<u>m</u>ark to create a mark to hold your place. You can also click the <u>P</u>rint button to print any help topic.

 Q&A

I had a Help window popped up, but when I switched away from WordPerfect, it disappeared when I came back. What gives?

WordPerfect Help is actually a program in its own right. Switching away from help is just like switching away from any other Windows application. Use Alt+Tab to cycle through your open programs to get help back. Or press Ctrl+Esc to display the Windows Task List, and select WordPerfect Help from the list.

(Tip)

> If you want to display your help topic alongside your work as you go through the steps of a task, click <u>H</u>elp, Always on <u>T</u>op on the Help dialog box menu. That puts the help window over your WordPerfect document. If the window gets in the way, click and drag an edge of the Help dialog box to change its size, and click and drag the title bar to move the dialog box to a different location.

Help is on the menu

<u>H</u>elp on the menu bar lets you get directly at the Coaches, Search dialog box, and How Do I topics. Click <u>T</u>utorial on the <u>H</u>elp menu for WordPerfect's built-in tutorial on basic WordPerfect operations.

If you've been using another word processing program, or if you've just upgraded from an earlier version of WordPerfect, take a look at the <u>U</u>pgrade Expert on the <u>H</u>elp menu.

Figure 3.10 shows the Upgrade Expert dialog box.

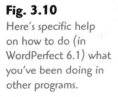
Fig. 3.10
Here's specific help on how to do (in WordPerfect 6.1) what you've been doing in other programs.

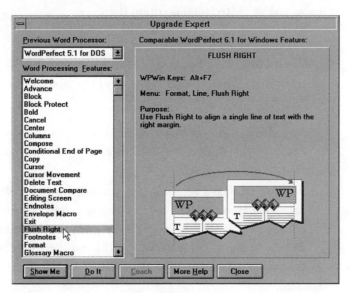

Choose what you previously used from the Previous Word Processor drop-down menu. Then select the feature you want to know about from the Word Processing Features list, and click the Show Me button. Your mouse pointer goes on auto-pilot and skitters straight to the WordPerfect 6.1 command for that feature.

Help in WordPerfect is not only helpful, it's also fun to play around with. Try it.

 Many dialog boxes in WordPerfect have their own help buttons. Click Help for specific help on that dialog box's topic.

Help you can talk to

WordPerfect's customer support by telephone is famous. You get real people at the other end of the line who can actually answer your questions. Amazing, but true—I've used it myself. If you can't find the answer in this book, the manual, or in WordPerfect Help, pick up the phone.

Click Help, Contents, Additional Help, Customer Support to view the various toll-free help numbers. You'll need to have sent in your registration card, and you'll also need your serial number (it's found on the registration card). If it's your first call to customer support, you'll be given a PIN (Personal Identification Number), which you use for subsequent calls.

There's a safe place to store both your serial number and your PIN in the program itself. Click Help, About WordPerfect, Edit Serial Number/PIN. Enter both numbers and click OK. The next time you call customer support, pop up the About WordPerfect dialog box for your serial and PIN numbers.

4 Good Writing Means Rewriting: Editing Text

What the food processor does for preparing food, the word processor does for editing text: it makes the job fast, fun, and accurate.

There are as many different writing styles as there are writers, but there's one thing every writer has in common. Whether it's a three-line memo or a three-volume novel, writing it usually requires some rewriting.

P.G. Wodehouse wrote over eighty novels at the typewriter (including those Jeeves and Wooster stories beloved by Masterpiece Theater). His style is famous for its witty ease; he called his stories musical comedies without the music. To get that effect, he wrote, and wrote again. Wodehouse sometimes rewrote a page eight times before he was satisfied. When he finished a page, he'd tape it to the wall at an angle. Each successive rewrite would be taped alongside at progressively less acute angles. When the page was right, it went on the wall perfectly straight.

WordPerfect spares us from having to use dodges like that. Rewriting, editing, and shifting text around is fast and easy. Our results might not read as effortlessly as Wodehouse's (nobody's do), but we'll have expended much less effort to get them.

Inserting, for everyday writing

Typing new text into a WordPerfect document is like shoving aside books on a shelf to make room for a new one. As you type, characters are entered at the insertion point, and any text that's already in the document gets pushed to the right.

That also goes for spaces, tabs, or blank lines—insert any of them into a document, and existing text is shoved to the right (or down, in the case of blank lines). Figure 4.1 shows where existing text moves when you insert more text and a blank line.

Fig. 4.1

Add new text, spaces, blank lines, or tabs; existing text moves aside to make room for it.

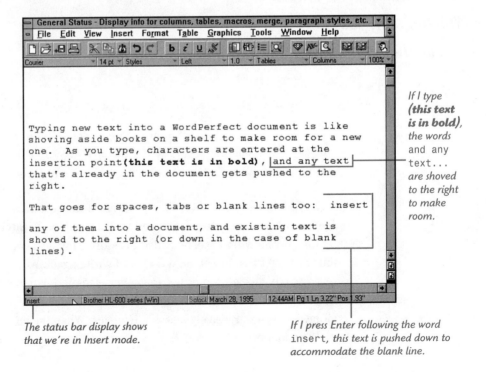

If I type (this text is in bold), the words and any text... are shoved to the right to make room.

The status bar display shows that we're in Insert mode.

If I press Enter following the word insert, this text is pushed down to accommodate the blank line.

How do I get the insertion point where I want it?

To move the insertion point to the "t" in the word "point" in figure 4.1, I put the mouse pointer I-beam next to the letter and clicked. That's a fast way of getting the insertion point from one place to another.

But if you need to move the insertion point past the current window of text, or if you don't want to lift your fingers from the keyboard, you've got the other options listed in table 4.1.

Table 4.1   Moving the insertion point around a document

To move the insertion point...	Press
One word to the right	Ctrl+Right Arrow
One word to the left	Ctrl+Left Arrow
To beginning of next paragraph	Ctrl+Down Arrow
To beginning of previous paragraph	Ctrl+Up Arrow
To end of line	End
To beginning of line	Home
To beginning of document	Ctrl+Home
To end of document	Ctrl+End
To top of next page	Alt+PageDown
To top of previous page	Alt+PageUp
To top of editing window	PageUp
To bottom of editing window	PageDown

 **{Note}**

When you move the insertion point past the current window, the display scrolls along with the insertion point. To scroll the display without moving the insertion point, use the scroll bars.

Typeover, an occasional option

When you start up WordPerfect, the program is in Insert mode—inserted text or spacing moves existing text down or to the right.

Double-click the status bar Insert button (refer to fig. 4.1), and WordPerfect switches to **Typeover** mode. The status bar displays Typeover, and any new text you type or spacing you add overwrites existing text instead of pushing it aside. Like a painter painting over an old canvas, existing text is blotted out as you type in the new.

Typeover might be handy for a quick, one-word editing job. Trouble is, if the new word is longer than the old one, the extra characters wipe out part of the next word on the line, too. It's safer to use Insert mode to add new text, and then delete any existing text you don't want.

 If you type over text by mistake in Typeover mode, you can restore the text by clicking the Undo button on the toolbar.

 To toggle between Typeover and Insert modes, press the Insert key on your keyboard.

Deleting text: no white-out needed

Remember all the gear we used to use to delete typescript? There was the bottle of white-out that always dried up, the strips of white correction tape that stuck to the fingers, and good old corrasable bond paper, guaranteed to smudge every time.

With WordPerfect, we can heave all that stuff out with the rest of the trash. Deleting in WordPerfect is cleaner and easier. Best of all, if you delete something and change your mind, you can get it back again.

Press the Delete key to delete one character to the right of the insertion point; press Backspace to delete one character to the left of the insertion point. The other deletion options are shown in table 4.2.

Table 4.2 Deleting text in WordPerfect

To delete...	Press
The word adjacent to or enclosing the insertion point	Ctrl+Backspace
From the insertion point to the end of the line	Ctrl+Delete
Any highlighted text	Delete

Changed your mind? Undelete

If you're a tough critic of your own writing, you'll find selecting and deleting text a great way to trim excess verbiage. If you're too tough, you might delete something you want back again.

That's no problem. Just click Edit, Undelete. The deleted text reappears highlighted at the insertion point. You also get the Undelete dialog box shown in figure 4.2.

Fig. 4.2
The highlighted line was deleted; it's about to be Undeleted.

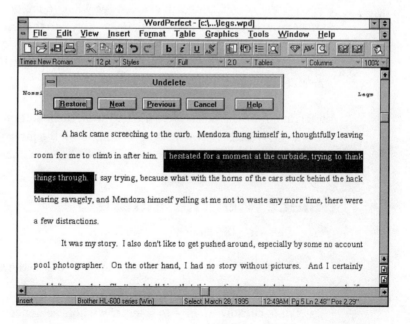

Click Restore to reinsert the deleted text at the insertion point.

Undelete can restore your last three deletions. Click Next or Previous to cycle through them until you find what you want to restore.

 (Tip)

> If the Undelete dialog box is blocking text you want to see, point at the dialog box title bar and drag the dialog box out of the way.

Selecting text for minor and major alterations

Editing in WordPerfect is speedy because the program lets you operate on as much of a document as you want at the same time. Whether you're moving, deleting, copying, or formatting, the basic idea is the same—select the text, then apply the command to the selection.

Select with the keyboard

Selected text is highlighted so you can see what you're doing. Pressing Shift+Arrow key selects text in whatever direction the arrow is pointing. Pressing Shift in combination with any of the insertion point movement commands in table 4.1 highlights everything from where the insertion point started to where the command moved it.

Shift+End, for example, selects the text from the insertion point to the end of the line. Ctrl+Shift+End selects everything from the insertion point to the end of the document. Figure 4.3 shows a selected line in a document.

Select with the mouse

You can also use the mouse to select text:

- Double-click a word to select the entire word to the beginning of the next word.

- Triple-click a sentence to select the whole sentence to the beginning of the next sentence.

- Quadruple-click a paragraph to select the entire paragraph to the beginning of the next paragraph.

Fig. 4.3
Selected text is high-lighted so you can see exactly what you're doing.

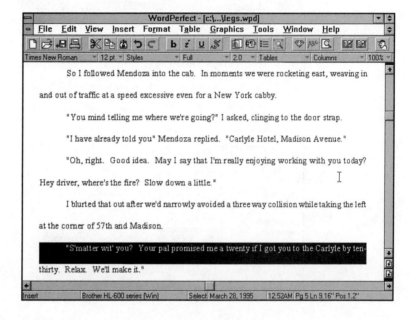

That triple-click to select a sentence is particularly handy. With some word processors, selecting a single sentence in a paragraph without unintentionally grabbing parts of the adjacent text can be tricky. The WordPerfect triple-click makes sentence selection foolproof.

(Tip)

> Another speedy selection option: move the pointer to the left margin. Point at a sentence with the white arrow and click to select it. Double-click to select the entire paragragh.

Select from the QuickMenu

If you find these click combinations hard to keep track of, or if you want to select a whole page, position the insertion point where you want to select text, and then move the pointer to the left margin. When the pointer changes from an I-beam to a white arrow, right-click for the QuickMenu shown in figure 4.4.

Fig. 4.4
Use this QuickMenu
to select text as an
alternative to the
keyboard or multiple
mouse clicks.

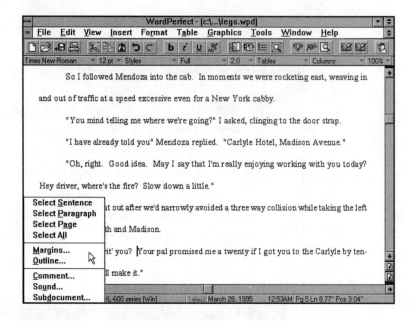

To deselect text, just press one of the arrow keys.

Selecting text is a drag

You probably won't remember all the click combinations and insertion point movement commands, at least when you first start using WordPerfect. That's okay, because you can also select text by dragging through it. Click at the beginning of the selection, hold down the mouse button, and drag until you get to the end of the selection.

> To add more to your selection without starting over after you release the mouse button, press Shift and drag again.

Go To, the insertion point express

When you know where you want the insertion point to go, and you want to get it there fast, click Edit, Go To or press Ctrl+G. Either method pops up the Go To dialog box shown in figure 4.5.

Fig. 4.5
Use the Go To dialog
box for fast insertion
point moves.

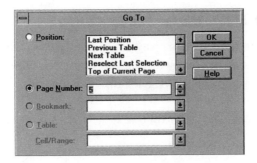

Click Page <u>N</u>umber, enter the page you want to get to, and click OK to go
straight to the beginning of that page. Click <u>P</u>osition and choose one of
the options on the list to move the insertion point to various spots in the
document.

What can I do with selected text?

You have a lot of different options for selecting text in WordPerfect. Once
selected, what do you do with it? The short answer is just about anything you
want to do. By now we know we can delete text by selecting it and pressing
Delete. But that's just for starters.

Cut and Paste it

You can put that glue stick and scissors in the same place where you put the
white-out. Cutting and pasting in WordPerfect is a push-button affair. To cut
text from one part of a document and paste it somewhere else:

1 Select the text by any of the various methods.

 2 Click the Cut button on the toolbar.

3 The cut text is moved to the Windows Clipboard and saved there until
you need it.

4 Move the insertion point to where you want the text to reappear.

 5 Click the Paste button on the toolbar. The text reappears at the insertion point.

This works for anything from a single character to an entire document.

Make a smudge-free copy

Copy and paste text the same way you cut and paste it. Just click the Copy button on the toolbar after selecting your text. Move the insertion point to where you want the copy, then click the Paste button.

You get a perfect copy every time!

Undo and Redo forgive mistakes, repeat successes

Everybody does it. Something about what you've just written bugs you. So you start to slice and dice, deleting words and moving sentences and paragraphs around with cut and paste. Then you look at it again and think, "This was better the way it was before."

WordPerfect lets you change your mind about your last several editing changes. Select Edit, Undo/Redo History for the dialog box shown in figure 4.6.

Fig. 4.6
Undo/Redo is a great tool for the editorially indecisive.

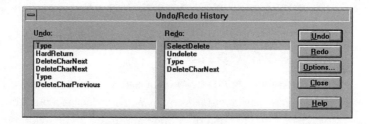

Your editing changes are displayed under Undo. Select an item, and all the preceding items are automatically selected, too. Then click the Undo button in the dialog box, and all the editing changes you've selected are reversed. Deleted text is restored, moved text is moved back to where it was originally, and even format changes are reversed.

 **{Note}** Undo is sequential. For example, you can't choose to undo only the fifth item in the list.

I want those edits back!

Any editing you've undone will appear under Re<u>d</u>o in the Undo/Redo History dialog box. If you change your mind again, select those edits under Re<u>d</u>o and click the <u>R</u>edo button in the dialog box. That restores the edits you've just undone.

 Undelete restores deleted text at the insertion point. Undo restores deleted text to its original location.

  To Undo or Redo just your last action, click the Undo or Redo button on the toolbar.

Undo and Redo let you edit fearlessly. Since anything you cut or move can be restored or moved back, you can tinker without worrying about doing permanent editorial damage to your document.

How many times can I change my mind?

Undo is very forgiving. WordPerfect starts you off with ten saved edits, but you can save up to three hundred editing changes for later undoing or redoing. You can even save the changes right along with the document.

Click the <u>O</u>ptions button in the Undo/Redo History dialog box and select the <u>N</u>umber of Undo/Redo items you want to keep.

 The more Undo/Redo items you save, the bigger your document. If you run into memory problems or find that WordPerfect is slowing down too much, try saving fewer Undo/Redo items.

Reveal codes take you behind the scenes

Actors doing their stuff on the stage look natural, but they're really just following stage directions. An actor walks off in a huff and it looks like part of the action. Actually, the director has told him, "Exit stage right." What you see is controlled by someone behind the scenes.

WordPerfect documents are peppered with "stage directions" called **codes**. Codes are instructions to WordPerfect on what to do with text. WordPerfect inserts some codes automatically, like the soft-return codes at the end of lines of text. Some codes are inserted when you type a keyboard command. Press Enter, for example, and you're actually inserting a hard-return code.

Just as you don't see the stage directions when you go to a play, you don't see the codes in the editing window. Instead, you view and edit them in the **reveal codes** window.

Opening the reveal codes window

Click <u>V</u>iew, Reveal <u>C</u>odes and the reveal codes window appears, as shown in figure 4.7.

Title bar description of the code

Fig. 4.7
The reveal codes window lets you view and edit WordPerfect's "stage directions" for text.

Hard-return code

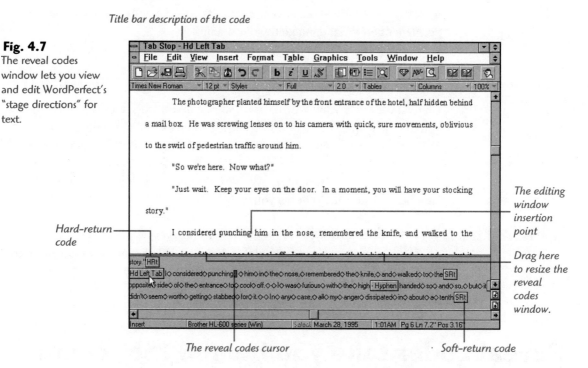

The editing window insertion point

Drag here to resize the reveal codes window.

The reveal codes cursor

Soft-return code

The text in the editing window is mirrored in the reveal codes window, but now you can see the codes that WordPerfect uses to control the text in documents.

Every code appears as a raised button. The reveal codes window cursor shown in figure 4.7 apes the editing window insertion point—as you move the insertion point in the editing window, the reveal codes window cursor moves through the text with it.

If you want to know what a code is for, point at it. A description appears in the title bar (refer to fig. 4.7).

And if you point at the border between the editing and reveal codes windows, the pointer changes to a double arrow. Drag the double arrow to resize the reveal codes window.

 (Tip)

> You can get the reveal codes window more quickly by pressing Alt+F3 or by clicking the right mouse button on the text area and choosing Reveal Codes from the QuickMenu.

Now that I can see the codes, what do I do with them?

Wonderful as they are, word processors like WordPerfect can sometimes drive you nuts. If you accidentally hit the Tab key, or lean on the spacebar, or make a similar but not too obvious mistake, your document might look odd. Those unnecessary spaces or tabs (I tend to hit the Return key when I don't want it) can give documents a curiously gap-toothed appearance.

It's hard to see extra tabs and blank lines in the editing window, so pop up the reveal codes window, move the insertion point next to the unwanted tab or hard-return code, and press Delete to get rid of it.

Using reveal codes to delete unwanted italics

The reveal codes window is especially useful for getting rid of formatting you don't want. In the editing window, it's not obvious where the formatting codes are, while they're easy to spot in the reveal codes window. Try the following example and you'll see what I mean.

1 Type **This line contains a needlessly italicized word.**

2 Double-click the word italicized to select it, and click the Italics button on the toolbar to italicize the word. Then click to the left of the word to turn off the highlighting.

3 Now click View, Reveal Codes. The result should look like figure 4.8.

Fig. 4.8
Clicking the Italics button causes WordPerfect to insert these italics codes.

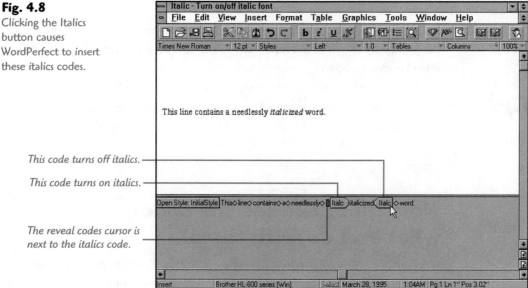

This code turns off italics.

This code turns on italics.

The reveal codes cursor is next to the italics code.

4 Move the reveal codes cursor so that it's adjacent to one of the italics codes.

5 Press Delete or Backspace, as necessary, and the italics vanish.

Get rid of unwanted codes fast by dragging them out of the reveal codes window. Drag a code in any direction; when you release the mouse button, the code is deleted.

Find and Replace: better than any lost and found

If I had to vote on the single handiest feature in WordPerfect, I'd pick the Edit, Find and Replace command. You use it to find every occurrence of a word or code in a document, automatically. You can then replace the word or code with whatever you substitute in its place. You can even get rid of every occurrence of the offending word or code by replacing it with nothing.

If you've just finished a three-hundred page novel and you decide that you hate your protagonist's name, use Find and Replace to change it to something better, wherever the name occurs. Or maybe you've written a long client letter, mentioned the client's name fifty times, and then realized that you've misspelled it every time. It takes only a few seconds to Find and Replace the misspelled name with the correct spelling.

First, Find it...

Suppose we have a short story on our hands, one of whose characters is an editor named Mel Shott. The name occurs many times throughout the story. After seeing the name "Mel" once too many times, we decide to replace it with "Oscar" throughout the document.

Select Edit, Find and Replace for the Find and Replace Text dialog box. Type **Mel** in the Find edit box and **Oscar** in the Replace With edit box, as shown in figure 4.9.

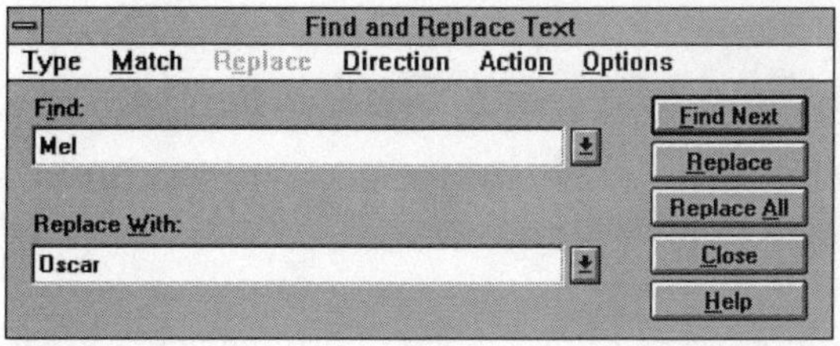

Fig. 4.9
Notice how the Find and Replace Text dialog box has its own menu bar to accommodate all the options.

 **{Note}** If you just want to find text or a code without replacing it, leave the Replace With box blank. Then click the Find Next button.

Although the Replace All button looks tempting, we won't use it. Clicking Replace All does indeed replace all occurrences of whatever you've typed in the Find edit box with whatever's typed in the Replace With edit box.

But Find can be too thorough. It'll find *every* occurrence of (in this example) the letters "mel," no matter what the context. Figure 4.10 shows how Find's thoroughness can lead to problems.

Fig. 4.10

Find has found the "mel" in "smelled." Replace All would have given us "soscarled" here!

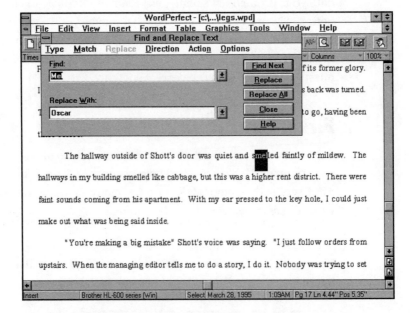

Getting specific with Find

Find's enthusiasm needs to be tempered with further instructions. Select Match for the following options:

- Whole Word is what we want here. Select it when you want to find a word like Mel, instead of the letters "mel" wherever they occur.

- Case matches either upper or lowercase, not both. Since we're only interested in occurrences of the proper name Mel, capital M, we'll select Case to further refine our search.

- <u>F</u>ont pops up the Font dialog box and lets you search for any font attribute you choose. For example, you can search for "Mel" in italics, or text in a specific typeface.

Remember those codes you saw in Reveal Codes? You can find any of them by selecting C<u>o</u>des to pop up the dialog box shown in figure 4.11. Double-click any code on the list to enter it in either the <u>F</u>ind or Replace <u>W</u>ith edit box. If you're hunting for specific codes in a document, this is a handy tool.

Fig. 4.11
The Codes dialog box lists WordPerfect formatting and wildcard codes.

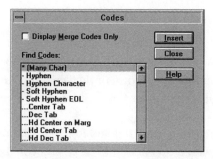

You can also use the Codes dialog box to search for words that contain unknown characters. Suppose you're looking for a word in the document, but you're not sure of the spelling. Type the first letter or two, then choose one of the **wild card** codes from the Codes dialog box.

Say you're looking for the word "bowdlerize" but you can't remember the exact spelling (I cheated and looked it up). Type **bow** in the F<u>i</u>nd edit box and double-click the *(Many Char) code highlighted in figure 4.11. <u>F</u>ind will stop at each occurrence of the **text string** bow, followed by several other characters. That would turn up bowdlerize, but you'd also find bowsprit and bow-chaser.

" Plain English, please!

A **text string** is a word or part of a word that you enter in a search. **Wild cards** are substitute characters that represent unknown characters in word or text string. The asterisk (*) represents a range of characters. For example, **mark*** finds market, marker, or marks. A question mark (?) represents just one unknown character. For example, **part?** finds parts or party, but not parties. **"**

Which way does Find search?

Find starts its search at the insertion point and continues to the end of the document. If the insertion point doesn't happen to be at the top of the document, click Options and choose Begin at Top of Document.

Wrap at Beg./End of Document starts the search from the insertion point and finishes back at the same place.

Finding, finding, found!

Suppose you're describing a local election to an English chum. Where we say "so-and-so ran for Congress," the English say "so-and-so stood for Congress." WordPerfect lets you find every form of the verb "run" in a document so that you can replace it with equivalent forms of "stand" for your transatlantic pal.

Select Type, Word Forms in the Find and Replace Text dialog box. Type **run** in the Find edit box and then click Find Next, and you'll come up with "run," "running," and "ran." Type **stand** in the Replace With edit box and you'll get "stood," "standing," and "stand" in the appropriate contexts.

 Word Forms won't find the noun "runner" in that example, though—just the tenses of the verb.

...then Replace it

Once you've specified exactly what it is you're finding and replacing, you have three choices for proceeding further:

- Click the Find Next button for the cautious approach. Find will stop at the first occurrence of the word and highlight it. Click the Replace button to replace it, or click the Find Next button to skip to the next occurrence of the word.

- Click the Replace button for the moderately cautious approach. That replaces the first occurrence of the word and stops at the next occurrence.

- Click Replace <u>A</u>ll and throw caution to the winds. It's a good idea to save your document first, in case you want to return to the original version after Find and Replace has finished.

Using Replace to delete words

To delete a recurring word in a document, type the word in the <u>F</u>ind box, leave the Replace <u>W</u>ith box blank, and click the <u>R</u>eplace button at each occurrence of the word. That replaces the word with nothing, which is the same thing as deleting it, at least as far as WordPerfect is concerned.

5

Formatting for Characters with Character

Documents, like people, make an impression. Format your text for eye-appeal, and your readers' first impression will be a good one.

In this chapter:

- I want to format text fast!

- When do I use italics? Underlining? Boldface?

- Just what is a font?

- I want to change fonts

- How do I know what font to use?

- Dropped caps create a nifty effect

Formatting refers to everything that has to do with the appearance of a document. So does it really matter? At least one fine American writer thought so. E. E. Cummings' great World War I novel, *The Enormous Room*, uses all kinds of formatting tricks to good effect. Cummings left out the spaces after commas to make his narrative livelier. He separated the lines in some of his dialogues with dashes to make the conversations more energetic. He capitalized certain words for emphasis. And Cummings did it all with a typewriter, which required a lot of inventiveness.

With WordPerfect, formatting text is easy and routine. There are also more formatting options in WordPerfect than you'll ever need. How might *The Enormous Room* have looked written in WordPerfect instead of at the typewriter? We can't know for sure, but one thing is certain: Cummings, and his readers, would have had a field day.

Formatting at the push of a button

Suppose the local gym decided to experiment with the soap and shampoo supplied in the shower room. The new stuff is awful. A strong memo is called for, something along the lines of the one in figure 5.1.

Fig. 5.1
Don't laugh—it can happen. Best to nip it in the bud with a memo that gets their attention.

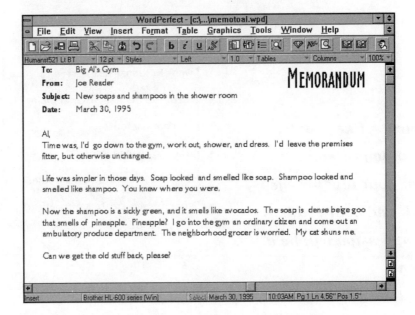

(Tip)

To create a memo in the format shown in figure 5.1, click the New Document button on the Toolbar, select Memo in the New Document dialog box, and double-click Memo-Cosmopolitan. Then follow the prompts.

Boldly go where no one else has gone

The memo in figure 5.1 expresses our feelings reasonably clearly, but we can pitch it a little stronger without rewriting.

Making text **bold** is an easy way of emphasizing key words or phrases. Select the text you want in boldface, then click the Bold button on the Toolbar. That's all there is to it.

We'll double-click the word soap in the memo to select it, then click the Bold button on the Toolbar. Figure 5.2 shows the result.

Fig. 5.2
Boldface makes text jump off the page.

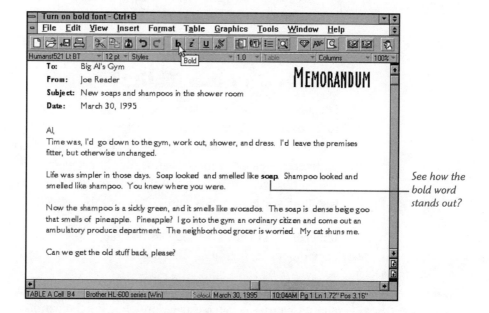

See how the bold word stands out?

To apply boldface to text you're about to type, you can click the Bold button on the Toolbar to turn on boldfacing, type the word, then click the Bold button again to turn off boldfacing. You might find it easier to use Ctrl+B to turn boldfacing on and off while you're typing.

Q&A

I pressed Ctrl+B for bold, and now everything I type is bold! What do I do?

You forgot to press Ctrl+B at the end of the text you wanted boldfaced. That turns off bold. To get rid of boldfacing on text, select the text, and either click the Bold button on the Toolbar or press Ctrl+B. This works for italics and underlining too—select the text, then click the appropriate Toolbar buttons to clear unwanted formatting.

(Tip)

To apply boldface to a single word, place the insertion point in the word, and press Ctrl+B. You don't have to select the word first. (This also works for italics and underlining.)

When do I use italics?

Like boldface, *italics* add emphasis, but give a subtler effect. You use italics for book, newspaper, or magazine titles, and for foreign language words in English text. Italics can also be used to express scorn, especially scorn for a particular choice of word or words. Book reviewers are fond of quoting awkwardly written or overwritten passages and italicizing them, as though to say, "Can you *believe* this trash?" Not nice, but effective.

Italicizing text works the same as boldfacing text. Just select the text, then click the Italics button on the Toolbar.

 Let's italicize the word Pineapple in the memo to emphasis our feelings about toiletries scented thusly. Double-click the word, and click the Italics button on the Toolbar.

Figure 5.3 shows the result.

Fig. 5.3
When bold might be too bold, try italics to get your point across.

Italics add emphasis

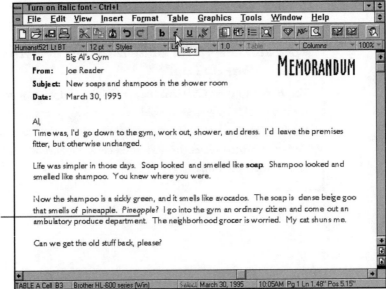

You can click the Italics button on the Toolbar to turn italics on and off while you're typing, or press Ctrl+I.

 Plain English, please!

Boldface, italics, and underlining are called the **attributes**, or, in WordPerfect, the **appearance**, of characters. **"**

Underline for emphasis

Underlining for emphasis is pretty obvious. It's even a figure of speech, as in "let me underline this point." No surprises in applying underlining: select the text and click the Underline button on the Toolbar.

 We'll double-click `please` in the last sentence of our memo to select it, then click the Underline button on the Toolbar for the result seen in figure 5.4.

Fig. 5.4
It's not exactly E. E. Cummings, but this memo now packs a little more punch.

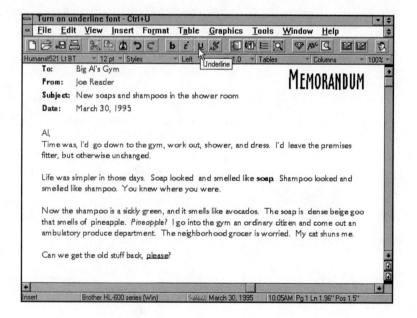

Applying underlining as you type works just the same as applying boldfacing or italics; click the Toolbar button to turn on underlining, type, then click again to turn it off. Or press Ctrl+U to turn underlining on and off.

What are fonts?

Build a house, and you might use stone, brick, and wood for the exterior. When you create a document, the exterior consists of **fonts**. Just as a builder might use one or a combination of materials, you create documents with one or more fonts and font sizes.

> 66 *Plain English, please!*
>
> You often see fonts and typefaces used interchangeably. Technically, there is a difference, although for most of us, it's not terribly important. **Typefaces**, or **font faces**, are those character types whose names you see on the Power Bar and in the Font dialog box. Times New Roman is a typeface and can be found in various sizes and with different attributes (bold, italic, and so on.) A **font** is just one size and style of a typeface. 99

WordPerfect makes it so easy to change fonts that you can wind up overdoing it. Too many fonts in one document distracts the reader's eye and makes for a cluttered page.

Figure 5.5 shows the distracting effect of too many different fonts on the page.

Fig. 5.5
The patchwork look gets in the way of the document's message.

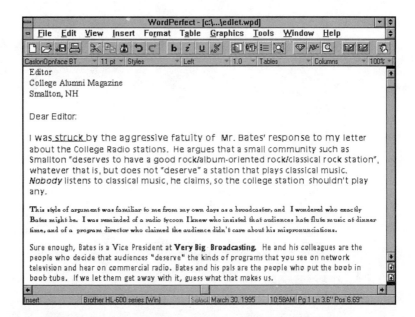

How do I change font faces and sizes?

WordPerfect comes with many different fonts. Windows has fonts of its own, and your printer has fonts, too. When you install WordPerfect, the program sniffs out all your fonts so that you can get at them right from WordPerfect.

When you start up WordPerfect, you get Times New Roman in 12-point size by default. You'll see Times New Roman and 12 pt displayed on the first two buttons at the left of the Power Bar. To switch to a different font face, click the Font Face Power Bar button for the drop-down list shown in figure 5.6.

Fig. 5.6

The first button on the Power Bar displays the current font face.

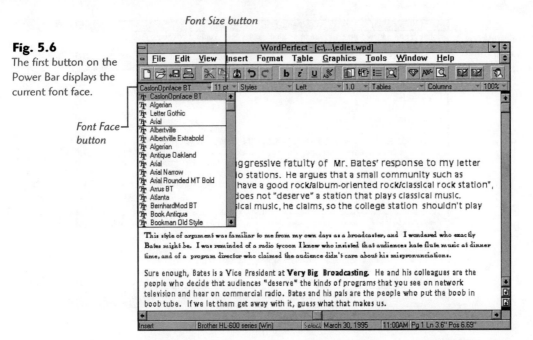

Font Size button

Font Face button

Click any of the font faces on the list, and all the text from the insertion point to the end of the document changes to the new face.

If you want to apply a font only to selected text, first select the text and then choose a new font face. This way, only the selection is changed. To change the font size, click the Font Size button on the Power Bar, and select a point size from the list. Either selected text or text from the insertion point on will be resized.

Figure 5.7 shows Times New Roman in different point sizes.

Fig. 5.7
WordPerfect lets your documents whisper or shriek with different-sized type.

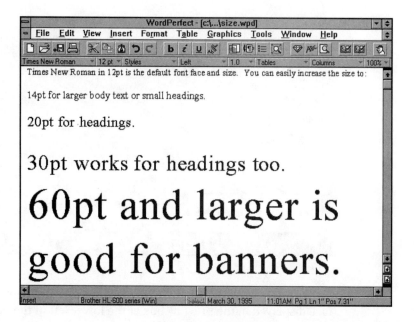

Plain English, please!

Point size is typesetter's jargon for the size, or height of the characters. There are 72 points in an inch; when a newspaper cranks up its headlines to a shriek, it uses 72-point, or one-inch, type.

How can I tell what those font faces look like?

The Power Bar makes changing font faces convenient and fast. But unless you know what each of those many faces looks like, how do you know what you're getting when you select one?

Click Format, Font for the Font dialog box shown in figure 5.8.

Fig. 5.8

Use the Font dialog box to preview and make font selections.

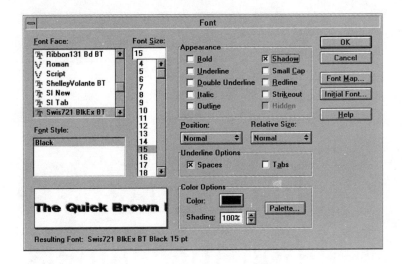

Make your selection from the Font Face list, and view the sample of the font face displayed in the preview box at the lower left of the dialog box.

The sample changes to reflect your choice of Font Size and Appearance, too. Experiment with Shadow and Outline for special effects. WordPerfect gives you a lot of flexibility, and if you don't like the results, you can always Cancel, or make other changes.

When you're finished with the Font dialog box, click OK; all the changes you've made take effect from the insertion point to the end of the document. If you've selected text, the settings affect only the selection.

Other font options

From the Font dialog box, apply any of these effects to new or selected text:

- Click the Position button for Superscript or Subscript. Text is displayed and printed at 60% of the selected size, above or below the line, like the "2" in H_2O.

- Relative Size changes text to preset ratios of the selected size. For example, Relative Size, Extra Large makes text twice as large (200%) as the selected point size.

- Click the Color button, and select a color from the color palette that pops up. The color will be displayed on the button, and the colored text will show in the preview window and on the screen. The Palette button lets you modify the color palette. Of course, having a color printer helps if you really want to print in color. However, some colors actually print in very nice shades of gray on a black and white printer.

- Click the Shading arrows and set a value between 0 and 100% for fainter or darker text.

I changed the font at the beginning of my document, but my page numbers and footnotes still use the old font. What am I doing wrong?

Each WordPerfect document has a "document initial font," or base font that affects not only text but also page numbering and footnotes, among other things. If you insert a font code in your document, you affect only text. To change the whole thing, choose the Initial Font button in the Font dialog box, and select the font you want to use.

WordPerfect has a font for every occasion

Changing fonts is easy. Picking the best font for a particular job is a question of taste and judgment. Trial-and-error is a fine way of proceeding until you get to know the various fonts, especially since your choices are always reversible.

These general ideas might help narrow your choices:

- **Serif** fonts are usually used in body text. Serifs are those little "tails" at the beginning and ends of characters like "T" or "M", in typefaces like Times New Roman. Because serifs guide the eye from one character to the next, serif fonts tend to be easier to read in the smaller sizes and in narrative type text. You're reading a serif font right now.

- **Sans Serif** fonts don't have the little tails—Arial is an example. In bigger sizes, they can have an insistent look, which is why sans serif fonts are often used for headlines. They say "look at me." For example, the heading for this section is printed in a sans serif font called High-lander Bold. In smaller text, sans serif fonts are less busy, and thus work well for lists or directories.

Other fonts, like Caslon or Shelly Volante, are more decorative and are usually used for special effects, such as in announcements or formal invitations. Figure 5.9 illustrates some of the choices among serif, sans serif, and decorative fonts.

Fig. 5.9
Experimenting with different fonts is the best way to find the right look for your text.

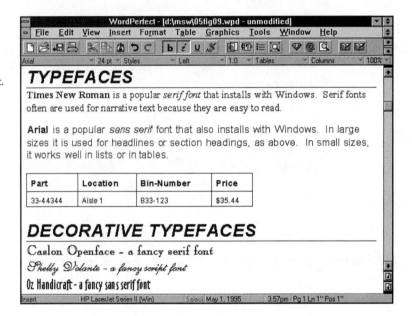

There are no hard and fast rules for any of this, however. **Typography**, the use and design of typefaces, is more art than science. Many newspapers use a famous serif typeface called Bodoni in headlines, for example, and you'll often see sans serif typefaces in body text.

WordPerfect makes it easy to experiment with font faces and their attributes. Go ahead and try different fonts. You can always change your mind later.

Drop caps, for characters with strong character

Drop caps, or dropped capital letters, are enlarged characters that are usually used at the beginning of the first paragraph in a chapter. Anyone who's read aloud to kids knows about drop caps—publishers of fairy tale books love them. There's also a place for drop caps in business reports. They can break up dense body text in an attractive way.

In the Middle Ages, monks would labor for months on magnificent decorated drop caps. WordPerfect lets you do the job in seconds.

How do I get a drop cap?

To create a drop cap, type your paragraph. Then move the insertion point to anywhere in the paragraph and click Format, Drop Cap.

That gives you an instant drop cap and the Drop Cap feature bar, both of which are shown in figure 5.10.

Fig. 5.10
You get a drop cap like this one with two clicks of the mouse.

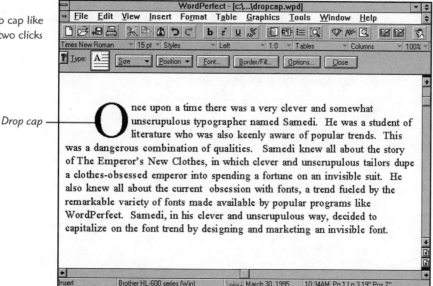

Drop cap

Click the feature bar buttons to change the size, font, and position of the drop cap. You can also select a predefined format for the drop cap from the palette you get by clicking the Type palette button.

Click the Border/Fill button and select Shadow from the Border Style list and 10% Fill from the Fill Style list for the effect shown in figure 5.11.

Fig. 5.11

You can get nifty effects in no time using the Drop Cap feature bar.

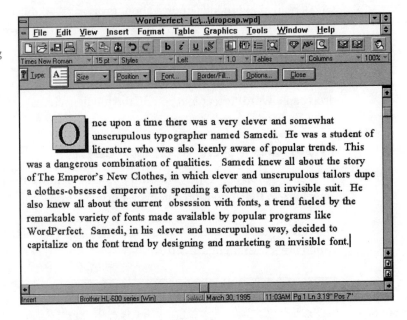

The result isn't exactly an illuminated manuscript. On the other hand, you get your results quite a bit faster.

6 What's My Line? Formatting Paragraphs for Precision and Punch

Pages need visual variety, so we use paragraphs. WordPerfect's paragraph formatting options add punch to pages.

A paragraph expresses a complete thought, or marks a break in a narrative or a discussion. Or does it? Henry James wrote paragraphs that go on for pages. He crammed more thoughts into a single paragraph than you sometimes find in other authors' novels. Colombian Nobel prize-winner Gabriel Garcia Marquez wrote a novel called *Autumn of the Patriarch* with no paragraphs at all.

In fact, there are no strict rules about what makes a paragraph. It's really just a formatting convention (of course, your Freshman Comp professor might disagree, but that's his or her job). Paragraphs break up a page to make it easier to read. Since WordPerfect shines at formatting text, you'd expect it to be pretty helpful in formatting paragraphs. And you'd be absolutely right!

How do I set the margins?

Paragraphs may vary in length and content, but all paragraphs are made up of lines. Formatting a paragraph begins with formatting lines. And since lines begin at the margin, that's where we'll start, too.

WordPerfect starts you out with one-inch left, right, top, and bottom margins. Those settings are fine for most uses, but there'll be times when you want to change the margins. If you're planning to put hole punches in your pages for a bound report, for example, you might want more than a one-inch left margin. Or you might be writing a document with densely packed text, like a contract. You might want less than one-inch margins in that case.

All the margin settings are easily changed, and WordPerfect gives you two different ways to do it:

- If you know what size margins you want, use the <u>M</u>argins command on the Fo<u>r</u>mat menu.

- If you want to see how your page looks with different margin settings as you change them, use the Ruler Bar.

Setting margins from the Format menu

You'll usually use the <u>M</u>argins command to set the margins for an entire page or document. Make sure the insertion point is where you want to change your margins, for example, at the top of the document, then click Fo<u>r</u>mat, <u>M</u>argins to pop up the Margins dialog box shown in figure 6.1.

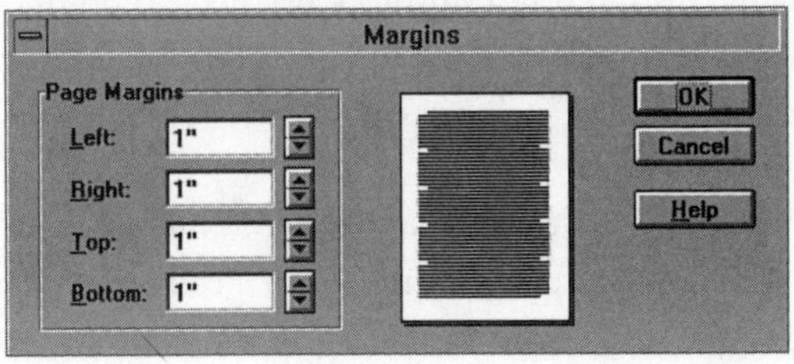

Fig. 6.1
The Margins dialog box gives you precise control over your margins.

Either type new values in the Left, Right, Top, and Bottom edit boxes, or click the arrows to change the settings. The measurements are in inches, from the edge of the page to the beginning of the text. As you change the margin settings, the sample page in the dialog box changes to reflect the new values.

Any changes you make affect the current paragraph (the paragraph where the insertion happens to be) to the end of the document, as shown in figure 6.2.

Fig. 6.2

These two-inch margins take effect in the current paragraph and below.

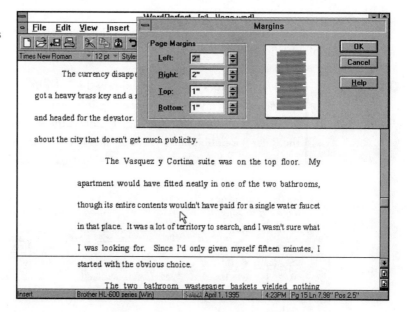

> **(Tip)**
>
> WordPerfect displays measurement in decimals, but you can just type in fractions if you want. For example, if you type in **1/4**, WordPerfect automatically converts that to **.250"**.

To change margins for the whole document, move the insertion point to the very beginning of your text. If you select text before popping up the Margins dialog box, only the margins for the paragraphs that contain the selected text are affected by new margin settings.

(Tip) A quicker way to get to the Margins dialog box is to move the mouse pointer to the left margin of the editing window. When the pointer changes from an I-beam to a white arrow, right-click for the QuickMenu and select Margins.

Setting margins from the Ruler Bar

If you want to experiment with different margin settings and see their effect on your text as you tinker, use the Ruler Bar.

To display the Ruler Bar, click View, Ruler Bar and your editing window will look like figure 6.3.

(Note) By default, WordPerfect doesn't display the Ruler Bar unless you call it up from the View menu. If you want to see the Ruler Bar all the time, select Edit, Preferences. Double-click the Display icon in the Preferences dialog box, click the Ruler Bar option button, choose Show Ruler Bar on New and Current Document, and click OK.

Drag the thick black line of the left margin marker to adjust the left margin.

Drag the equivalent right margin marker to set the right margin.

Fig. 6.3
The Ruler Bar is handy for trial-and-error margin settings.

These triangles are tab stops; drag them to adjust the tabs.

The broken line indicates where the margin is on the page.

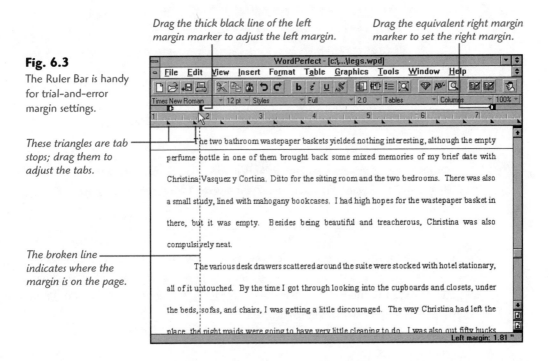

Drag the thick black left and right margin markers to adjust the margins. When you release the mouse button, the text snaps into alignment with the new margin settings. If you don't like the way it looks, drag the markers to a new position.

?Q&A

How do I get the original one-inch margins back after dragging these Ruler Bar markers all over the place?

If you just made the change, use Undo to reverse the changes. If you made a lot of changes, open the Reveal Codes window (<u>V</u>iew, Reveal <u>C</u>odes) and delete any margin setting codes you see there.

!(Tip)

You can also get the Margins dialog box by double-clicking the left or right margin marker on the Ruler Bar.

How do I get rid of tab stops?

It's sometimes convenient to clear tab stops. For example, you might want to tab from the left margin to the right margin with one press of the Tab key.

To clear individual tab stops, just drag the tab markers off the Ruler Bar.

To get rid of all the tab stops, right-click the lower part of the Ruler Bar for the QuickMenu and select Clear <u>A</u>ll Tabs.

That Ruler Bar keeps getting in my way

To put away the Ruler Bar, right-click the Ruler Bar and select <u>H</u>ide Ruler Bar.

Everything you always wanted to know about indents

Paragraphs break up a page of text to make it easier on the eyes, but a long document with paragraph after paragraph of the same type can get a little wearisome, too. It's like sneaking away from your desk for an ice cream. A welcome break, but a choice of one flavor would get old fast.

Variety is good for ice cream flavors and for paragraphs. WordPerfect lets you create all kinds of different paragraphs, easily and quickly. You don't want to overdo it; too many different kinds of paragraphs in a document might lead to visual indigestion.

But the occasional indented, double-indented, or hanging-indented paragraph adds variety to the pages and emphasis to key paragraphs. WordPerfect gives you a choice of four indented paragraph formats:

- Ordinary paragraphs begin with a tab and end with a hard return.

- Indented paragraphs shift all the lines in the paragraph from the left margin to the first tab stop.

- Double-indented paragraphs shift all the lines in the paragraph from the left margin to the first tab stop and an equivalent distance from the right margin.

- Hanging-indented paragraphs begin the first line in the paragraph at the left margin and indent each succeeding line to the first tab stop.

Figure 6.4 shows these four basic types of paragraphs.

Fig. 6.4

Use the different indenting options to add emphasis and break up the page.

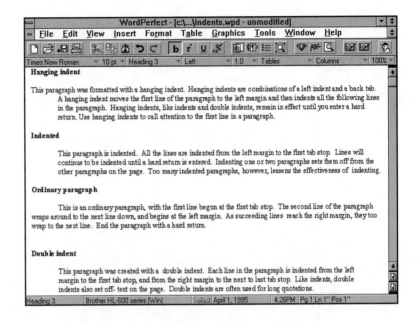

Pick your indent option from the Format menu

You can get at all the indenting options from the menu bar. Select Format, Paragraph for the menu shown in figure 6.5.

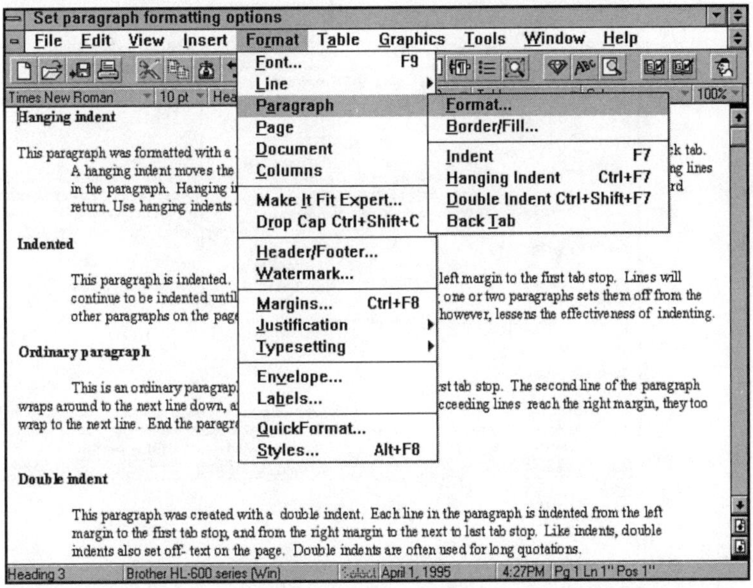

Fig. 6.5

Choose your indent option from the Format menu.

To start a new paragraph, click the menu option you want, then type to indent new text. Or move the insertion point to the beginning of an existing paragraph and make your choice to format text you've already typed.

{Note}

> You can create a hanging indent in an indented paragraph. Put the insertion point at the beginning of the first sentence in the paragraph, then select Format, Paragraph, Back Tab. That slides the first sentence one tab stop to the left.

The Format Toolbar makes indenting easy!

I find the Format Toolbar a lot handier than the menu. It gives you convenient buttons for all kinds of formatting options, including the different kinds of indents.

To get the Format Toolbar, point at the Toolbar and right-click for the QuickMenu shown in figure 6.6.

Fig. 6.6

Pop up the Toolbar QuickMenu by pointing at the Toolbar and right-clicking.

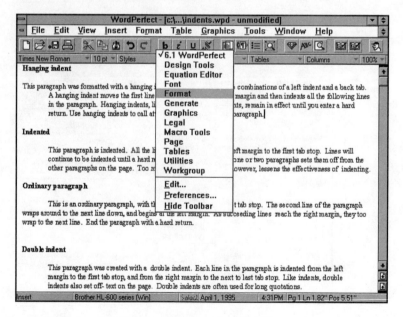

Select Format from the Toolbar menu, and you get the new crop of buttons on the Toolbar (see fig. 6.7).

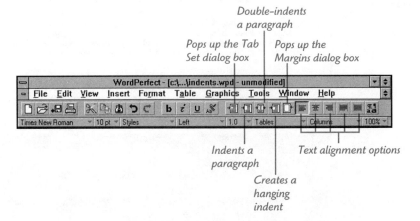

Double-indents
a paragraph

Pops up the Tab
Set dialog box

Pops up the
Margins dialog box

Fig. 6.7

Click the formatting
buttons to align your
paragraphs.

Indents a
paragraph

Text alignment options

Creates a
hanging
indent

Point at a button for the QuickTip button name and read the corresponding description in the title bar.

The buttons work just like the menu commands. To format existing text, put the insertion point at the beginning of the paragraph and click a button.

For new text, click a button and type. The paragraph will be indented, double-indented, or hanging-indented depending on what you select. Pressing Return at the end of the paragraph turns off the button.

How do I get rid of paragraph formatting?

Hate the way those formatted paragraphs look? Move the insertion point to the beginning of the paragraph and open the Reveal Codes window by pressing Alt+F3.

Press Delete or Backspace to delete the formatting codes, then use the mouse to drag the formatting codes out of the Reveal Codes window. The hanging indent codes are shown in figure 6.8.

Fig. 6.8
Use the Reveal Codes
window to delete
unwanted formatting
codes.

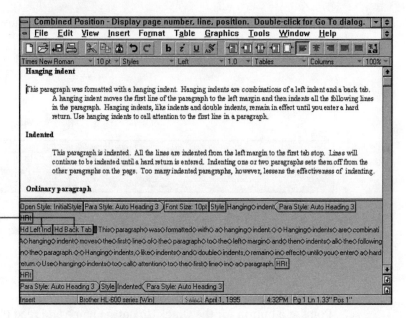

Delete both codes to
get rid of hanging
indents.

Q&A

> ### *I clicked one of the Format Toolbar buttons, and now my paragraph looks awful! What did I do?*
>
> Chances are, the insertion point was in the middle of the paragraph when you hit the button, instead of at the beginning of the paragraph. The format codes are inserted wherever the insertion point happens to be. Use Undo to start over again, or use the Reveal Codes window to delete the codes.

Left, right, or center— justifying text beats politics

Some politicians are adept at slipping from left to center to right as political winds shift. But not even the slipperiest politician changes position with the ease of text in WordPerfect. Whether you've got a title to center or text to align from the right margin, a click of the mouse places your text exactly where you want it.

Plain English, please!

In printing and page-layout jargon, to **justify** means to align exactly, either between the margins or with either margin. In WordPerfect, however, we use justify only to refer to alignment of *sections* of text. Single-line alignment is simply called left align, center, and flush right.

Bringing titles front and center

Centered text stands out from the rest of the text on the page. Titles and headings are often centered for that reason. Centered text also gives the page a balanced look.

To center a single line, simply position the insertion point at the beginning of the line and press Shift+F7. If you can't remember that, you can always click the right mouse button to get the QuickMenu, then choose Enter from the QuickMenu. Quick and easy—no muss, no fuss! To return to the left margin, simply press Enter.

If you want to center a bunch of text, WordPerfect offers two quite different kinds of centered text with a click of the Power Bar:

- Justify Center centers text between the left and right margins. Spacing between words and characters in the text isn't affected.

- Justify All also centers text between the left and right margins. Character and word spacing are adjusted so that text stretches evenly all the way across the line (see fig. 6.10).

To center titles with either Justify Center or Justify All:

1 Put the insertion point at the beginning of the text you want centered.

2 Click the Justify button on the Power Bar for the drop-down list shown in figure 6.9.

Fig. 6.9
The Power Bar button displays the current justification option.

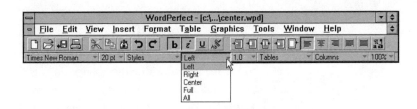

3 Select either Center or All. For new text, click a Power Bar Justify option first, then start typing. Click the option and choose Left to return to normal, left-aligned text.

⊛ {Note} The justification options are also available from the Format Toolbar. Point at the Toolbar and right-click for the Toolbar menu. Select Format for the Format Toolbar.

Figure 6.10 shows both normal center justification and a line that is all justified.

Fig. 6.10
Create centered titles with a click on the Format Toolbar.

This title is centered with Justify All.

This title is centered with Justify Center.

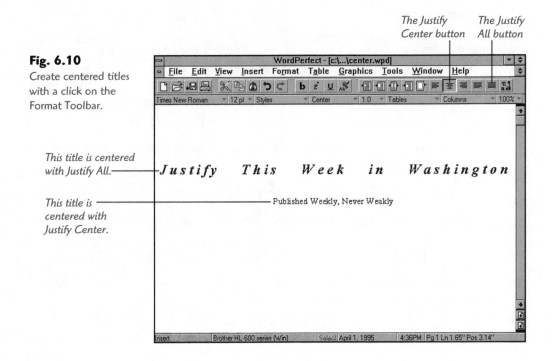

You can also select text and either click the Justify Center or Justify All button or use the Power Bar to center the paragraphs that contain the selection.

You can also get all the centering and justification options from the menu bar. Select Format, Justification and take your pick from the menu; the menu also shows the Control key combinations for these features. Between the Power Bar, the Format Toolbar, the menu, and the keyboard, you have four ways of doing exactly the same thing. WordPerfect tries to please everyone—so pick the method that suits you best.

Flush right and left

When you start typing text in WordPerfect, each new line is aligned with the left margin. That's called left align. You can also align text with the right margin, for flush right text. Dates in letters or memos are sometimes aligned flush right, as are headings.

To flush right single lines of text, simply press Alt+F7 (or choose Flush Right from the QuickMenu). Text you type then aligns at the right margin until you press Enter.

To align a section of text flush right, put the insertion point at the beginning of the text and click the Right option on the Power Bar Justify button list. For flush left text, click Left on the Power Bar Justify button list.

Both the Left and Right justification options work for selected or new text. Select the text and click the button, or click the button and type. Figure 6.11 shows flush right and flush left headings.

Fig. 6.11

Flush right text is often balanced by flush left text on the next line.

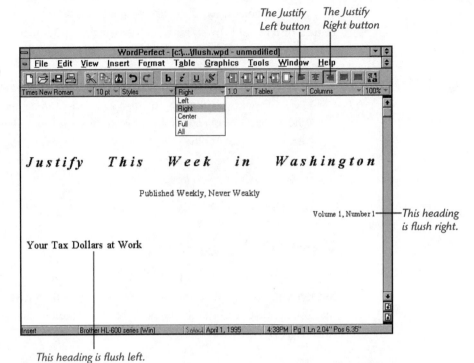

The Justify Left button *The Justify Right button*

This heading is flush right.

This heading is flush left.

Don't forget to select Left Justification to return to normal, left-aligned text.

Want some really cool dots?

A common use of left and right justification on the same line is a directory or table of contents. In a directory you have a person's name at the left and his or her phone number at the right, with a line of dots, called **dot leaders**, in between.

It's a snap to get this effect. First, at the left margin, type the person's name. Then click the right mouse button on the text area to get a QuickMenu, and choose Flush Right. Choose Flush Right again from the QuickMenu and the dot leader appears. Type the phone number and press Enter. If you want to use the keyboard for Flush Right instead of the QuickMenu, simply press Alt+F7.

How do I justify my work?

Text that is aligned left, the default alignment in WordPerfect, has what's called a ragged right margin. Each line of text begins at the left margin, but ends wherever a hard or soft return is inserted. Text in this book has a ragged right margin.

You get that irregular look on the left margin of a line aligned flush right, too.

Full justified lines have fully aligned left and right margins. Each line begins and ends at exactly the same horizontal position on the page. Full justified lines are like lengths of string cut neatly with scissors at both ends. They give the page a more formal look.

 To fully justify text, click the Full option on the Power Bar Justify button list. Justification starts at the insertion point; or select text and click Full to justify the paragraphs that include the selection. Figure 6.12 shows a paragraph of text formatted with full justification.

Fig. 6.12
Full justification
produces even left
and right margins.

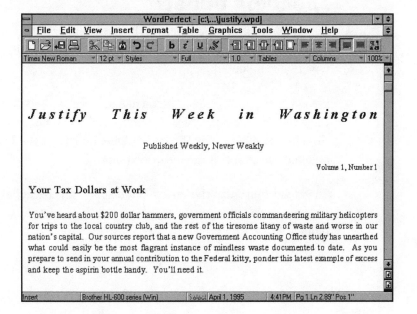

Bullets and numbers add punch to paragraphs

The idea behind paragraph formatting, whether it's indenting or justifying, is to add variety to the page and emphasis to key points in a document. WordPerfect's Bullets and Numbers feature is a convenient way of painlessly doing both for certain types of paragraphs:

- Bullets, small graphics at the beginning of lines, hammer home successive points in an argument and draw attention to important sections of a document. You're reading bulleted text right now.

- Numbers at the beginning of lines outline successive steps in a series of directions or in a procedure. Numbers are also useful to list a series of distinct items.

Speeding bullets

 For fast bullets, choose Insert, Bullets & Numbers, then double-click the bullet style you want to use. WordPerfect creates a bullet, and any text you type is also indented.

To add succeeding bullets, first make sure the default Toolbar is displayed. Click the Toolbar with the right mouse button and choose `6.1 WordPerfect` from the list. Then click the Insert Bullet button on the Toolbar to add a bulleted paragraph at the insertion point.

The Styles button on the Power Bar displays a vertical bar. Click the button for a list of bullet types and sizes you may have already used, as shown in figure 6.13.

Fig. 6.13
Use the Power Bar to change bullet styles and sizes.

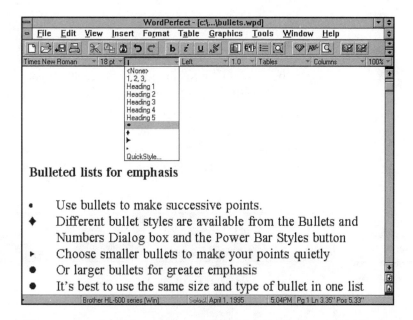

Click any of the bullet types on the Power Bar list to change the bulleting style for the current line.

You've got it on a numbered list

To create a numbered list, click Insert, Bullets & Numbers. That pops up the Bullets & Numbers dialog box shown in figure 6.14.

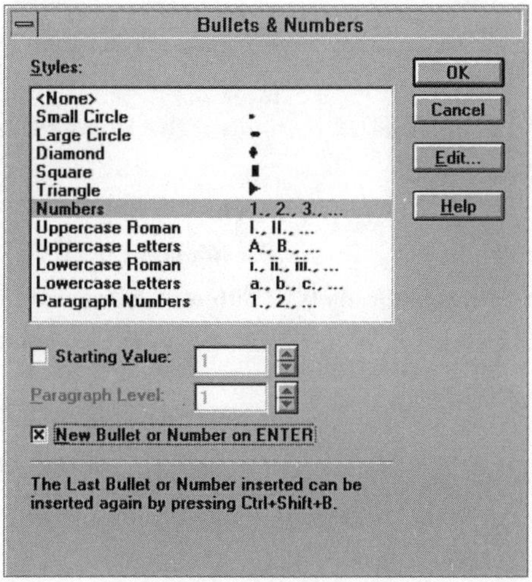

Fig. 6.14
Select bullet and numbering styles from the Bullets & Numbers dialog box.

In the Styles list, select Numbers. Select the New Bullet Or Number On ENTER option to add a number to each successive line.

The numbers will be incremented automatically. If you want the list to start from a number other than 1, click the Starting Value box and enter a new value. Click OK when you've made your selections.

The Power Bar Styles button displays numbering, along with any other numbering or bullet styles you may have previously used, as shown in figure 6.15.

Fig. 6.15
The Styles button list on the Power Bar displays new features as you select them.

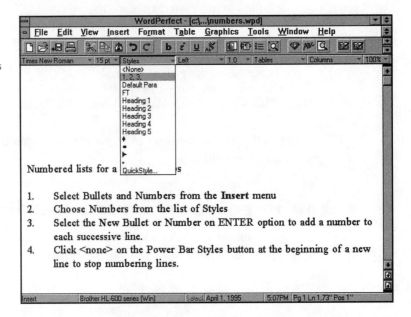

To stop line numbering, click <None> on the Power Bar Styles button list at the beginning of a new line.

 **{Note}** The Styles button on the Power Bar is a great tool! As you select different formatting features like bullets of different types and numbers, the button's list displays each new feature. Just click the list item to switch to a different style.

You can also number or bullet text you've already typed. Select the text, then choose your option from the Power Bar Styles button list, or from the Bullets & Numbers dialog box.

7

Setting Up the Page

In this chapter:

- How do I number my pages?
- I want something fancier than plain numbers
- What's a header (or a footer)?
- My second page needs to look different
- How do I keep my text together?
- This page needs more white space!

Like a picture frame, a well-organized page draws the reader's eye to your text and adds focus to the words.

Good writing is clear writing. And if a writer is hard to read, it's because his thinking is muddy. At least, that's what Lord Chesterfield argued, two hundred or so years ago.

In Chesterfield's day, it was okay to make pronouncements like that and then drop the subject. Nowadays, we'd insist on some practical suggestions for clearer writing.

WordPerfect is one practical place to start. Easy-to-read writing begins with good page layout. WordPerfect supplies plenty of page-layout tools to sharpen a document's focus and to help make your meaning clear. Lord Chesterfield would have approved.

The Page Toolbar, for page setup at your fingertips

The Page Toolbar is the handiest way to get at page setup options. Point at the Toolbar, right-click for the Toolbar menu, and select Page. The Page Toolbar buttons appear on the Toolbar, as shown in figure 7.1.

Force Page ensures that the current page always has an even or odd page number.

Subdivide Page lets you break up the page into columns or rows.

Center Page from top to bottom.

Page Border lets you put a border around the page.

Paper Size adjusts page settings for different sizes of paper.

Fig. 7.1
For big or small page setup jobs, pop up the Page Toolbar.

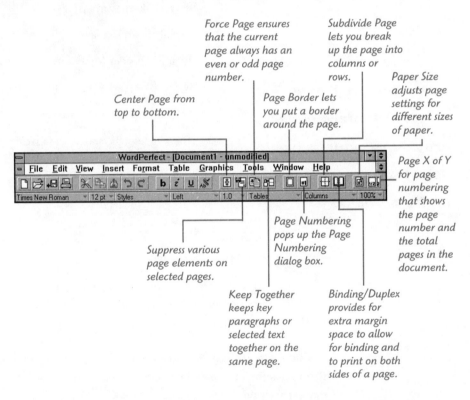

Page X of Y for page numbering that shows the page number and the total pages in the document.

Suppress various page elements on selected pages.

Page Numbering pops up the Page Numbering dialog box.

Keep Together keeps key paragraphs or selected text together on the same page.

Binding/Duplex provides for extra margin space to allow for binding and to print on both sides of a page.

Most often, the page setup commands are available from the Format, Page menu, but you might find the Page Toolbar more convenient.

The Page Toolbar is especially useful when you're first setting up a document. If you want the regular Toolbar back again when you're finished formatting the pages, right-click the Toolbar for the Toolbar menu and select WordPerfect 6.1.

Pick a number, any page number

The easiest way to add focus to a page is to identify it with a page number. Instead of saying "see the page with all that stuff about x, y, and z on it," it's much crisper to say "see page 3."

Numbering pages in WordPerfect is a snap. As with most WordPerfect features, you get different page-numbering options, and you also have different ways to get those options.

 **{Note}** _____

> When you fill a page with text, WordPerfect automatically flows text to another page. The page number is displayed on the status bar, but those numbers won't print. For page numbers that print, you have to use Page Numbering.

Where on the page should the page number go?

 To add page numbers to a document, first position the insertion point on the page where you want numbering to begin. Then click the Page Numbering button on the Toolbar (or select Format, Page, Numbering) for the Page Numbering dialog box. Click and hold the Position button to display a pop-up menu of page number position choices.

Once you pick your page number position, the Sample Facing Pages window displays a sample of your choice. Figure 7.2 shows the Top Center option.

Fig. 7.2
Choose the position of page numbers in the Page Numbering dialog box.

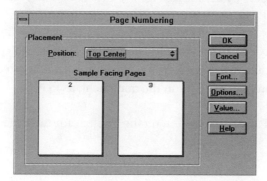

Putting your page numbers at the top center of every page is usually a safe choice. If you plan to bind or staple your document, consider the Alternating Top or Alternating Bottom options. Both put the page number at the outside edge of every page, where the numbers are easy to read when the inside edges are bound together. Books often use alternating page numbers for that reason.

Once you've made your choice, click OK. Each page of your document will be numbered automatically, reflecting the actual page number of your document. And if you don't like the way your choice of position turns out, click the Page Numbering button on the Toolbar and try again.

?Q&A

How come I can't see my page numbers?

You're viewing the editing window in Draft mode. WordPerfect page numbers are placed in the margins at the top or bottom of the page. Margins are not displayed in Draft mode. Select View, Page to flip to Page mode to display page numbering.

❋{Note}

Even though you can't see your page numbers in Draft mode, they'll print just fine.

Dress up that page number: use the canned format...

Page numbers by themselves look a little bare. Surround a page number with text, and it'll be more decorative and more informative.

The Page X of Y button on the Toolbar is a built-in choice for more informative page numbers. It gives you page numbers with both the current page and the total number of pages in the document, as in Page 4 of 10.

Click the Page X of Y button on the Toolbar for the Page X of Y dialog box.

 **{Note}** The Page X of Y dialog box is titled Page X of Y Macro. A **macro** is a series of keystrokes recorded by the program, which are then played back whenever the macro is run. The Page X of Y "feature" is actually a macro written by WordPerfect's programmers. You can write your own, too. See Chapter 12 for more about macros.

The Position button has the same page-positioning options as its cousin in the Page Numbering dialog box. The Format list offers the choice of text and numbering formats shown in figure 7.3.

Fig. 7.3
Choose a format for page numbers that also shows the total number of pages in the document.

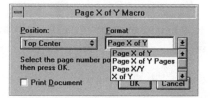

Take your pick of formats and click OK. The text prints on every page, and the page numbers will be incremented automatically. WordPerfect tallies the "Y," or total number of pages, for you.

The Page X of Y numbering style is especially useful in long documents with many sections and no obvious conclusion. Contracts spring to mind. The reader of such a document might not know he's missing a page or two unless the pages are numbered in the Page X of Y format. It's also handy for long faxes, where pages sometimes have a way of vanishing mysteriously into the ether.

<Caution> Page X of Y counts the total number of pages at the time you run the feature. If you subsequently make changes to the document that affect the total number of pages, that initial count will be off. Run Page X of Y again if that happens, or wait until you're ready to print the document before inserting Page X of Y numbering.

...or create your own page numbering format

You might have your own ideas about what text you want to accompany page numbers. You can ornament your page numbers with simple dashes; "- 2 -," for example. Or you could have the document title repeat with every page number, as in Sales Report, Page 2.

To add your own text to page numbers, first position the insertion point on the page where you want the numbering style to change, then follow these steps:

1 Click the Page Numbering button on the Toolbar or select Format, Page, Numbering.

2 Select a Position for your page numbers, then click the Options button in the Page Numbering dialog box.

3 In the Page Numbering Options dialog box, you'll see the [Pg #] code in the Format and Accompanying Text edit box. Type your text in the edit box on either side of the code, as shown in figure 7.4.

Fig. 7.4
I've added the text
- Sales Report,
Page -.

```
┌──────────────────────────────────────────────────────────┐
│ ⊖              Page Numbering Options                      │
│ ┌─Number Type──────────────────────────┐    ┌─────────┐  │
│ │ Format and Accompanying Text:         │    │   OK    │  │
│ │ ┌──────────────────────────┐ ┌──────┐│    ├─────────┤  │
│ │ │ - Sales Report, Page [Pg #] - │ │Insert ▼││    │ Cancel  │  │
│ │ └──────────────────────────┘ └──────┘│    ├─────────┤  │
│ │                                        │    │  Help   │  │
│ │ Page:      │ Numbers      ▲▼│          │    └─────────┘  │
│ │ Secondary: │ Numbers      ▲▼│          │                 │
│ │ Chapter:   │ Numbers      ▲▼│          │                 │
│ │ Volume:    │ Numbers      ▲▼│          │                 │
│ └───────────────────────────────────────┘                 │
│                 Sample Facing Pages                        │
│    ┌──────────────────┐  ┌──────────────────┐             │
│    │ Sales Report, Page 2 │  │ Sales Report, Page 3 │             │
│    │                  │  │                  │             │
│    │                  │  │                  │             │
│    │                  │  │                  │             │
│    │                  │  │                  │             │
│    └──────────────────┘  └──────────────────┘             │
│  □ Insert Format and Accompanying Text at Insertion Point  │
└──────────────────────────────────────────────────────────┘
```

4 The Sample Facing Pages windows show you a preview of the way your page numbering will look. Click OK when you're done, then click OK again in the Page Numbering dialog box. Your page number and text will appear on each document page in the position you've specified.

②Q&A

I accidentally deleted the [Pg #] code in the Page Numbering Options dialog box! What do I do?

Put the insertion point in the Format and Accompanying Text edit box at the spot where the code should be. Click the Insert button and select Page Number. This reinserts the code for you.

How come I can't see a preview of my page number text in the Sample Facing Pages windows?

Before typing accompanying text in the Page Numbering Options dialog box, you have to select a Position in the Page Numbering dialog box. If you don't, the default Position option of No Page Numbering remains in effect.

These page numbers need a facelift

You might want your page numbers in a font face that's different from the face you're using for body text. That adds variety to the page, and it makes the numbers more obvious or less obvious, depending on what face you choose. Just click the Font button in the Page Numbering dialog box to pop up the Page Numbering Font dialog box. Take your pick of face, size, and appearance; and click OK when you're done.

What if I want the page numbers to start at something other than 1?

By default, WordPerfect numbers pages beginning with page 1. That's perfectly logical, but on occasion you'll want to number your pages starting with a different number.

You might have several preface pages. Or you might have different sections of a report in different WordPerfect files, but you want to number all the pages in the report consecutively.

To start each file with a different page number:

1 Click the Page Numbering button on the Toolbar.

2 Click the Value button in the Page Numbering dialog box.

3 Click the Page Settings, New Page Number arrows until you get the page number you want, or just type the number into the edit box, as shown in figure 7.5.

Fig. 7.5
Starting documents with a page number other than 1 is easy in WordPerfect.

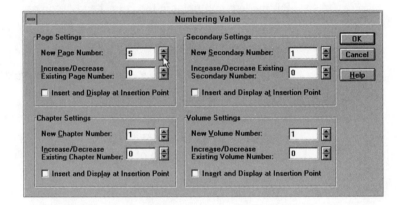

4 Click OK when you're done, and then click OK in the Page Numbering dialog box to insert the new page number.

What's a header (or a footer)?

We don't record answering machine greetings every time we receive messages. We record them once, and the greeting is repeated as often as needed. **Headers** and **footers** in documents work the same way—enter the information once, and it's repeated on every page. Like the greeting on your answering machine, headers and footers convey important, but repetitive, information.

Document titles, chapter titles, and author names are good choices for headers and footers. You can even put page numbers in headers or footers. Headers and footers add a balanced look to the page.

Where do the header and footer go?

Create a header, and WordPerfect sticks it right below the top margin of the page. Footers go just above the bottom margin of the page.

You can have up to two different headers and two different footers per page. WordPerfect calls them Header A and Header B, and Footer A and Footer B.

To create a header, position the insertion point on the page where you want the header to begin, then:

1 Click Format, Header/Footer for the dialog box shown in figure 7.6.

Fig. 7.6
Use the Headers/ Footers dialog box to create and edit headers and footers.

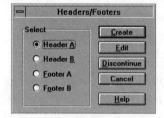

2 Select Header A and click the Create button. The Header/Footer feature bar appears automatically, as seen in figure 7.7.

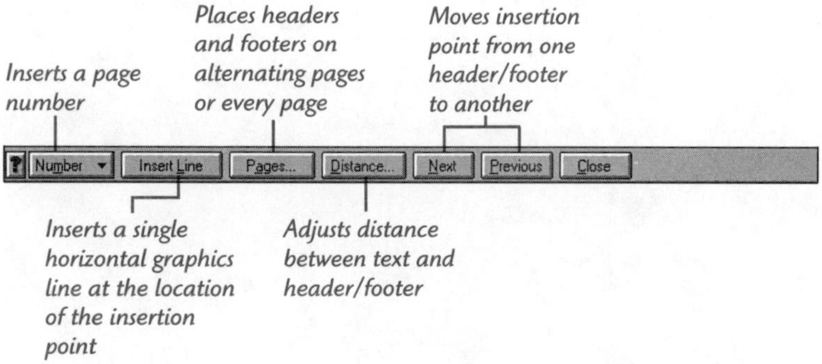

Inserts a page number

Places headers and footers on alternating pages or every page

Moves insertion point from one header/footer to another

Fig. 7.7
The Header/Footer feature bar springs up when you create or edit a selected header or footer.

Inserts a single horizontal graphics line at the location of the insertion point

Adjusts distance between text and header/footer

3 Type the text you want in the header. Use any of WordPerfect formatting options, just as you would in body text. Click Number, Page Number on the feature bar to stick page numbers in your header.

{Note}

If you've added page numbers with the P̲age, N̲umbering menu command and picked one of the top-of-the-page position options before creating a new header, the page number will also print along with the header. This may result in a jumbled mess, so be careful not to use both page numbering and headers at the same location.

<Caution>

The top-left page number position should be avoided if you plan on creating a header. Header text at the left margin will type right over the page number!

4 Click the Insert L̲ine button to insert a horizontal graphics line at the position of the insertion point. Click the P̲ages button and select O̲dd Pages or E̲ven Pages if you want the header to appear on alternating pages. By default, headers go on every page.

5 Click the C̲lose button when you're done. Figure 7.8 shows a header with a previously added top-center page number, a line inserted from the Header/Footer feature bar, and italicized text.

(Tip)

If you want to quickly create a header or footer, put the mouse pointer in the top margin area, right-click, and select H̲eader/Footer from the QuickMenu that appears.

Fig. 7.8

Headers and footers add information and give the page a professional look.

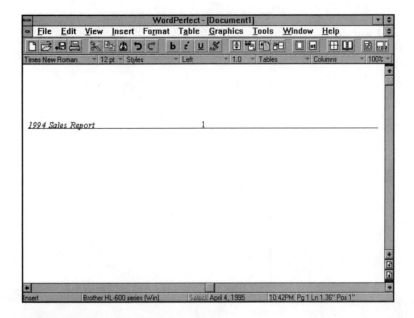

How do I add a second header?

The header in figure 7.8 shows the page number and document title, but suppose you want to add the author's name? That blank space against the right margin would be a perfect spot for flush right text. We can add a header B and format the text with the Power Bar Justify button to get that effect.

To add a header B:

1 Move the mouse pointer in the top margin, and right-click for the QuickMenu shown in figure 7.9.

Fig. 7.9
Right-click in the top margin for the QuickMenu.

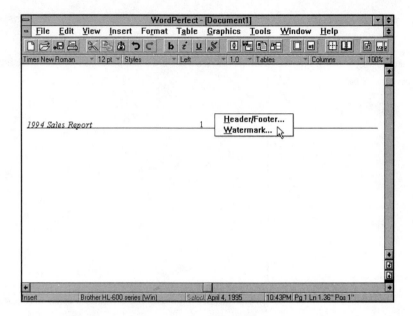

2 Select <u>H</u>eader/Footer from the QuickMenu for the Headers/Footers dialog box. Click Header <u>B</u> and select <u>C</u>reate.

3 Click the Justification button on the Power Bar, and select Right.

4 Type the text for header B, and click <u>C</u>lose on the Header/Footer feature bar when you're done. The two headers might look something like figure 7.10.

Fig. 7.10
Adding a header B is easy to do, and lends more balance to the page.

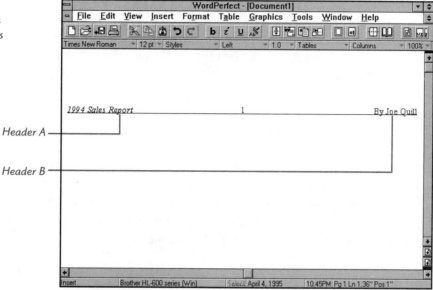

Header A ───────
Header B ───────

Put your footer down on that page

The same steps that concocted headers A and B create footers A and B. Just select Footer A or Footer B from the Headers/Footers dialog box. Figure 7.11 shows a footer A with center justification on the same page as our two headers, zoomed to 40% so you can see the headers and footer.

Fig. 7.11
Footers convey additional repetitive information and round off your pages.

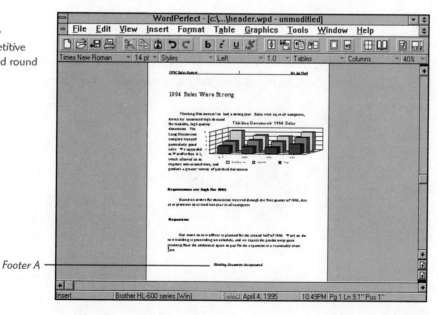

Footer A ───────

How do I edit headers?

You can edit header A in Page view by clicking it. To get at header B, click Format, Header/Footer for the Headers/Footers dialog box. Select Header B and click Edit. Check WordPerfect's title bar to see which header you are editing. If your header B is aligned flush right, press the End key to move the insertion point to the header text. Then edit the text with all the usual WordPerfect editing tools.

 {Note}

If you want a different header or footer on another page, move the insertion point to that page and create the new header or footer. The new ones replace the old ones from that point on in the document. Even better, use the A header or footer for part of the document, and the B header or footer for other parts, such as alternating pages.

I don't want all this stuff on every page

By convention, page numbering and headers and footers usually don't appear on the first page of a document. Or you might create a letterhead in a header on the first page, but you don't want the letterhead to appear on page two. You can suppress headers, footers, and page numbering on the first page or any current page.

 Move the insertion point to the page where you want to suppress page-formatting features. Click the Suppress button on the Page Toolbar, or select Format, Page, Suppress for the Suppress dialog box shown in figure 7.12.

Fig. 7.12
Stop any of these page-formatting elements from displaying or printing on the current page.

Suppress
Suppress on Current Page
☐ Header A ☐ Watermark A
☐ Header B ☐ Watermark B
☐ Footer A ☐ Page Numbering
☐ Footer B ☐ All
OK   Cancel   Help
☐ Print Page Number at Bottom Center on Current Page

Select the features you want to suppress, and click OK. Any headers, footers, or page numbering will be unaffected on the other pages in the document.

If you want to suppress these elements on other pages, you have to repeat the above steps on each page. However, if you simply want to discontinue a header or footer, you can select Format, Header/Footer, select the header or footer you no longer want, and choose Discontinue.

How do I double-space this page?

Pages that are densely packed with text can be hard to read. Want a quick way of adding white space to the page? Change the line spacing. By default, WordPerfect **single-spaces** the lines on a page. Lines display and print one line below the other.

That's easily changed. Select Format, Line, Spacing for the Line Spacing dialog box shown in figure 7.13.

Fig. 7.13
Automatically insert blank lines between lines of text in the Line Spacing dialog box.

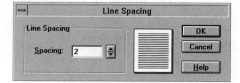

Click the arrows or type a new value in the Spacing edit box. Line spacing is measured in numbers of lines, and you can enter any number, or fraction of a number—for example, **1.3 or 1 3/8**. For **double-spaced** lines, enter **2** in the Spacing edit box. The preview window in the dialog box changes to reflect the new spacing value.

My page looks unbalanced

You've written a short letter, printed it, and all the text is scrunched up at the top of the page.

Centering the page is a quick fix. Click the Center Page button for the Center Page(s) dialog box. Take your pick of centering options—you can center the Current <u>P</u>age, or the Current and <u>S</u>ubsequent Pages.

Either option automatically centers the text on the page between the top and bottom margins, as shown in figure 7.14.

Fig. 7.14
Short letters are good candidates for page centering.

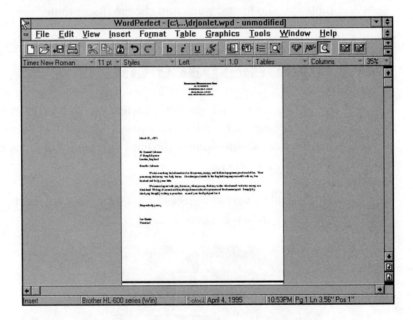

I want to keep my text together

Let's face it. Books on the subject of word processors, admirable though they may be, don't lend themselves to high drama. So when you see references to block protection and widows and orphans, don't expect crime stories or gripping tragedy.

 Plain English, please!

When you fill up a page of text, WordPerfect automatically starts the next line on a new page. A **widow** is the last line of a paragraph that appears by itself at the top of the next page.

An **orphan** is the first line of a paragraph that winds up by itself at the bottom of a page. The rest of the paragraph has been moved to the top of the next page.

How to prevent widows and orphans

In WordPerfect, widows and orphans are produced not by devastating wars or natural disasters, but by the way the program automatically flows text from one page to the next.

 These minor tragedies are easily avoided. Put the insertion point at the beginning of a multipage document and click the Keep Together button on the Page Toolbar. Or select Format, Page, Keep Text Together.

Either way, you get the Keep Text Together dialog box shown in figure 7.15.

Fig. 7.15

Keeping widows and orphans together in WordPerfect is no trouble at all.

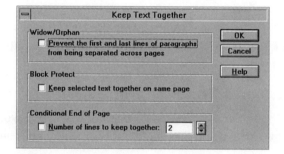

Click the Prevent the first and last lines of paragraphs from being separated across pages selection box under Widow/Orphan in the Keep Text Together dialog box, then click OK. The name of that dialog box is so long, that the "dialog" is more like a one-sided conversation! No first or last lines of paragraphs will be widowed or orphaned for the rest of the document.

Block protection: lock up text, not doors

Keeping widows and orphans together is enough to keep text together in most situations, but there may be times when you'll want to keep entire paragraphs together. Tables, for example, or numbered lists might look peculiar if they're separated on two pages.

Block protection keeps selected blocks of text together on the same page. To keep any block of text together on the same page:

1 Select the text you want to keep together.

(Tip)

> To select an entire paragraph, put the insertion point anywhere in the paragraph, and quadruple-click (click four times in rapid succession).

2 Click the Keep Together button on the Page Toolbar, or select Format, Page, Keep Text Together.

3 Click the Keep Selected Text Together On Same Page selection box under Block Protect in the Keep Text Together dialog box (see fig. 7.15).

4 Click OK.

No matter what editing changes you make, on the page or throughout the document, the selected block of text will now stay together.

What is conditional end of page?

The third option in the Keep Text Together dialog box works like Block Protect, except that you keep only a specific number of lines together.

Suppose you have a title, then a blank line, and then a paragraph. You don't want the title to end up at the bottom of a page by itself. By keeping the first three lines of the paragraph together, the title and the paragraph won't be separated.

8

Choose Your Words...Easily!
(Spell Them, Too.)

Writers tear their hair out trying to find, spell, and use the right word. They'd save a few follicles if they'd use WordPerfect's handy writing tools.

The French are so fussy about French that they have laws against misusing the language. Americans are more freewheeling. E.B. White, by anyone's reckoning a master of American English, compared correct American usage to crossing the street—getting to the other side is mostly luck.

H.W. Fowler wrote the book on English usage. His *A Dictionary of Modern English Usage* is the writer's bible. Here's what he says about grammar: "What are generally recognized for the time being as its conventions must be followed by those who would write clearly and agreeably."

WordPerfect has some nifty tools to help us follow the conventions of "clear and agreeable" English.

Spell Checker is handy, but not infallible

With over a hundred thousand words at its command, unfailing persistence, and, within limits, perfect accuracy, WordPerfect's Spell Checker makes a great adjunct to proofreading. Not a replacement—copy still has to be read with care. You just won't have to worry about routine misspellings anymore.

Spell Checker corrects typos and misspellings

Spell Checker compares the words in your document to the words in its built-in dictionary. If your spelling doesn't match its spelling, WordPerfect highlights the word and suggests a correction.

To check the spelling of your document:

1 Save the document before you run the Spell Checker.

They just don't spell like they used to

Not so long ago, spelling in English was largely a matter of taste. Writers winged it, and the spelling of the same word varied from writer to writer. The first modern dictionary of the English language, written in 1755 by Dr. Samuel Johnson, changed all that. Johnson's great tool helped to standardize the spelling of English words. Trouble is, knowing that a word should be spelled a particular way doesn't help us with knowing how to spell it. WordPerfect's Spell Checker goes a long way towards solving that little problem. You still need a good dictionary, though. Spell Checker says nothing about pronunciation, for one thing. Good dictionaries do. Johnson's dictionary, although dated now, was also famous for using quotations to show how words are used in context. Good dictionaries still do that. That's often the best way of getting at a word's meaning.

 *{Note}*

Spell Checker is a program in its own right. You can run it from WordPerfect, or from another Windows application (by clicking the Spell Checker icon in the Program Manager). Running more than one program at a time puts a strain on PCs, and can sometimes lead to unpredictable results. To avoid losing valuable work, always save your documents before running Spell Checker, the Thesaurus, or Grammatik.

2 Click the Spell Check button on the Toolbar. The Spell Checker dialog box pops up, and Spell Checker immediately highlights the first misspelling in the document, as shown in figure 8.1.

Fig. 8.1
Spell Checker doesn't waste time. Click the Spell Check button and it goes right to work.

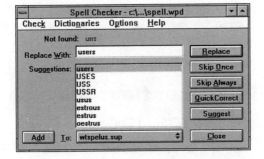

3 In figure 8.1, Spell Checker has seized on the typo "usrs." It has guessed that we meant to type "users," and displays the word in the Replace With edit box. Click the Replace button, and Spell Checker replaces "usrs" with "users."

4 Spell Checker then goes on to check the rest of the document. As each incorrect word is found, choose to replace it with the word in the Replace With edit box. If that's not the word you wanted, look at the list of Suggestions. Select any of them; the word you click is placed in the Replace With edit box. Click the Replace button to substitute the selected suggestion for the word in your document.

5 If there are no suggested replacements for a word that you know is incorrectly spelled, just type the correct spelling in the Replace With edit box and click Replace. When the spell check is completed, you're asked if you want to close Spell Checker. Click Yes to shut down Spell Checker and return to your document.

(Tip)

> To make editing changes in a document while Spell Checker is running, click outside the Spell Checker dialog box. That moves the insertion point back into the document. Edit, then click the Resume button in the Spell Checker dialog box to continue with the spell check.

{Note}

> Don't forget to save the document again when Spell Checker is finished. The corrections Spell Checker makes aren't permanent until you save them.

Spell Checker flags some correctly spelled words, too!

Spell Checker will also seize on legitimate words that don't happen to be in its dictionary, as shown in figure 8.2.

Fig. 8.2
Pentium isn't in the Spell Checker dictionary, but it's spelled correctly.

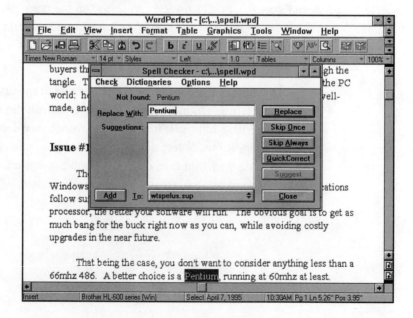

Some proper nouns, nicknames, and specialized terms that are spelled correctly will be marked by Spell Checker. You have several options when that happens. Click any of these buttons in the Spell Checker dialog box to do the following:

- Skip Once will ignore the word this time, but Spell Checker will stop if the word is found again.

- Skip Always is a better choice if it's a recurring word. Words that you skip Always will be ignored throughout the document. You can even close Spell Checker, then rerun it, and words you've skipped Always continue to be ignored. But when you close the document, always is over. Always, at least in this case, only lasts for as long as the document is open.

- In the case of a correctly spelled word in common use that Spell Checker doesn't recognize ("Pentium" might be one choice), add it to the Spell Checker supplementary dictionary. Click Add, making sure that To WTSPELUS.SUP is selected, to add the word. Whenever you run Spell Checker again, the added word will be ignored, just like the other correctly spelled words in your document.

- Some documents might have uncommon words peculiar to the subject of the document—a technical paper, for example, or an essay on Chaucer. As Spell Checker highlights each correctly spelled but unrecognized word, select Document Dictionary from the list on the Add button, and click Add. That adds the words to a supplementary dictionary that'll be used for that document only. Fiction writers fond of unusual character names find this feature especially useful.

- If the list of suggestions seems rather limited, click Suggest to get a more extensive listing of suggested replacements.

Spell Checker finds all kinds of errors— even non-errors

Here's a mistake I'm prone to making. Maybe you do it too. I'll type "the the" when all I want is "the." Spell Checker catches double words like that and suggests replacing them with a single word. Spell Checker needs to be carefully monitored, though, as shown in figure 8.3.

Fig. 8.3

Some double words are really needed, but Spell Checker doesn't make the distinction.

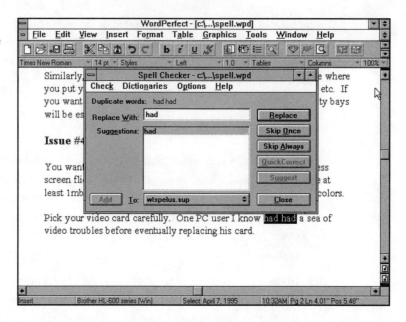

Spell Checker doesn't distinguish between "the the" and "had had." Just click the Skip Once button in situations like that.

Spell Checker catches other mistakes that aren't always mistakes:

- Words with numbers are flagged, as in the tax form 1040ES.

- Words with irregular capitalization are also flagged. If you're in the habit of typing "EveryWhere," Spell Checker will catch the mistake. But Spell Checker warns you that "MacDonald" is a capitalization error, even though it's correct. (Oddly enough, Spell Checker won't bug you about "O'Brien" unless you type "O'brien," in which case it suggests the correct form of the name.)

These features, helpful in the case of errors, are minor irritations when the document isn't in error. If they become major irritations, you can control the kinds of errors Spell Checker hunts down.

Click Options in the Spell Checker dialog box for the menu shown in figure 8.4.

Fig. 8.4
The Options menu
gives you a measure of
control over Spell
Checker.

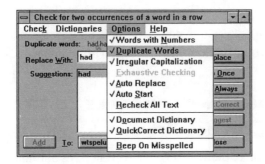

Menu items that have a check mark beside them are flagged. Click checked
menu items to have Spell Checker ignore those sorts of "errors." Spell
Checker is a great tool, but it needs to be watched.

Proofread, to catch what Spell Checker misses

Spell checkers and automobile air bags are sometimes knocked for the same
reason: both can give you a false sense of security. Consider the sentence
"A Pentium is fast, well-made, and expendable."

The word "expendable" is correctly spelled, so Spell Checker will ignore it.
But it's the wrong word entirely in this context. Expandable is what's meant
here, not expendable. A one-letter difference between words, but a big
difference in meaning. It's a common, and easily made, error.

Spell Checker is no help for mistakes like that. Only a human proofreader
will catch correctly spelled words that are just plain wrong in the context.
But in spite of its limitations, Spell Checker has something else in common
with air bags: we'd much rather have them than not.

QuickCorrect corrects as you type

At the back of every glittering parade is someone with a broom and dustpan
cleaning up the debris. That's pretty much how QuickCorrect works: it
corrects common typos and capitalization errors as soon as you hit the
spacebar to move to the next word.

Try it. Type **THe**, press the spacebar, and watch the error get corrected to **The**, automatically. Same thing with **wierd**; type it and QuickCorrect transforms it to **weird** without your having to lift a finger.

Add your own mistakes to the QuickCorrect list

To see a list of all the words QuickCorrect fixes automatically, select <u>T</u>ools, <u>Q</u>uickCorrect for the QuickCorrect dialog box shown in figure 8.5.

Fig. 8.5
The left-hand column might look familiar—those are all common typos and misspellings.

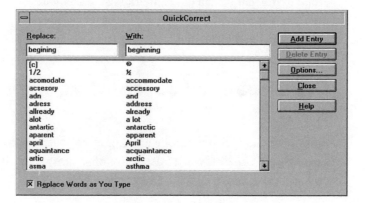

I often type "**begining**" when I want "**beginning**," so I'm adding it to the QuickCorrect list in figure 8.5. To add your own common typos to the list:

1 Pop up the QuickCorrect dialog box by clicking <u>T</u>ools, <u>Q</u>uickCorrect.

2 Type your typo in the <u>R</u>eplace edit box. In figure 8.5, I've typed **begining**.

3 Type the correction, **beginning**, in the <u>W</u>ith edit box, as shown in figure 8.5.

4 Click <u>A</u>dd Entry and <u>C</u>lose when you're done. From now on, whenever I misspell "beginning," QuickCorrect will correct it for me.

Make sure that R<u>e</u>place Words as You Type is checked in the QuickCorrect dialog box or corrections won't be made automatically.

Click the QuickCorrect button in the Spell Checker dialog box when you find common errors during a spell check. That adds the error and the correction to the QuickCorrect list.

What else does QuickCorrect correct?

Click the Options button in the QuickCorrect dialog box for the QuickCorrect options shown in figure 8.6.

Fig. 8.6
QuickCorrect fixes other common mistakes besides typos and irregular capitalizations.

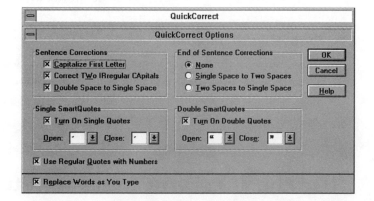

If you're spacebar-happy and tend to add two spaces after words instead of one, QuickCorrect can fix that for you as you type. Also single spaces at the end of sentences and omitted capitals at the beginning of sentences. You can even make sure you use "tcqm" (typographically correct quote marks.)

And if any of these automatic corrections are irritating rather than helpful, just deselect them.

?Q&A

QuickCorrect is driving me nuts! Can I turn it off?

You're right. QuickCorrect can be somewhat disconcerting at first. You'll probably get used to it, but if you can't, just deselect the Replace Words as You Type checkbox in the QuickCorrect dialog box. Errors will still be caught when you run Spell Checker, but they'll be left alone as you type.

I can't think of the right word!

You're sitting at your desk, typing away at a report. It's due at the end of the day, but you're making fast progress. Then you hit a roadblock—the dreaded writer's block. What's the word for...? The word for what you're trying to say just won't come to mind. Or maybe you've used a word three times already and you need another word to say the same thing.

You could stare out the window and rack your brain for the answer. Or you can use WordPerfect's Thesaurus to find the word for you.

Plain English, please!

A **thesaurus** is a dictionary of **synonyms** (different words with the same or similar meaning) and **antonyms** (words with opposite meanings). The original meaning of the Greek word "thesaurus" is treasury or storehouse, and a thesaurus can indeed be a treasury of words.

Use the Thesaurus to say it better

If you're having a hard time thinking of the right word, first type or place the insertion point on one you think is close to what you mean, then click Tools, Thesaurus to pop up the Thesaurus dialog box, as shown in figure 8.7.

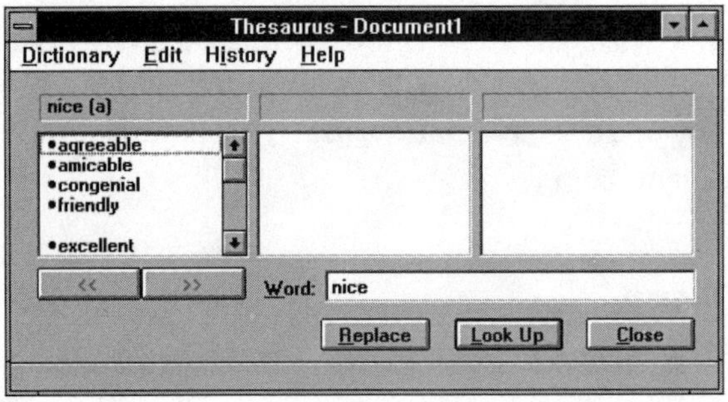

Fig. 8.7
The Thesaurus is a storehouse of word choices.

1 The Thesaurus automatically looks up the word at the insertion point. If you want some other word, type a word close in meaning to the word you want in the <u>W</u>ord edit box. We want synonyms for "nice" in the example in figure 8.7.

2 Click <u>L</u>ook Up. A list of synonyms appears in the first column. Scroll down to the bottom of the list for antonyms.

3 Each of the words in the column has a corresponding list of synonyms and antonyms associated with it. Browse the list, and double-click the word that's closest in meaning to what you're trying to say. That gives you another list of synonyms and antonyms in the second column, as shown in figure 8.8.

Fig. 8.8
Double-clicking
pleasant produces
another list of
synonyms and
antonyms in the
second column.

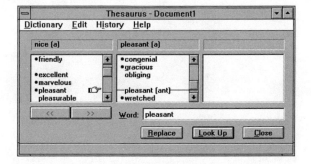

4 If nothing in the second list appeals to you, double-click any of the bulleted words to fill up the third column with yet another list of synonyms and antonyms.

 **{Note}** The Thesaurus groups the forms of both the words you look up and the words it finds for you in these categories: (v) is a verb; (n) is a noun; and (a) is an adjective.

Chances are, you'll find a better word amongst all those choices.

Put the Thesaurus to work on your document

The Thesaurus is also handy for improving a document. A letter dashed off in a hurry, like the letter in figure 8.9, might not be as clear as we'd like. For example, "no good" in the first paragraph sounds vague. An antonym for "good" might help. We'll select the word, then click Tools, Thesaurus, as shown in figure 8.9.

Fig. 8.9
Sometimes the right antonym can sharpen the focus of your writing.

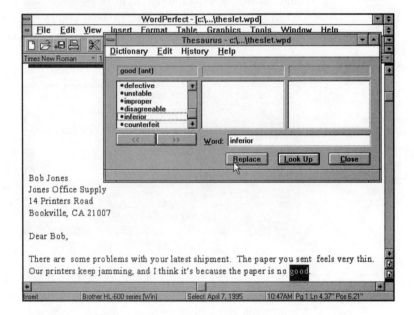

Replacing "no good" with "inferior" would be an improvement. Click Replace to substitute "inferior" for "good," then select "no" in the document and delete it. You can edit a document while the Thesaurus is running; just click in the document to move the insertion point to the desired spot. Click the Thesaurus dialog box again when you're done editing. Note that the Thesaurus automatically looks up the word at the location of the insertion point.

We've also got the word "wrong" in both sentences in the second paragraph. Click the second occurrence, then click Look Up in the Thesaurus dialog box, as shown in figure 8.10.

Fig. 8.10
The Thesaurus is helpful in the case of an overused word.

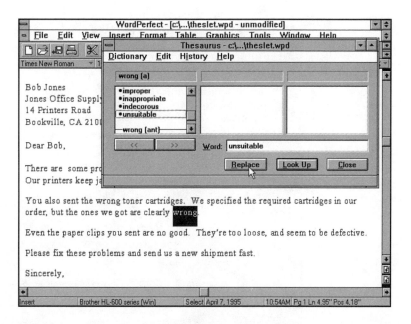

"Unsuitable" is a good substitute for "wrong" in this context. Select the word in the Thesaurus dialog box, then click Replace to pop it into the document in place of "wrong."

Our changes don't result in a masterpiece, but it's a distinct improvement over the original.

It's English, but is it Grammatikal?

Who can forget those reports and term papers we labored over in school? It was always a relief to hand them in, but the relief was short-lived. They usually came back covered in the teacher's red ink, peppered with annotations like "awk," or "run on."

WordPerfect's Grammatik feature is your old English teacher revisited. Grammatik goes through your documents line by line, pointing out errors in grammar and usage along the way. Grammatik has one major advantage over your old teacher: you can adopt its corrections, or ignore them completely. My teachers never gave me that choice.

How do I use Grammatik?

Let's turn Grammatik loose on our corrected letter to Jones Office Supply.

1 Open the document, then click the Grammatik button on the Toolbar.

2 The Grammatik dialog box pops up and immediately seizes on the first word it doesn't recognize, as shown in figure 8.11.

Fig. 8.11
Grammatik flags words it doesn't find in its dictionary.

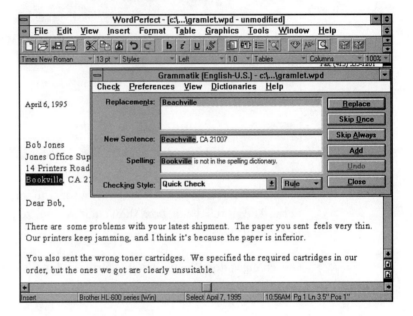

3 Grammatik has its own dictionary. It doesn't recognize the place name "Bookville" (which doesn't exist, as far as I know, because I made it up). I guess it does think there is a Beachville, however. But this isn't an error, so we'll click Skip Always and carry on.

You can add words to the Grammatik dictionary. Click Add in the Grammatik dialog box, and the highlighted word is added to the default supplementary dictionary, WTSPELUS.SUP, the same one used by Spell Checker.

4 Grammatik jumps on "clips," as in paper clips, as shown in figure 8.12.

Fig. 8.12
Grammatik can be overzealous. It's prone to finding errors where none might exist.

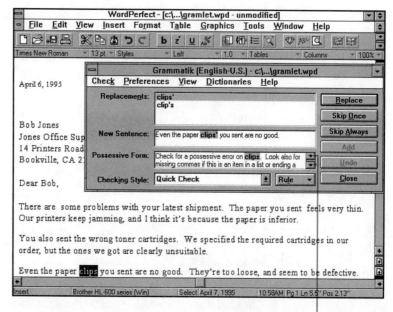

Click these arrows to scroll through Grammatik's error message.

5 Grammatik suspects that `clips` is missing the possessive apostrophe, as in `clip's`. That's clearly an incorrect assessment in this case. However, if you think that Grammatik is really on to an error, you can get more information about the grammatical rule or term in question. Click the underlined words in green in the grammatical rule box for definitions and explanations of Grammatik's rules. You'll get a Grammatik Grammar and Writing Help window like the one in figure 8.13.

Fig. 8.13

Grammatik gives definitions and explanations of grammatical rules and terms on demand.

Click the under-lined words in green in the rule box for a Help window.

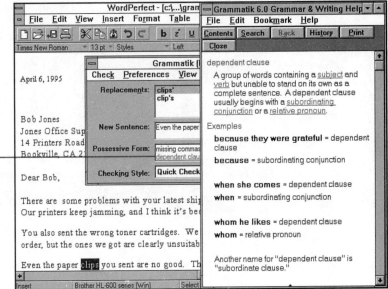

6 Clicking Skip Once brings us to the next problem in our letter. Grammatik finds the object pronoun "you" following the noun "clips" to be awkward (see fig. 8.14). Here, Grammatik offers no Replacements; had it done so, we could have selected the replacement and clicked Replace to replace our word with Grammatik's. We could replace "the paper clips you sent" with "the paper clips that you have sent to us" on our own. But we won't bother. This letter's tone is informal, and the original formulation is fine.

7 Clicking Skip Once again gets us to the end of the grammar check. Although Grammatik didn't have much to offer in the way of improvements for our letter, we did learn something about a few grammatical terms.

My letter is informal. Can I tell Grammatik to lighten up?

Grammatik can be more useful if you adjust its Checking Style. By adjusting the severity of Grammatik's application of grammatical rules, you can better tailor it to particular documents.

Click the Checking Style arrow for the drop-down list shown in figure 8.14.

Fig. 8.14

Grammatik varies checking criteria, depending on your choice in this list.

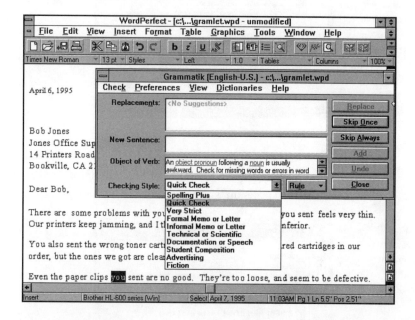

Grammatik offers a lot of interesting information

You may or may not find Grammatik to be a useful tool. It's certainly worth putting through its paces; if nothing else, you'll learn a fair amount of English grammar.

For those who like to put their writing under a powerful lens, Grammatik has some nifty options.

When Grammatik highlights a potential problem, click View on the Grammatik dialog box menu bar and select Parts of Speech. Your sentence is broken down into its component parts, as shown in figure 8.15.

Fig. 8.15
If grammatical analysis appeals to you, explore Grammatik's View choices.

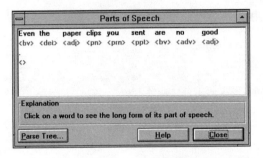

For a diagram of the indirect and direct objects in your sentence, click the Parse Tree button in the Parts of Speech dialog box. A display like the one in figure 8.16 pops up, showing the relation between the words in the sentence.

Fig. 8.16
If you're wondering about agreement questions, the Grammatik Parse Tree can supply answers.

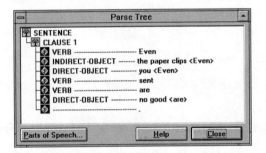

All I really want is a word count for this document

There are plenty of situations where you'll need an accurate word count of your document. If you submit a document for publication, for example, you'll probably be required to give a word count. If you're a high school student writing a 500-word essay, you'll want to know exactly when to stop. Or you might just be curious as to how many hard-won words you've actually set down.

To get a word count, and quite a bit more besides, select File, Document Info while your document is open. This pops up the Document Information dialog box shown in figure 8.17.

Fig. 8.17
The Document Information dialog box tells you everything you want to know about your document.

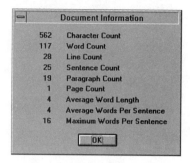

The Printer's Craft

Any writer gets a charge out of seeing her words in print. Nothing gets lost in translation when you print from screen to page in WordPerfect.

The best gadget for storing information is completely portable, easily searchable, and conveniently viewable. What is it? The printed page. It's still easier to read text in print than text on the screen. Carrying a document is much handier than lugging a computer, no matter how diminutive the machine.

Printed text isn't just convenient. Readers tend to treat print with respect. There are always exceptions—Charles Darwin used to rip big books in half to make them easier to handle. But putting words in print gives them authority, and dignity, too. It's no accident that the printer is the most common computer accessory.

All of WordPerfect's formatting and editing features are designed to produce accurate and readable pages. So when it's time to put those pages on paper, most of the work is already done. That makes the rest of the job—actually getting a printout—very easy.

Pick your printer

Before Windows came along, setting up a printer to work with your software was a job fraught with obscure commands, arcane terminology, and gray hairs. Nowadays, Windows handles the job for us. Before printing a document in WordPerfect, we just need to make sure that the current printer is the printer we want to use.

Glance at the WordPerfect status bar; if the displayed printer isn't the printer you want, double-click the status bar printer button for the Select Printer dialog box shown in figure 9.1

Fig. 9.1
The Select Printer dialog box lets you switch printers.

Click here for a list of available printers.

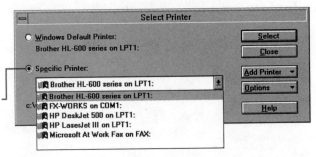

Click the Specific Printer arrow for a list of your installed printers, select the one you want, then click Select.

If you have a fax/modem installed in your computer, a fax printer may be listed among other available printers. Select the fax printer to send your fax (it will print to a file on disk or directly to your fax software rather than to a printer). Remember to reselect a regular printer for your other print jobs.

How do I print this document?

You've finished writing your document. It's formatted and edited and spell-checked. Print a copy, and you can go home. Or maybe you're still working on your document, and want to print what you've done so far. Many people, including me, find that reading hard copy makes editing easier.

 Either way, save your work with a click of the Save button on the Toolbar. Then, to print the active document:

 1 Click the Print button on the Toolbar. That pops up the Print dialog box shown in figure 9.2.

Fig. 9.2
Click the Toolbar Print button to summon up the Print dialog box.

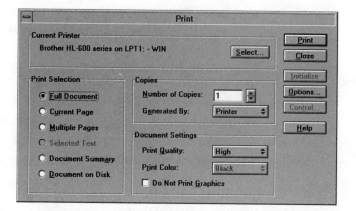

2 There are plenty of options in the Print dialog box, and all the important ones are already selected for you. If you want to print one copy of all the pages of your document, and print it on the printer displayed as the Current Printer in the dialog box, don't change anything. Just click Print.

3 That's all there is to it. WordPerfect displays a message that it's preparing the document for printing, the dialog box disappears, and the printout emerges from your printer.

How come the pages of my printout aren't numbered?

The status bar displays page numbers as you move around in the document, but those numbers won't print. For printed page numbers, select Format, <u>P</u>age, <u>N</u>umbering. Choose a <u>P</u>osition in the Page Numbering dialog box, and click OK. See Chapter 7 for more information about page numbers.

Look before you leap: previewing your document layout

WordPerfect shows you what you're doing as you do it. When you change fonts, or apply boldface or italics to text, the editing window displays your changes. WordPerfect's ability to do that is called **WYSIWIG** (say it as "WIZZY-wig), an acronym for What You See Is What You Get. It's a common feature of Windows programs.

The trouble is, what you see in the editing window is not exactly what you'll get on the printout. It's tough to gauge how margin settings will look on paper, for example, just by looking at the display on the screen. Since the editing window only displays about a third of the page at a time, you can't really tell how the whole page will look in print.

 Although you can display the two pages, side by side, by selecting <u>V</u>iew, T<u>w</u>o Page, there's a much easier way to get around the editing window's limited field of view: Page/Zoom Full. To zoom out to a full page view, simply click the Page/Zoom Full button on the Toolbar. That shows you one entire page at a time, at reduced magnification. Figure 9.3 shows the editing window in full-page view.

Fig. 9.3

Use the Page/Zoom Full button for a preview of the printed page.

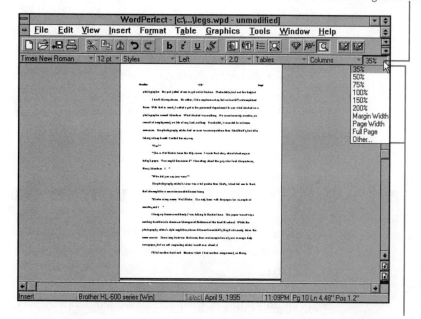

Click the Zoom button and select a different magnification from the list.

In the full-page view shown in figure 9.3, you can see how your margin settings and text placement will look in print. To see more or less detail, use the Power Bar Zoom button.

All the editing and scrolling commands are available in full-page view, so you can move from page to page, change margins, and even edit text. This view is particularly handy if you're adjusting graphics or other large elements on the page.

Click the Page/Zoom Full button again to return to the normal editing view.

Q&A

> *I'm looking at my document in full-page view, and the text is all scrunched up toward the top of the page. And there's lots of white space at the bottom of the page! What do I do?*
>
> The quick fix: center the text on the page. Press Ctrl+Home to move the insertion point to the top of the document. Then Click Format, Page, Center. Then choose Current Page, and click OK to center the text.

I don't want to print the whole document

There'll be plenty of occasions when you'll want to print only a few pages of a long document, or only the page you're working on, or even just a section of one page.

To print only some of the pages in a document:

1 Click the Print button on the Toolbar for the Print dialog box.

2 Select Multiple Pages under Print Selection.

3 Click Print for the Multiple Pages dialog box shown in figure 9.4.

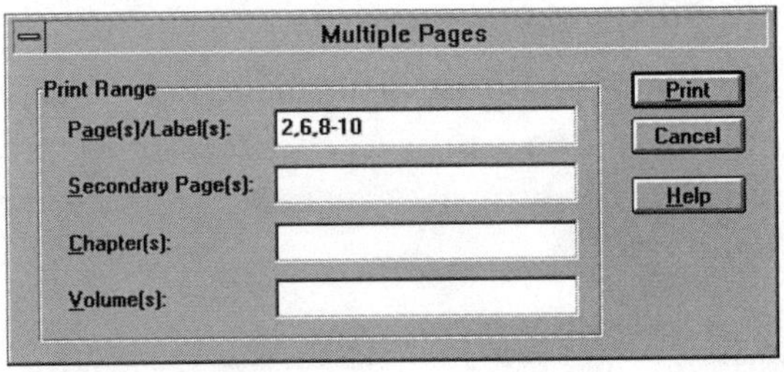

Fig. 9.4
This range prints pages 2, 6, and 8 through 10.

Multiple Pages	
Print Range	Print
Page(s)/Label(s): `2,6,8-10`	Cancel
Secondary Page(s):	Help
Chapter(s):	
Volume(s):	

4 By default, all is the choice in the Page(s)/Label(s) edit box. Click inside the Page(s)/Label(s) box to put the insertion point there, delete all, and then type in the range of pages you want to print. Use commas to separate page numbers if you want to print individual pages, and hyphens to define ranges to print.

Table 9.1 Defining print ranges

Type this...	To print page(s)
2	2 only
2,4,6	2 and 4 and 6
2-6	2 through 6
-6	From beginning of the document to page 6
6-	From page 6 to the end of the document

 **{Note}** If you just want to print individual pages *and* a range, use a combination of hyphens and commas: 6,8,9-12 prints pages 6 and 8, and pages 9 through 12.

5 Once you've entered the range of pages you want, click <u>P</u>rint.

Q&A

The Print button on the Toolbar is grayed out! What happened?

If the insertion point is inside a header or footer, the Print button is grayed out. Click anywhere outside the header or footers to restore the Print button.

All I want to print is one section of a page

You may want to see how a heavily formatted paragraph looks in print without printing the whole document.

 Select the text you want to print, and click the Print button on the Toolbar. WordPerfect chooses the Se<u>l</u>ected Text option in the Print dialog box for you; just click <u>P</u>rint and your selected text goes right to the printer. Note, however, that the selected text appears at its original location on the page, not at the top of the page as you might expect.

How do I print more than one copy?

With a computer and a printer, you can save yourself a trip to the photo-copier. WordPerfect lets you print multiple copies of a single page, a range of pages, or a whole document. To print multiple copies:

1 Click the Print button on the Toolbar for the Print dialog box.

2 Click the arrows, or type in a number in the Number of Copies box.

3 For collated copies (copies in the document's page order), select Generated by WordPerfect; for multiple copies of individual pages (2 or more copies of page 1, page 2, etc.), select Generated by Printer.

4 Select Full Document, Current Page, or Multiple Pages.

5 Click Print. If you chose multiple pages, you get the Multiple Pages dialog box; define the range of pages you want, then click Print. If you chose Current Page, you get only the page where the insertion point currently resides.

If you're using a laser printer, you almost always want to let the printer make multiple copies, especially when printing tables or graphics. The printer acts like a photocopy machine: once it gets the original image, it can quickly make copies of that image. WordPerfect is slower because it has to generate the image over again for each copy it makes.

Other nifty print options

One of my printers is an inkjet model that's nice and quiet. It has one big disadvantage. Print jobs come out with the pages face up. That puts the first page at the bottom of the pile, with the last page on top. Reverse page order. I used to reorder the pages by hand, but now I get WordPerfect to do it for me.

WordPerfect can print documents in reverse page order, so that on some printers the first page winds up at the top of the output pile, the last page at the bottom.

To print in reverse page order, click the Print button on the Toolbar. In the Print dialog box, click Options. That gets you the Print Output Options dialog box shown in figure 9.5.

Fig. 9.5
Printing in reverse order is handy for printers that output in reverse order.

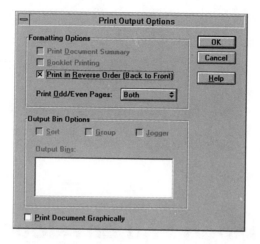

Select Print in Reverse Order (Back to Front), click OK, then click Print. The last page of your document will come out of the printer first, then the next to last page, and so on. If you print long documents on printers with reverse order output, this option will save you a lot of paper shuffling.

Here's a paper saver: print on both sides of the page

Some printers can print on both sides of a sheet of paper at the same time. That's called **duplexing**, a neat trick that my printer certainly can't do, and yours probably can't either.

WordPerfect lets you print on both sides of the page, even if your printer doesn't do duplexing:

1 Click the Toolbar Print button for the Print dialog box.

2 Click the Options button in the Print dialog box.

3 Click and hold the Print Odd/Even Pages button and select Odd.

4 Click OK, then Print to print your document's odd-numbered pages.

5 Put the stack of printed pages back in the printer, making sure the correct side is facing up, and repeat these steps to print the document's even-numbered pages; make sure to select Even in step 3.

This will work, but depending on how your printer feeds paper and the order in which it prints pages, you might have to experiment with re-feeding the pages for the even-numbered pages part of the print job. Try printing a few pages first. A little trial and error work will ensure success here.

✳ **{Note}** Booklet Printing prints pages that are divided into columns in the correct order for a booklet bound at the spine. See Chapter 14 for more information on booklet printing.

How do I print labels and envelopes?

I always get a kick out of receiving a beautifully laser-printed letter, formatted to perfection, but mailed in an envelope addressed by hand. The sender obviously gave up on trying to master the intricacies of envelope printing. Same thing with labels; with some software, fitting the text on to a label is just more trouble than it's worth.

Not with WordPerfect, though. Envelopes and labels are as easy to print as ordinary pages.

Perfect envelopes, fast

No matter how nice and crisp your letter looks, something is lost if you have to address the envelope by hand, or even with a typewriter (if you still have one). With WordPerfect, your envelopes will look just as nice as your letter:

1 Insert an envelope in your printer. With the letter still as the active document, click Format, Envelope. That pops up the Envelope dialog box shown in figure 9.6.

Fig. 9.6
The Envelope dialog box grabs the mailing address right from the letter.

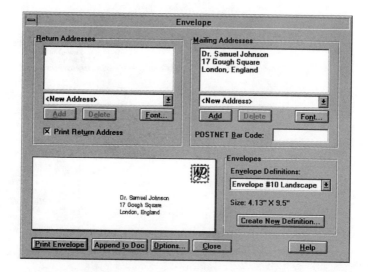

2 If you've typed the mailing address on the letter, WordPerfect grabs it and automatically puts it in the Mailing Addresses edit box. You also can select a specific address before choosing Format, Envelope. Otherwise, just click the edit box and type it in yourself. To add the address to the WordPerfect address book for future re-use, click Add.

3 Click the Return Addresses edit box and type in the return address. Click Add to add the return address to the WordPerfect address book; the next time you print an envelope, save yourself the chore of typing the return address by selecting it from the Return Address drop-down list shown in figure 9.7. Make sure the Print Return Address box is checked, or the return address won't print.

Fig. 9.7
Store mailing and
return addresses in the
WordPerfect address
book.

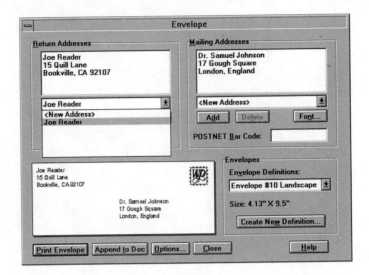

4 Select the correct envelope type and size from the Envelope Definitions drop-down list. The default is a #10 envelope, the standard size.

5 Click Print Envelope to print.

Q&A *I did all this and my envelope's still not printing! What gives?*

WordPerfect assumes that you're feeding envelopes into the printer manually. Press the appropriate button on the printer to continue printing. It varies from printer to printer, but usually it's some variation of form-feed or Continue.

{Note} To print USPS bar codes on your envelope, click Options in the Envelope dialog box, and select one of the USPS bar code position options. WordPerfect automatically translates your typed 5-, 9-, or 11-digit ZIP code into a bar code.

Printing labels is easy, too

You need to answer one crucial question before trying to print labels in WordPerfect: what kind of labels do you have? Once you've got the make and model number of your labels, you're set. In this example, we're going to print an Avery 5162 Laser Printer Label, a standard address label sheet available at any office supply store. Check your label package for the make and model number of your labels.

With that vital information in hand, let's create and print a label:

1 Click Format, Labels for the Labels dialog box shown in figure 9.8.

Fig. 9.8
Scan the list of label types in the Labels dialog box for your make and model.

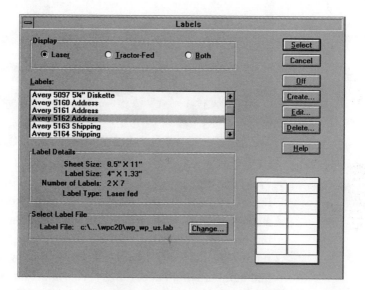

2 If you're printing laser sheet labels, click Laser under Display. That trims the very long list of labels to manageable proportions. Otherwise, leave the Both option selected to see all the label types.

3 Scroll down the list of Labels, and select your make and model number. In the example, we're using Avery 5162 Address labels.

4 Click <u>S</u>elect, and the editing window changes to display the first blank label on the sheet. If you're printing the first label on the sheet, type the information you want on the label. It looks like figure 9.9.

Fig. 9.9
Type the address or any other information you want on the blank on-screen label.

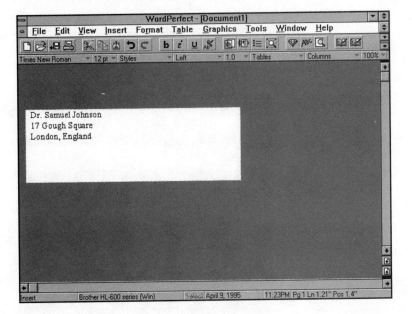

5 Press Ctrl+Enter to move the insertion point to the next label, and type the information for that label. As you move from label to label, the status bar page number indicator changes. Click the Page/Zoom Full button on the Toolbar to see the whole sheet of labels at once (see figure 9.10). WordPerfect considers each individual label a **logical** page and numbers them accordingly. This sheet has 14 labels on it, so there are logical pages 1-14 to choose from. The whole sheet is called a **physical page.**

Fig. 9.10
As you add labels, the physical page begins to fill with completed labels.

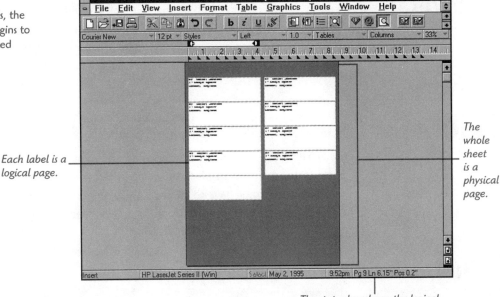

Each label is a logical page.

The whole sheet is a physical page.

The status bar shows the logical page location of the insertion point.

6 Click the Zoom/Page Full button again to return to 100% view, so that you can see what you're doing. Continue typing your label information until you are done.

7 Insert the sheet of labels in your printer, click the Print button on the Toolbar, and select Print to print your labels.

Labels are expensive. You can print labels to regular sheets of paper first, and then—when you're satisfied with the result—you can insert the sheet of labels and print the final copy.

If you don't want to waste unused labels on a sheet of labels, fill the blank ones with return addresses that can be used on packages, for example.

✳{Note} To print only certain labels on the sheet, click <u>M</u>ultiple Pages in the Print dialog box, then click <u>P</u>rint for the Multiple pages dialog box. Enter each label's logical page number, separated by commas (or a hyphen for ranges) in the P<u>a</u>ges(s)/Label(s) edit box, then click <u>P</u>rint.

❓Q&A

How come my label's not printing?

Just as with envelopes, WordPerfect assumes you're manually feeding sheets of labels. Unless you actually place the label sheets in your paper tray like regular sheets of paper, you'll have to go over to your printer and press the appropriate button to continue printing from the manual feed.

❗(Tip) If you want a whole sheet of the same label, type the information in the first label on the sheet, then copy and paste the information into all the other labels on the sheet. Press Ctrl+Enter to move the insertion point from label to label. See Chapter 13 for information on automatically merging address information to labels.

❗(Tip) You can format your labels the same way you format pages and paragraphs. Click Fo<u>r</u>mat, <u>P</u>age, <u>C</u>enter to center the text on the label, for example. You can change fonts, add borders, or any other formatting touches you like.

Can I print several documents at once?

Want to print a document without bothering to open it? Or maybe you've got several chapters, each in a different file, and you want to print them all at once. Either way, click the Open button on the Toolbar.

Click the file you want to print; for more than one file, click the first file, then hold down the Ctrl key and click additional files (release the Ctrl key when you've selected all the files you want).

Then click the File Options button, and select Print.

Figure 9.11 shows the Open file dialog box with several files chosen, and the File Options, Print command selected.

Fig. 9.11

Print one file or many from the Open File dialog box without the bother of opening them first.

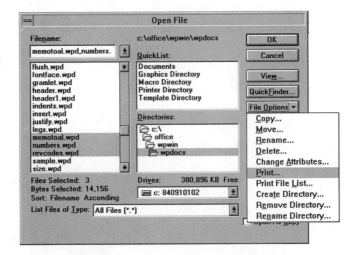

10

Templates for Fancy Documents, Fast

Like a mold for clay or a pattern in sewing, templates shape your text for professional-looking results.

There's nothing quite like the image of a major-league pitcher poised on the mound. Against the backdrop of cropped green grass and neatly uniformed teammates, he's a stirring sight. Now, imagine the same pitcher in blue jeans and a tee shirt, tossing a pickup game in a vacant lot.

The setting matters for documents as much as for pitchers. Plain, unadorned text might get the job done, but without much impact. Set the text in a perfectly formatted document, and it gains instant visual power. WordPerfect's templates give you just that sort of setting. Templates take documents right from the sandlot to the major leagues.

What exactly is a template?

Just like a cookie cutter with raw dough, a **template** gives shape to your text. Each template is a collection of formatting commands saved in a special file. Opening the file gives you a ready-made, precision-formatted document. Just add text, and you're done. There are dozens of WordPerfect templates to choose from, for everything from greeting cards to purchase orders.

Templates save you the bother of choosing fonts, setting margins, or making other tricky formatting decisions.

When do I use templates?

Templates provide everything you need for complex documents like newsletters, but they're easy enough to use even for a simple memo.

In fact, dashing off a quick memo using one of the memo templates takes less time than trying to set it up yourself, and the results will be a lot more impressive. To write a memo using a template:

1 Click the New Document button on the Toolbar for the New Document dialog box, which lists all the WordPerfect templates. From the <u>G</u>roup list for the general template categories select **memo**. WordPerfect then displays memo-type templates, as shown in figure 10.1.

Fig. 10.1
Each Group heading has several associated templates from which to choose.

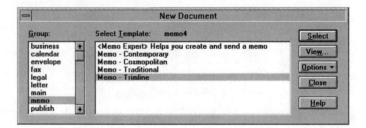

2 Double-click Memo-Trimline. WordPerfect's gears whir for a moment as the program creates the document, then the Template Information dialog box pops up. Enter the name(s) of your memo's recipient(s) and the subject, as shown in figure 10.2.

Fig. 10.2
Completing a template
is like filling in the
blanks on a form.

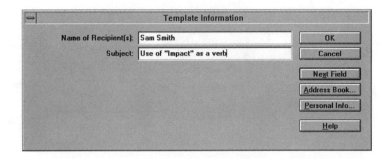

 *{Note}*

If this is the first time you have used a template, WordPerfect asks you to fill in some personal information about yourself. Not *that* personal, mind you, but information you should fill in carefully because it will be used in this and other templates you create.

3 If the memo recipients are often on your mailing list, add their names to the Template Address Book. Click Address Book, then click Add in the Template Address Book dialog box. Enter the information, as shown in figure 10.3, and click OK. Next time you send that person a memo or a letter, just grab the name off your Address Book list. Click Select to insert the address information in the Template Information dialog box.

Fig. 10.3
Add names of frequent
correspondents to the
Template Address
Book.

4 By now, you'll probably have entered your Personal Information. If you haven't, or if you want to review your entries, click the Personal Info button. Make any additions or changes in the Enter Your Personal Information dialog box shown in figure 10.4.

Fig. 10.4

Information stored
here is used in all the
templates.

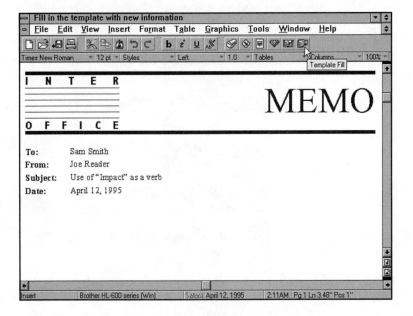

Fig. 10.5

The memo template
includes the current
date, one more item
you needn't bother
about adding yourself.

5 If you want the entered information to be used in all the templates, and
you probably do, click Save as Default. Click OK in the Template
Information dialog box.

6 WordPerfect takes the information you typed in the Template Information dialog box and puts each item in the appropriate spot in the
document. Any relevant data from Personal Information is also in-
cluded. Here, we've got the name of the memo's sender, plucked
directly from Personal Information. Figure 10.5 shows the memo so far.

The memo has everything—date, subject, recipients, and sender—except the
body text. Type that in, save the memo with the File, Save As command, and
you're done.

Figure 10.6 shows the completed memo.

Fig. 10.6
Memos get added
punch when they have
the professional look
of a WordPerfect
template.

*The title and template
information is called
the* **masthead***.*

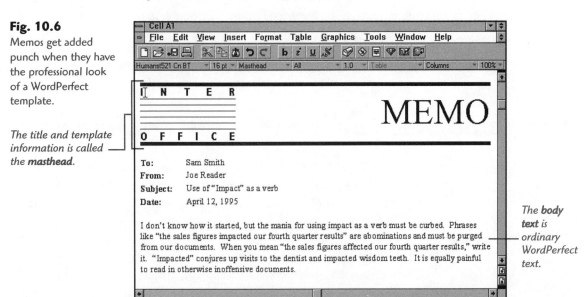

The **body
text** *is
ordinary
WordPerfect
text.*

Can I edit template information?

Maybe you misspelled one of the memo recipient's names. Or you might want
to change the subject title. Whatever your editing changes, just put the
insertion point where you want to edit, and fire away. Documents created
with specialized templates can be edited with all the usual editing commands.

You can also pop up the Template Information dialog box again and fill in the
blanks for changes in your memo information. Click the Template Fill button
on the Toolbar to return to the Template Information dialog box.

The Template Fill button appears on the Toolbar, along with other new
buttons depending on the template, after you fill in the blanks and click OK
in the Template Information dialog box.

The title bar shows `Cell A1`. What's that all about?

You'll notice the title bar display references like `Cell A1` when you move the
pointer into the masthead of the memo, as shown in figure 10.6. That's

because WordPerfect sometimes sets up the heavily formatted parts of templates, such as the masthead in the this memo, in a table grid.

For editing purposes, just ignore the cell references. They're covered in detail in Chapter 17, where you can find out more about WordPerfect tables.

Use templates for (nearly) instant letters

Everybody gets stuck with writing them. Those often dreary standard letters, in which you have no personal involvement and little real interest. Routine thank you notes and acknowledgments come to mind. You wind up saying the same thing every time, but they still have to be written.

Why waste your time trying to vary the usual boilerplate-style language? WordPerfect supplies you with ready-made boilerplate instead. Add the correct names, change a word or two, and the job is done, right down to the envelope.

 Plain English, please!

A **boilerplate** is a type of word template. It has standard wording or paragraphs, such as in a rental agreement or even a governor's proclamation. You choose which paragraphs you use, and supply any missing details.

Opening WordPerfect's box of canned letters

Here's an especially tedious correspondence chore: responding to job applicants. We'll use WordPerfect's Letter templates and boilerplate letters to take the tedium out of the task:

1 Click the New Document button to pop up the New Document dialog box. Under <u>G</u>roup, select letter.

2 Double-click a letterhead choice on the Select <u>T</u>emplate list. We'll try Letter-Trimline Letterhead. The letterhead appears briefly, then the Letter dialog box pops up.

(Tip)

If you're using your own printed letterhead stationary, double-click the Blank Letterhead template in the Select Template list.

3 Enter the Recipient's Name and Address and the Salutation. The Letter Format options offer a choice of paragraph indenting styles, as shown in figure 10.7.

Fig. 10.7
The sample letter shows the indenting style when you take your pick of letter formats.

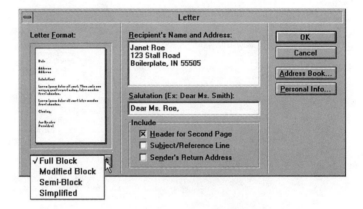

4 Click OK. That gives us the bare bones of our letter: letterhead with data taken from the Personal Information file, date, salutation, and margin and font settings. Click OK in the Letter Formatting Complete message box that appears next (see fig. 10.8).

Fig. 10.8
In order to see the entire letter, the masthead has scrolled up off the screen.

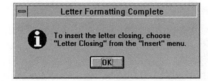

 5 The insertion point should be where we want the letter's body text to begin. Click the Insert Pre-Written Letter button on the Toolbar. That gives us the Insert File dialog box shown in figure 10.9.

Q&A ─────

Where's the Insert Pre-Written Letter button?

If the various letter buttons don't appear on the Toolbar as you create your letter, point at the Toolbar, right-click for the menu, and select Default. That puts all the letter tools on the Toolbar.

Fig. 10.9

The file names describe the pre-written letters; for more detail, select one and click View.

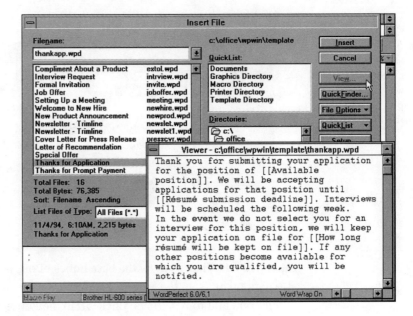

6 Double-click Thanks for Application in the File<u>n</u>ame list. The WordPerfect message `Insert File Into Current Document?` appears. Click <u>Y</u>es. That dumps the text shown in figure 10.10 right into our letter.

7 The only changes we need to make in the body of the letter are set off by double brackets. Delete the double-bracketed text, insert our own, and the tedious letter is written.

 8 Press Ctrl+End to move the insertion point to the end of the letter. Then click the Letter Closing button, make a selection from the Complimentary Closing list in the Letter Closing dialog box, and click OK.

Fig. 10.10
Not exactly deathless prose, but we didn't waste time writing it.

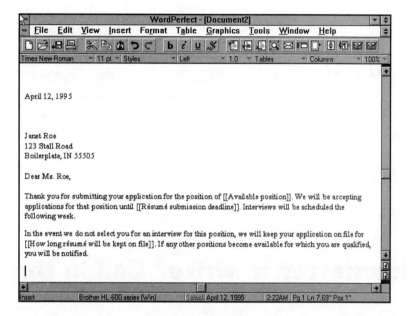

9 Click the Envelope button for the Envelope dialog box. There isn't much to do here; the Mailing Address is filled in from the letter, and if you've used the Envelope feature before, the Return Address is also filled in, as shown in figure 10.11.

Fig. 10.11
If you haven't visited the Envelope dialog box before, just type in the return address.

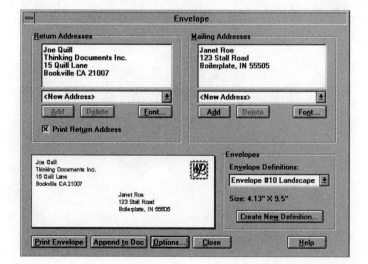

10 Click Append to Doc to put the envelope at the end of our letter document, and we're done.

⊛ **{Note}** — When you print the document, WordPerfect first prints the letter. But unless you have a separate envelope bin on your printer, you'll have to feed the envelope manually to complete the print job.

❶ **(Tip)** — Although templates work well for one or two letters, you can really speed up mass mailing by using the Merge feature. See Chapter 13 for details.

Newsletter to write? Call in the expert

Newsletters are a great way to keep colleagues informed. Anyone who's had to write a newsletter knows that the actual text is the easy part; formatting the newsletter is the real chore. Not with WordPerfect, though. The Newsletter Expert takes care of all your formatting worries, leaving you with the quick job of writing the text.

Click the New Document button and select the Publish Group. Double-click the <Newsletter Expert> for the Newsletter Expert dialog box shown in figure 10.12.

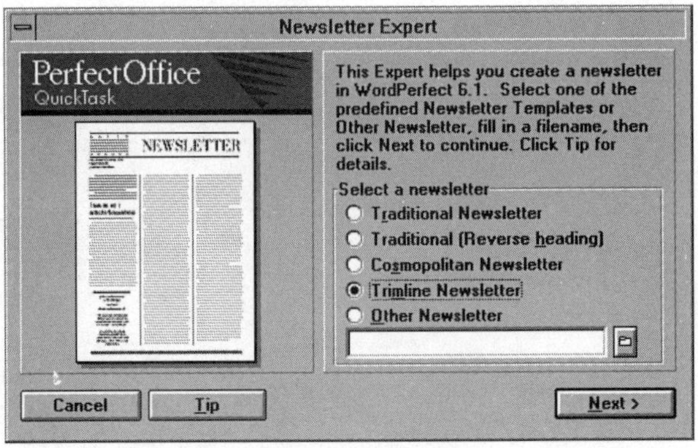

Fig. 10.12
The Newsletter Expert offers four choices of newsletter styles.

Click the different newsletter styles and preview them in the sample window. Figure 10.12 shows the Trimline Newsletter. Click <u>N</u>ext when you've made your choice.

Then let the Newsletter Expert guide you through the creation of a newsletter:

1 Fill in the blanks in the Template Information dialog box that pops up. You'll need a newsletter title; add a subtitle, volume number, issue number, and date if you like.

2 Click OK when you're done, then <u>N</u>ext in the Newsletter Expert dialog box. You get a prefabricated newsletter like the one in figure 10.13.

Click the Article Heading button before writing the title of each article. *The Table of Contents button generates contents from the article headings.* *Click the Thesaurus button for help in finding the right word.*

Fig. 10.13

The formatting is all in place; just as with the other templates, all you add is text.

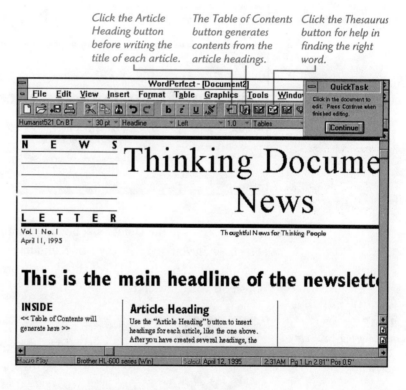

3 Click inside the document for the insertion point, then move the insertion point to replace the instruction text with your own copy. Start with the insertion point next to the main headline. Just delete template text and substitute your own.

4 Click the Article Heading button before writing each heading; the headings are formatted in a uniform style.

5 When you've finished writing the articles and headings, click the Table of Contents button. That automatically generates a table of contents drawn from the article headings and puts it in the first column. Figure 10.14 shows the newsletter taking shape.

Fig. 10.14

The Newsletter Expert helps you automatically create a table of contents from your article headings.

6 Click Continue in the QuickTask box at the upper right corner of the screen when you're finished writing, and have the Newsletter Expert perform any of the final chores shown in figure 10.15. Click Finish to polish off your newsletter.

Fig. 10.15

Newsletter writing has never been this easy!

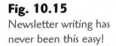

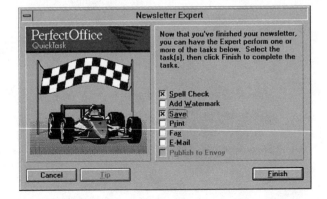

Can I create my own template?

Once you've created a document based on a template, it's easy to modify the template's formatting. Change the fonts, for example, or shift the margins. If the results appeal to you, save your modifications as a new template for future use.

Figure 10.16 shows the newsletter created in this chapter with some quick font changes.

Fig. 10.16
Customizing existing templates is easy with a few font changes.

Save your customized newsletter with a new file name, and close it. We'll call this effort NEWSLET1. To save the customized newsletter as a new template:

1 Click the New Document button and select Options, New Template in the New Document dialog box. The template feature bar, shown in figure 10.17, displays.

2 Click the Insert File button, then find and double-click the file name of your customized template document. Click Yes to insert the document and Yes again to overwrite existing styles.

Fig. 10.17

The template feature bar provides the tools for building your own template.

3 The customized newsletter appears in the editing window. Click Exit Template, and then click Yes to save the changes.

4 The Save Template dialog box appears (see fig. 10.18). Enter a Description of the template, the Template Name, and click the Template Group to which you want to add the new template. That'll be Publish in this case.

Fig. 10.18

Saving new templates preserves them for future use.

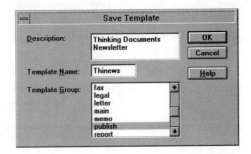

5 Click OK and the template is saved. To reuse it, just select it from the list in the New Document dialog box.

There are plenty of other templates in WordPerfect 6.1. So many, in fact, that you may never need to create your own.

Documents with Style(s)

In this chapter:

- Can I copy formatting from one paragraph to another?
- QuickFormat really is quick!
- Borders and fill make for stylish paragraphs
- How can styles save me time?
- I want my own style

Plain text is like white bread: functional, but not too exciting. WordPerfect's formatting tricks are fresh raspberry jam for text.

Lord Chesterfield, the eighteenth century wit, was an authority on elegance and style. "Style is the dress of thoughts," said Chesterfield, as neat a definition as we're ever likely to get. Of course, not everyone agreed that Chesterfield's was the last word on style. A great stylist of a different kind, Dr. Samuel Johnson, said he'd thought Chesterfield "a lord among wits; but I find he is only a wit among lords."

True style is as hard to come by as it is to pin down, but not in WordPerfect. WordPerfect **styles** are collections of formatting commands you assemble yourself. Use them to dress up your text, and you'll find that stylishness is easily achieved.

QuickFormat provides instant style

Styles are one or more formatting commands that you name, save, and apply to your text. You don't have to create styles to format text. They're just time and trouble savers, and they do help you maintain a consistent style throughout your document.

But if you're really in a hurry, or if you have a small formatting job on your hands, use QuickFormat instead of creating a style.

QuickFormat grabs the formatting you've applied to text and paints it over unformatted text. It's just like mixing paints on a palette to get a particular shade, then dipping a brush in the paint and applying it to a plain surface.

QuickFormat starts with formatting

QuickFormat is especially handy for headings in a short report or newsletter.

The headings shown in figure 11.1 are on the plain side. We'll format the first heading, then use QuickFormat to copy the formatting to the other headings on the page.

Fig. 11.1
Headings should call attention to the text, but these could use some work.

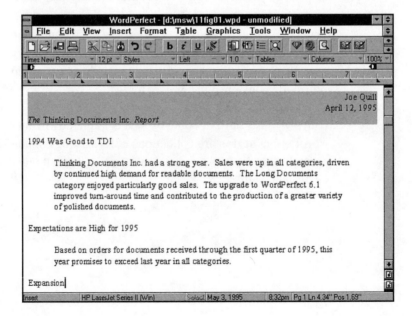

1 Triple-click the heading to select it. Click the Power Bar Font Face button, and select Arial to change fonts.

2 Click the Size button and choose 14 point, and choose the Bold button on the Toolbar to apply boldface. Plain, sans serif fonts like Arial work well in headings, and large, boldface makes them stand out.

3 To copy the formatting to the other headings, put the insertion point anywhere within the formatted heading. Then click the QuickFormat button on the Toolbar. That pops up the QuickFormat dialog box, shown in figure 11.2.

Fig. 11.2
With the insertion point in a heading, QuickFormat automatically selects Headings in the dialog box.

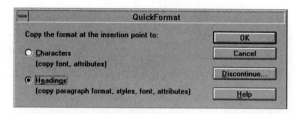

4 With Headings selected in the QuickFormat dialog box, click OK.

5 The pointer grows a little paint roller. Put the pointer inside the heading you want to format, then click to apply the formatting, as shown in figure 11.3.

Fig. 11.3
While the pointer sports that little paint roller, you can keep applying the copied formatting.

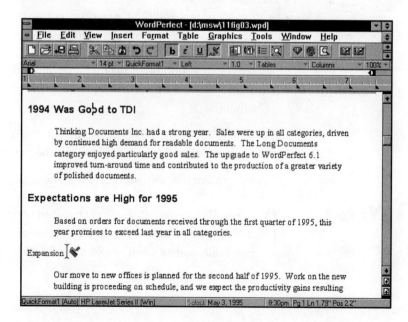

5 Click your other headings, too, if you want them formatted the same way. When you're finished, click the QuickFormat button on the Toolbar to turn off QuickFormat.

> When you copy formatting with QuickFormat, WordPerfect names the formatting QuickFormat1. Use QuickFormat a second time, and you get QuickFormat2, and so on. Those named QuickFormats appear in the Power Bar Select Style button list. You can apply the QuickFormats to the current paragraph by clicking their names on the Power Bar Select Style button list.

Because these headings are formatted by a single style, if you change the format of one heading, all the others change, as well. For example, place the insertion point inside any of the headings, and click the Italic button on the Toolbar. Note that the entire heading changes to italic, as do all the other headings formatted with this style.

Can I copy formatting from character to character?

QuickFormat also works for individual characters, words, or sentences. In the example, we want to make all of the initial capitals of Thinking Documents Inc. 28 points and bold. After formatting the first character, use QuickFormat to quickly format the other characters:

1 Place the insertion point inside the formatted text or select it, and click the QuickFormat button to display the QuickFormat dialog box. Select Characters.

2 Click OK; the pointer I-beam acquires a little paint brush (see figure 11.4. Notice that this isn't the same as the paint roller in figure 11.3.).

3 Drag through the text you want to format, as seen in figure 11.4.

> You "paint" character attributes to characters using this procedure, but the characters are not formatted with a QuickFormat style. Therefore, they do not automatically update when one of the characters is changed.

Fig. 11.4
When you QuickFormat text instead of paragraphs, the pointer acquires a paint brush.

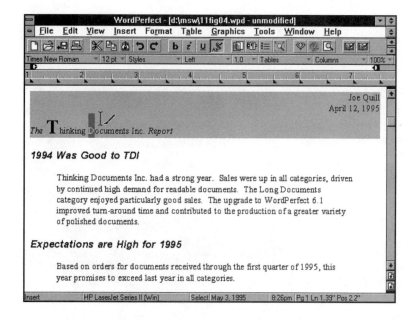

4 When you release the mouse button, the formatting you've copied with QuickFormat is applied to the text.

What is fill, and how do I use it?

Are you wondering how to get that gray background (known as fill) seen in the heading in figure 11.4?

 Plain English, please!

Fill is a pattern that you can apply to paragraph backgrounds or to characters in the paragraph foreground. Fill can be different levels or shades of gray, or designs made up of dots and lines. **Borders** are lines in different thicknesses above, below, or around text. Borders also include shadow effects. 99

To add a gray fill to the top three paragraphs (lines, in this case) of your document, follow these steps:

1 With the insertion point in the paragraph you're formatting with fill, or with multiple paragraphs selected, select Format, Paragraph, Border/ Fill.

2 In the Paragraph Border dialog box, click the Fill Style button, and select a fill style (for example, solid gray) from the palette shown in figure 11.5.

Fig. 11.5

Click the Fill Style button for a palette of fill patterns. The Border Style palette displays various border lines.

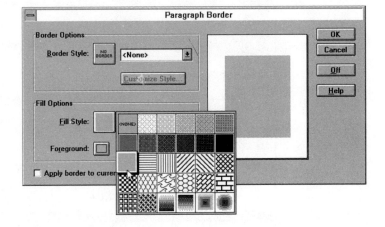

3 Click OK; the fill is applied to the selected paragraph.

Applying borders works just like applying fill. Click the Border Style button in the Paragraph Border dialog box for the many border options.

To get rid of fill or borders: put the insertion point in the paragraph you've formatted with either one, select Format, Paragraph, Border/Fill and click <None> on the appropriate drop-down lists.

Just what is a style?

Like a QuickFormat, **styles** are used to apply formatting commands to text. There's one big difference: Styles name the formatting you've assembled and save it for future use.

Instead of mixing paints on a palette to get a special shade, styles are like mixing the paints right in the can. Name your creation, label the can of paint, and—the next time you want that shade—you just grab the can off the paint shelf. Styles have names too. There's even a shelf to store them on.

What can I do with styles?

Create styles for any headings or titles that need to be formatted the same way every time. Newsletter headlines are good candidates for a style; also report titles, section headings, and chapter titles.

You can apply several different styles in the same document for a consistent, professional look from one document to the next.

QuickStyles, for styles the quick way

There are two ways of getting paint. You can go hiking to collect ores, grind them up for pigment, mix them with a liquid, and hope that you wind up with something usable. Or you can go to the hardware store and buy a can.

You've got a similar choice with styles. You can make them from scratch, or you can use QuickStyles.

QuickStyles grab formatting from your document and turn it into a style. Figure 11.6 shows a chapter title formatted with Albertville Extrabold 12 pt and a paragraph shadow border.

{Note} In these examples, we use the Albertville font. The font you use in your styles depends on the fonts you have installed in Windows on your computer.

Fig. 11.6

If you like the way your formatting creation looks, preserve it as a style.

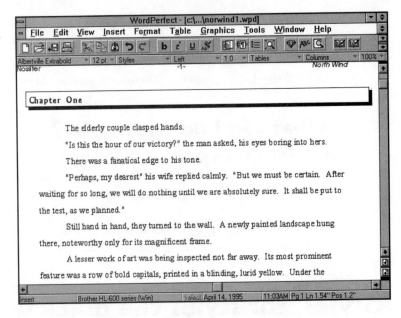

To make a QuickStyle out of that chapter-title formatting:

1 Put the insertion point in the paragraph whose formatting you're turning into a style, click the Power Bar Select Style button, and select QuickStyle, as seen in figure 11.7.

Fig. 11.7

The Select Style button list displays all the styles in use.

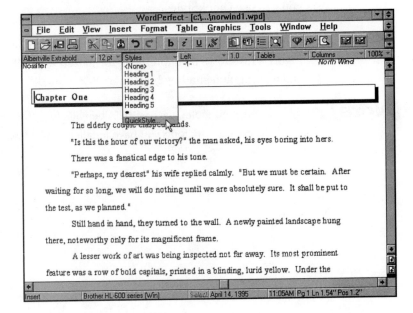

2 That pops up the QuickStyle dialog box. Type a name for your style, and add a brief description, as shown in figure 11.8.

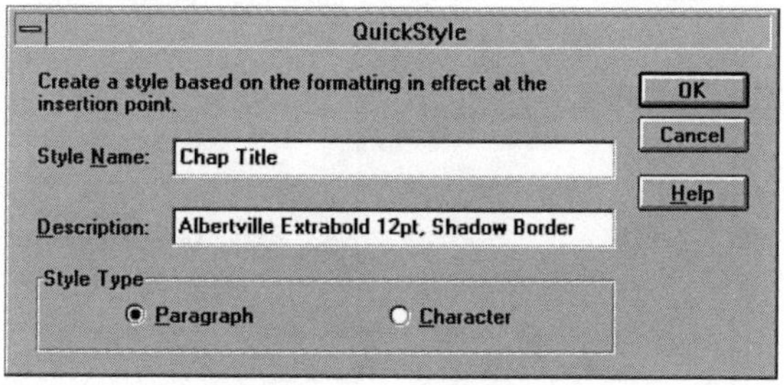

Fig. 11.8
Give your paragraph
style a short name and
a longer description.

3 Click OK. The style name is added to the Power Bar Select Style button list, and it's displayed on the button.

You can create QuickStyles for entire paragraphs, single characters, or any selected text, exactly as we've created the chapter title style here.

How do I apply my new style?

Creating a QuickStyle is quick, applying it is even quicker:

1 Put the insertion point in or next to the paragraph you want to apply the style to and click the Power Bar Style button. In figure 11.9, we'll style that plain-looking chapter title.

2 Click the style you want, Chap Title here, and the paragraph is instantly formatted in that style, as shown in figure 11.10.

?Q&A

I tried to create a QuickStyle from a paragraph with two fonts, but only the first font shows up when I quit the QuickStyle dialog box. What gives?

Styles can only save one formatting attribute—font face or size, border style, etc.—per paragraph. You have to create a different style for each attribute. Any one style can hold several formatting elements though—one font size and face, a border style, a fill style, and so on.

Fig. 11.9

Once your style is created, apply it with two clicks.

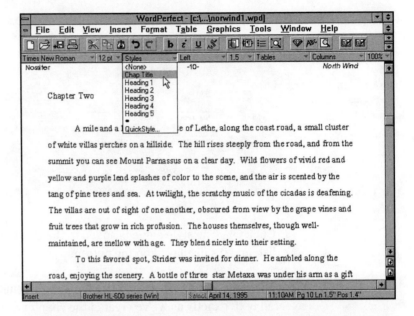

Fig. 11.10

Styles are the best way of creating consistent headings within documents and from one document to another.

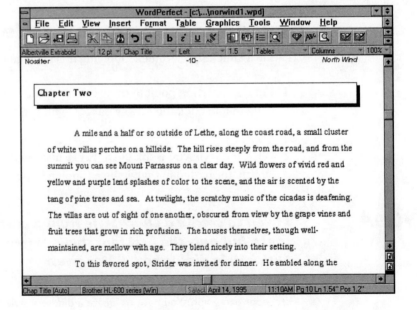

I hate this style. How do I get rid of it?

To change or remove a paragraph style, put the insertion point in the paragraph, click the Power Bar Select Style button, and select <None> or some other style from the list.

If you hate the style so much you never want to use it again, select Format, Styles to see the Style List dialog box shown in figure 11.11.

Fig. 11.11

Manage styles in the Style List dialog box.

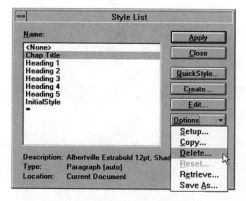

Select the offending style from the list of Names, click Options, and choose Delete.

You get two choices in the Delete Styles dialog box:

- Include Codes deletes the style throughout the document, and removes the formatting codes that go along with the style, too.

- Leave Codes removes the styles codes but leaves the formatting codes in the document.

?Q&A

I accidentally applied a style to a paragraph. How do I get rid of the style?

If you catch the mistake immediately, simply click the Undo button on the Toolbar. Or you can position the cursor in the mistakenly styled paragraph and select None from the Styles button on the Power Bar. You also can delete the Para Style: Auto code from the Reveal Codes windows.

This style needs restyling

Even if you don't hate your style enough to delete it, you may find it mildly unsatisfactory. You might want to change a font, for example, or add or remove a border. If that's the case, just edit your style.

Click Format, Styles, Edit for the Styles Editor dialog box, shown in figure 11.12.

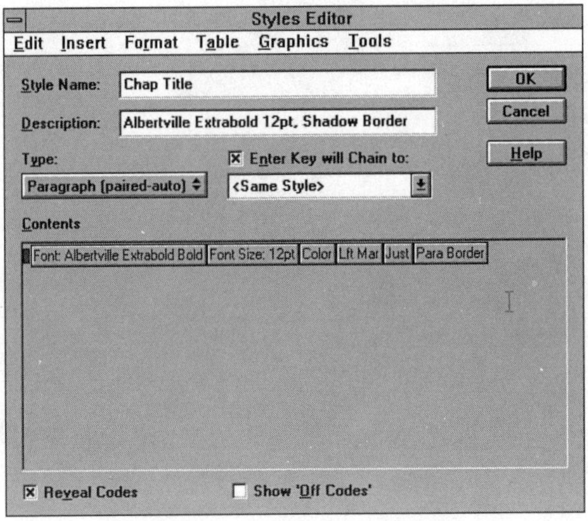

Fig. 11.12
Edit the formatting codes or add formatting commands from the Styles Editor menu bar.

In the Styles Editor dialog box, you can make any changes you like to your style. Get rid of formatting codes by dragging them with the mouse out of the reveal codes (content) window. Add codes by using the menu-bar commands, which put all the WordPerfect formatting features at your disposal.

The Styles Editor dialog box also has a useful option for controlling the way styles are applied to your text as you type.

By default, if you select a style and begin to type, the style stays on until you turn it off (by selecting <None> or a different style from the Power Bar). If you want to turn off a style at the end of the paragraph (when you press Enter), select Enter Key will Chain to: <None>.

Concoct your style from scratch

If you know exactly what you want from a style, make it from scratch. Select Format, Styles, Create for the Styles Editor dialog box. Choose any formatting commands you like from the dialog box menu bar. The codes appear in the Contents (reveal codes) window when you make your choices. Name and describe the style, and click OK to save it.

You might find it easier to create styles from formatted text with the QuickStyles command we've look at already. You wind up with the same thing: a named style to apply to text. And with QuickStyles, you can get your style just right by experimenting on text first.

I want this style in another document

Styles you create in one document are saved with the document. They're also only available in that document. You might want to apply a style created in one document to text in other documents, too.

To grab a style from one document so you can use it in the current document, select Format, Styles, Options, Retrieve for the Retrieve Styles dialog box shown in figure 11.13.

Fig. 11.13
Share styles among documents by retrieving them into the current document.

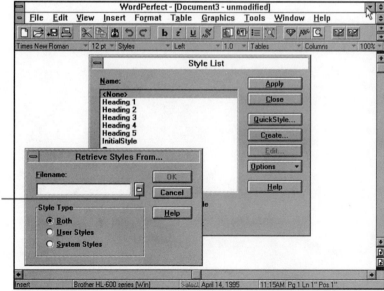

Click this button for the Select File list of all your WordPerfect files.

Either type the file name of the document with the style you want, or click the Select File button, and select the file from the list.

Choose the User Styles option button, and then click OK. The style now appears on the Power Bar Select Style button in your current document.

If WordPerfect prompts you to Overwrite Current Styles, answer No, or you may lose other styles in your current document.

12

WordPerfect's Labor-Saving Devices

Time spent on chores like typing is time stolen from thinking (or golf). WordPerfect has great gadgets to free you from routine jobs.

Monday morning in the Age of Gadgets. The automatic alarm goes off. The automatic coffeemaker goes on. Electric hair dryers compete with electric razors for air time. Toast springs eternal from electric toasters; less easily identified foodstuffs emerge from microwave ovens. Automatic garage doors open for our favorite mechanical marvel. Gadgets aren't necessities, but just picture Mondays without them.

WordPerfect's labor-saving devices aren't necessities, either. But if you value your hair dryer and coffeemaker, take a minute to learn about macros and abbreviations. Put them to good use, and you'll have more time to figure out that VCR.

Save typing with abbreviations

Mr., Mrs., Dr. These abbreviations are so common that we don't even think about them. Glance at Mr. on the page, and your mind automatically expands it to Mister. That's exactly what WordPerfect does with abbreviations.

Create an abbreviation, type it in a document, and press Ctrl+A to instantly expand it—that's all there is to it! Use abbreviations for words or phrases you type all the time. If you type your company name or address frequently, abbreviate it. Editors given to repeating phrases like "This is not clear," can abbreviate it to "tnc" and save themselves time.

To create an abbreviation:

1 Select the text that you want to abbreviate and click Insert, Abbreviations, Create. Figure 12.1 shows selected text and the Create Abbreviations dialog box.

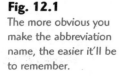

Fig. 12.1
The more obvious you make the abbreviation name, the easier it'll be to remember.

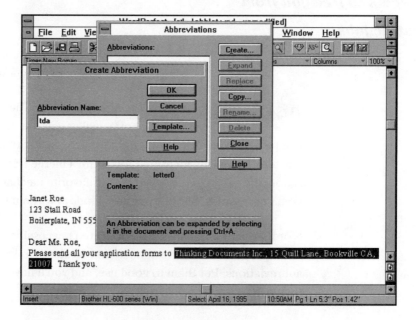

2 Type the abbreviation in the Abbreviation Name edit box shown in figure 12.1 and then click OK. Make the abbreviation as easy to remember as possible, using an obvious combination of letters. I've typed **tda** for Thinking Documents address.

⊛ {Note}

Abbreviations are **case-sensitive**, which is a fancy way of saying that if you name the abbreviation TDA with uppercase letters, you'll have to type **TDA** every time you use it. So, **tda**, in lowercase, won't work.

Because entries in Abbreviations are case-sensitive, you can use both **TDA** and **tda** as abbreviation names. That's handy if you want to abbreviate both the Thinking Documents address and "Theodore Delano Asquith."

❓Q&A

I'm typing my lowercase abbreviation at the beginning of a sentence and it doesn't work! What's going on?

QuickCorrect is the culprit. QuickCorrect automatically capitalizes the first letter of a sentence, making lowercase abbreviations inoperable. You can out-persist QuickCorrect; it gives up after one, or sometimes two, corrections. Press Del or Backspace to get rid of the incorrectly capitalized letter, then retype the lowercase letter. Repeat the procedure if QuickCorrect corrects you again.

⊛ {Note}

If you find deleting and retyping a nuisance, you can also turn off QuickCorrect's automatic capitalization: select <u>T</u>ools, QuickCorrect, <u>O</u>ptions for the QuickCorrect Options dialog box. Uncheck the <u>C</u>apitalize First Letter checkbox and click OK.

3 Click the <u>T</u>emplate button in the Create Abbreviations dialog box to see the Abbreviation Location dialog box shown in figure 12.2.

Fig. 12.2
Make an abbreviation available to only one template or to all your documents, depending on your choice here.

4 If you only want the abbreviation available to the current template, select <u>C</u>urrent Template. To make it available to all your documents, select <u>D</u>efault Template. Click OK when you're done.

5 Click OK in the Create Abbreviation dialog box. Your new abbreviation is added to the list in the Abbreviations dialog box. Select the abbreviation on the list, and the dialog box displays the template where it's saved, and the word or phrase you've abbreviated, as shown in figure 12.3.

Fig. 12.3
The Abbreviations dialog box displays the abbreviation and what it stands for.

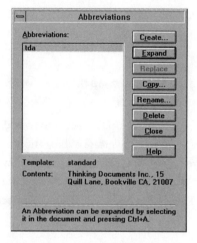

Click <u>C</u>lose, and we're through. For a quick reminder of your abbreviations, just select <u>I</u>nsert, <u>A</u>bbreviations to pop up the Abbreviations dialog box. Select an abbreviation and read the Contents to jog your memory.

Abbreviate your typing chores: use abbreviations

Once you've created an abbreviation, just type it wherever you want the word or phrase it represents. With the insertion point in or adjacent to the abbreviation, press Ctrl+A. The abbreviation is instantly expanded.

Q&A

Why can't I get this #$@! abbreviation to work?

Chances are, you're typing a space after the letters of the abbreviation. Hitting the spacebar after typing a word is the natural thing to do, but it makes abbreviations non-functional. The insertion point has to be in or adjacent to the abbreviation before Ctrl+A can expand it.

Click Insert, Abbreviations for the Abbreviations dialog box to do any of the following:

- Delete abbreviations: select the abbreviation from the list, and click Delete, Yes.

- Rename abbreviations: select the abbreviation from the list, and click Rename. Type a new name in the Rename Abbreviation dialog box and click OK.

- Replace the text the abbreviation stands for: select the new text, then click Insert, Abbreviations and choose the abbreviation from the list. Click Replace, Yes to replace the old text with the new selection.

I want this abbreviation in another template

You might create an abbreviation in a letter template, but you need to use it in a report template. To copy an abbreviation from one template to another:

1 Click Insert, Abbreviations for the Abbreviations dialog box.

2 Click the Copy button for the Copy Abbreviation dialog box.

3 Select the abbreviation you want to copy from the Select Abbreviation to Copy list.

4 Click the Template to copy to drop-down arrow, and select a template, as shown in figure 12.4.

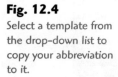

Fig. 12.4
Select a template from the drop-down list to copy your abbreviation to it.

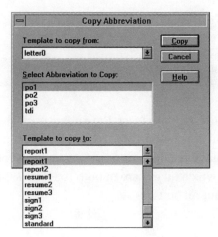

5 Click Copy and then Close in the Abbreviations dialog box.

(Tip)

> If you want to make the abbreviation for all of your new blank documents, copy the abbreviation to the STANDARD template.

How about expanding all my abbreviations at once?

Once you've created a collection of abbreviations, you can put your typing on the express train. Figure 12.5 shows a memo full of abbreviations (they're in boldface so you can see what's going on).

Fig. 12.5
Abbreviations save time; combined with a button to expand them, they'll save even more time.

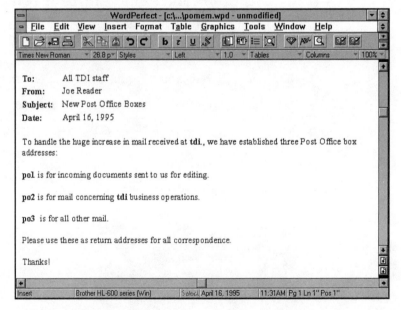

Typing the abbreviations is fast. Expanding each abbreviation as you work might slow you down. And going back and expanding each one is a nuisance. WordPerfect has a handy button that expands all your document's abbreviations at once, which takes care of both roadblocks. To get, and use, the Toolbar Expand All button:

1 Right-click the Toolbar for the Toolbar QuickMenu and select Utilities.

2 Click the Expand All button on the Toolbar. That expands all the abbreviations at once, as shown in figure 12.6.

Fig. 12.6

Point at the other buttons on the Utilities Toolbar for their names and descriptions of what they do—some are pretty handy.

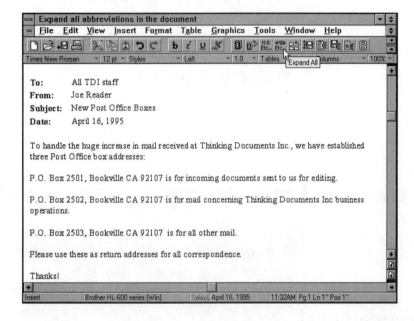

3 To get the regular Toolbar back, right-click the Toolbar, and select 6.1 WordPerfect on the QuickMenu.

(Tip) If you like this feature, you can add the Abbreviations Expand All button to your main Toolbar.

What's a macro?

As useful as they are, household and office gadgets are only tools to help us get the job done. They can't do the job for us. The fax machine is a terrific device, but if we want to send a fax, we still have to load the document, dial a number, and press a button to send it.

We'd rather have an assistant on call all the time to do chores like faxing for us. The kind of assistant who'll remember how to do any job just by watching us do it once. An assistant who then does the job flawlessly whenever we want it done.

We have a helper like that in WordPerfect: a **macro**. The Expand All button we used earlier is a macro supplied with WordPerfect. One click, and it executes many expand abbreviation commands, saving us the bother.

 Plain English, please!

A **macro**, in computer lingo, is a single command that executes a large, or macro, number of other commands.

How can I create my own macro?

Macros are great for any repetitive task. If you find yourself doing the same WordPerfect chore all the time, create a macro to do it for you. Turn on the macro recorder, do your chore, then turn off the macro recorder. Creating a macro is no harder than doing the chore itself. Even if it involves dozens of steps, a macro will take care of the whole job with one command.

Here's one repetitive chore not covered by an existing WordPerfect feature: setting up a generic document header. Let's create a macro called HEADER.WCM to create a generic header for us:

1 Click Tools, Macro, Record for the Record Macro dialog box shown in figure 12.7.

Why is it called a macro?

Macro, the opposite of micro, comes from the Greek. As a prefix, macro-means large or long. Think of microscopic—too tiny to see; and macroscopic, meaning large enough to be visible to the naked eye. If your newly promoted colleague gets big-headed on you, he's macrocephalic, meaning big-headed. And if an author is putting you to sleep, he's becoming macrostylous, or long-styled.

Fig. 12.7
The Record Macro dialog box displays a list of all the macros that come with WordPerfect and that you have recorded.

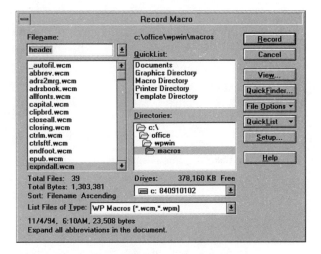

⊗<*Caution*> If you record a macro after already starting a document, it's a good idea to save your work before you start recording the macro. You're unlikely to run into memory or program glitches while recording macros, but on those rare occasions when you might, you don't want to risk losing your work.

2 Type a name in the Fil<u>e</u>name text box. WordPerfect supplies the .WCM extension, so we needn't bother. We'll call this macro **header**, as shown in figure 12.7.

3 Click <u>R</u>ecord to turn on the macro recorder. The dialog box disappears and the macro feature bar pops up. Until we turn the macro recorder off again, every mouse click we make and command we execute will be recorded.

⊛{*Note*} You can't select text or move the insertion point with the mouse while recording a macro. That's why the pointer turns into the circle with a line across it (the international "NO" symbol). Instead, use the arrow keys to move the insertion point and the Shift+arrow key combination to select text while recording macros.

4 With the macro recording, we'll start doing our chore. Click Fo<u>r</u>mat, <u>H</u>eader/Footer, select Header A, and click <u>C</u>reate.

5 We'll stick our company name in here, **Thinking Documents Inc.**, formatted in PC Brussels 9 pt italics. You can use your company name, your own name, a font of your own choosing, or whatever other text you want in the header.

6 Tab to the center of the header, and click Nu<u>m</u>ber, <u>P</u>age Number on the header feature bar to insert page numbering.

If you make a typing mistake while recording a macro, correct it and carry on, just as if you were editing an ordinary document. It's the end result of your typing and corrections that matters.

7 Borders work well in headers. Instead of using the feature bar Insert <u>L</u>ine command, we'll click Fo<u>r</u>mat, <u>P</u>aragraph, <u>B</u>order/Fill for the Paragraph Border dialog box and something more decorative.

8 Click the <u>B</u>order Style button for the palette of borders shown in figure 12.8.

Fig. 12.8
The Paragraph Border dialog box offers more variety than the header feature bar Insert Line button.

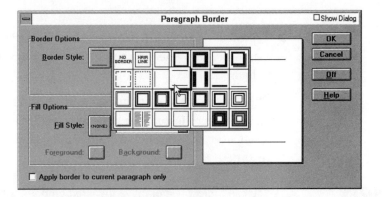

9 Select the Thin Top/Bottom border, the fourth button on the second row, and click OK.

10 Click <u>C</u>lose on the header feature bar, and click the Stop Macro button on the macro feature bar shown in figure 12.9.

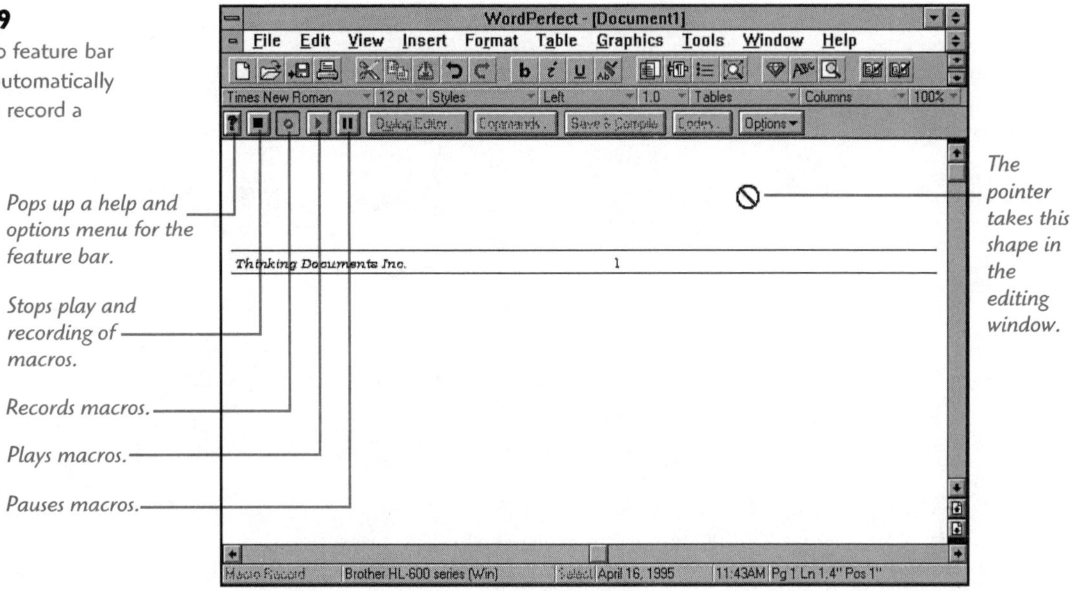

Fig. 12.9

The macro feature bar pops up automatically when you record a macro.

Pops up a help and options menu for the feature bar.

Stops play and recording of macros.

Records macros.

Plays macros.

Pauses macros.

The pointer takes this shape in the editing window.

That's it. HEADER.WCM is born. It took a dozen or so steps to create this simple header. The next time we want it, a couple of clicks will take care of the whole thing.

Macros aren't confined to creating headers—any similar chore can be automated with a macro. Once you start creating macros, you'll wonder how you ever got along without them.

How do I play it back?

Recording a macro is only as complicated as performing the task you record. Playing a macro back is always a snap, no matter how complex the underlying chore.

To play the HEADER macro you just created, first go to a new blank document, then:

1 Click Tools, Macro, Play for the Play Macro dialog box shown in figure 12.10.

Fig. 12.10

Macros are stored in files that can be renamed, deleted, and moved from the dialog box.

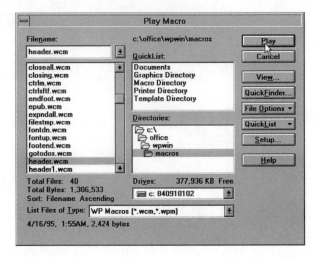

2 Select a macro from the Filename list; to play the macro we just created, scroll down to HEADER.WCM, and select it.

3 Click Play. All the typing we did and commands we issued while recording the macro are played back in the blink of an eye. The header pops into place on the page, and you're ready to write your document.

The macros on the Filename list in the Play Macro dialog box are handy time-savers supplied by WordPerfect. Any of them can be run from Toolbar buttons, like the EXPNDALL.WCM macro we used to expand abbreviations. You can also play them from the Play Macro dialog box. Just select a macro, and click Play.

The Tools, Macros menu displays the last four macros you've used. Click one, and then click OK to run it.

As you select WordPerfect's macros, read the description of what they do at the bottom of the Play Macro dialog box. To see a list of descriptive names, instead of the file names displayed in figure 12.10, click Setup for the Open/ Save As Setup dialog box. Click the Show button and select Descriptive Name, Filename for the display shown in figure 12.11.

Fig. 12.11
Displaying WordPerfect macros' descriptive names gives you a better notion of what they do.

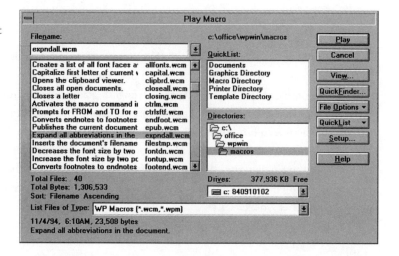

 (Tip)

> If you find a macro that's particularly useful, add it to your customized Toolbar. That way it'll never be more than a mouse click away.

This macro could use a few alterations

When you record your keystrokes and mouse clicks in a macro, some pretty amazing things go on behind the scenes. Macro recording sets in motion a kind of United Nations simultaneous translation team. As you perform them, your actions are translated, or **compiled**, into WordPerfect's macro language.

It's a language with its own vocabulary, punctuation, and syntax that's used to talk directly to WordPerfect. Normally, you communicate with the program through menus and buttons; the macro language bypasses the menus and issues commands directly to WordPerfect.

Plain English, please!

Macros consist of commands that WordPerfect understands. When you record a macro, WordPerfect arranges all the commands in the proper order, using correct syntax. We know syntax in English grammar as the rules that govern sentence construction. English isn't necessarily strict about syntax; writers break the rules all the time and call it poetic license. WordPerfect is more exacting. Macros require correct syntax in order to run. You can write macros, programming the commands yourself, as long as you use the proper syntax. WordPerfect's translation team ensures that our actions are recorded with the proper syntax.

Can I edit my macros?

Although macros are saved in the macro language, in other respects, macro files are like ordinary WordPerfect files. All the program's editing features can be used in macro files. And, although macro language isn't English, it's close enough so that we don't have to learn it in order to edit it.

Why would you want to edit a macro in the first place? If you don't like the way it turns out, you can always delete the macro and start again. But if you just have a few minor alterations to make, editing the macro is often faster than re-recording the whole thing.

To edit a macro:

1 Click Tools, Macro, Edit for the Edit Macro dialog box.

2 Select the macro from the Filename list in the Edit Macro dialog box, and click the Edit button. That puts the macro in the editing window and pops up the macro feature bar, as shown in figure 12.12.

Fig. 12.12

This is what the HEADER.WCM macro looks like in macro language.

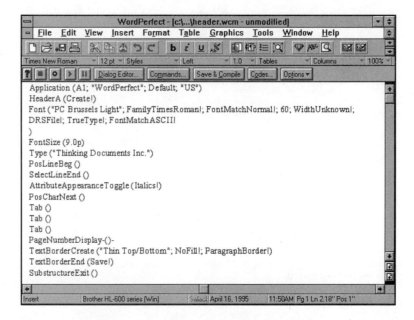

```
WordPerfect - [c:\...\header.wcm - unmodified]
 File   Edit   View   Insert   Format   Table   Graphics   Tools   Window   Help

Times New Roman    12 pt   Styles        Left        1.0    Tables        Columns        100%

Application (A1; "WordPerfect"; Default; "US")
HeaderA (Create!)
Font ("PC Brussels Light"; FamilyTimesRoman!; FontMatchNormal!; 60; WidthUnknown!;
DRSFile!; TrueType!; FontMatchASCII!
)
FontSize (9.0p)
Type ("Thinking Documents Inc.")
PosLineBeg ()
SelectLineEnd ()
AttributeAppearanceToggle (Italics!)
PosCharNext ()
Tab ()
Tab ()
Tab ()
PageNumberDisplay-()-
TextBorderCreate ("Thin Top/Bottom"; NoFill!; ParagraphBorder!)
TextBorderEnd (Save!)
SubstructureExit ()

Insert            Brother HL-600 series (Win)      Select  April 16, 1995      11:50AM Pg 1 Ln 2.18" Pos 1"
```

3 Most of your macro edits are likely to be changes in the text you typed while the macro was recording. Typed text appears within quotation marks inside parentheses preceded by Type and a space, as in Type ("Thinking Documents Inc.") on line seven in figure 12.12.

4 If you want to change Inc. to Incorporated, just place the insertion point after the "c" in "Inc.," delete the period, and type **orporated**. Be careful not to move or delete any of the punctuation marks around the text.

5 When you've finished editing your macro, click the Options button on the feature bar and select Close Macro and click Yes to save the changes.

WordPerfect has an on-line macro guide

If you're inclined that way, WordPerfect has a complete on-line guide to macros. Click Help, Macros to access it. There's help for problem macros, and what amounts to a language manual for the macro language.

13

Merges, for Letters by the Bushel

In this chapter:

- What happens in a merge?
- Data files? Form files? Explain, please
- How do I set up a data file?
- Form files are very flexible
- Can merges really be that easy?

Merges mass-produce documents on the assembly line principle, yet each finished document looks hand-made.

Merging is a risky business, and recent history is full of mergers gone awry. Which isn't to say that mergers are always flops. When Maria Sklodowska (Marie Curie) married Pierre Curie, their merger resulted in the discovery of radioactivity and a shared Nobel prize in Physics.

Word processor merges used to be seen as risky procedures, akin to hitching a big manufacturer to an investment bank. In WordPerfect, merges are more like the collaboration of the Curies: a sure thing.

What happens in a merge?

A WordPerfect merge produces documents on an assembly line. Henry Ford pioneered the idea when he built the Model T: you start with an empty shell of a car, systematically add parts from a supply bin, and end up with a finished automobile.

WordPerfect merges have the same three-part setup:

- The empty shell is called a **form file.** The form file is a document with blanks, such as a letter missing the recipient's name and address.

- The parts bin is called a **data file.** It's a document containing the items needed to fill-in-the-blanks in the form file; names and addresses, for example.

- **Merging** takes the data from the data file and sticks it in the appropriate blanks in the form file to produce finished documents.

When do I use a merge?

Like Henry Ford's assembly line, merges mass-produce finished products quickly and with little effort. Whenever you have more than a couple of documents to produce, and the documents vary only slightly one from the other, use a merge.

With a merge, you can:

- Write one letter and send it to dozens of recipients, each letter personalized with the recipient's name and address.

- Produce labels by the gross, using one formatted label and a list of names and addresses.

- Create and update phone books by merging lists of phone numbers and a blank phone book setup.

Once you see how easy merges are, you'll think of plenty of other applications.

Merges start with a data file

Here's a common chore: sending out letters announcing a change of address to your clients. A generic "Dear Client" letter is fine, but maybe you'd like to personalize the letters to your best clients.

It's the perfect opportunity for a merge. The body text is identical in each letter: the details of your new address. The only variations are the names and addresses of each client.

We'll start by assembling a data file of the clients' names and addresses. **Data files** are made up of two building blocks: records and fields.

- **Records** are like Rolodex cards. Each record contains all the information you want to use to fill in the blanks in a form file. For a data file like the one we're creating here, a record has the name and address of each client.

- **Fields** are separate items of data in a record. Last names, first names, company names, and street addresses are all distinct fields. You can break a record down into as many fields as you choose.

Generally speaking, the more fields you include, the more flexible your records will be. Instead of one field for a name, for example, use separate fields for last names and first names. A little advance planning at this point can save you time and effort later on.

 (Tip)

> One rule of thumb for designing records: make each field the smallest item of information you're likely to use. You might want separate fields for ZIP code, city, and state, for example. You can then sort and search your data on any of those individual items.

How do I create a data file?

A **data file** is a collection of records, and each record consists of several fields. Once you identify each field with a name—"last name" and "street address," for example—WordPerfect makes the job of filling in each record easy. A handy data entry form pops up automatically. Just enter the information for each field, and you'll be knocking off records in record time.

To build a data file:

1 Click Tools, Merge for the Merge dialog box shown in figure 13.1.

Fig. 13.1

The three parts of a merge begin in the Merge dialog box.

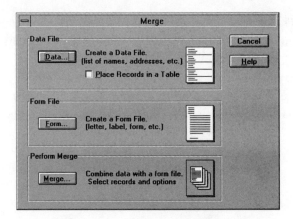

2 In the Merge dialog box, click the Data button. The Create Data File dialog box pops up (see fig. 13.2).

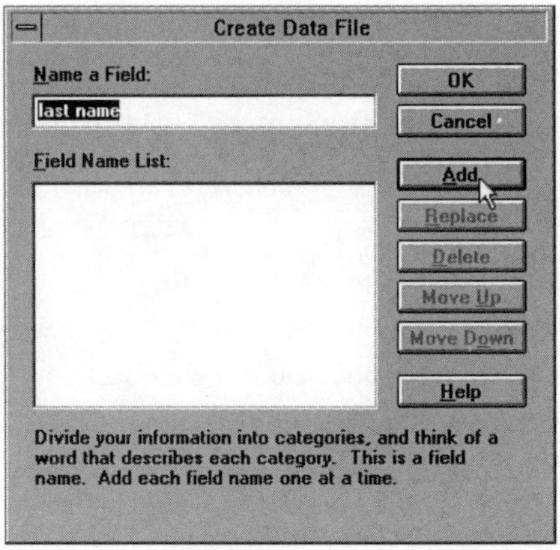

Fig. 13.2

The Create Data File dialog box is where you name each field.

3 Type the name of the first field in the Name a Field edit box and click Add, or just press Enter. Repeat the process for each of the fields in the record, and you'll wind up with something that looks like figure 13.3.

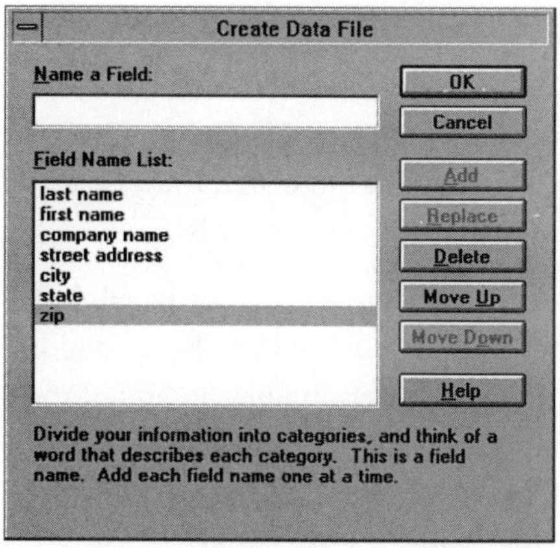

Fig. 13.3

If your records contain something more esoteric than addresses, planning your field names now will ease data entry later.

4 Use the buttons in the Create Data File dialog box to change the order of your field names, edit the names, or delete them. Select a field name from the list, then click a button.

5 Click OK, and the Quick Data Entry dialog box (WordPerfect's automatic data-entry form) pops up. Each of the fields we named in the Create Data File dialog box shows up here, with a blank edit box beside it for data entry.

6 Just start typing! When you finish with one field, press Enter or Tab, or click Next Field to move to the next one. The Back Tab key (Shift+Tab) or Previous Field takes you back, one field at a time. Figure 13.4 shows a completed record in the Quick Data Entry dialog box.

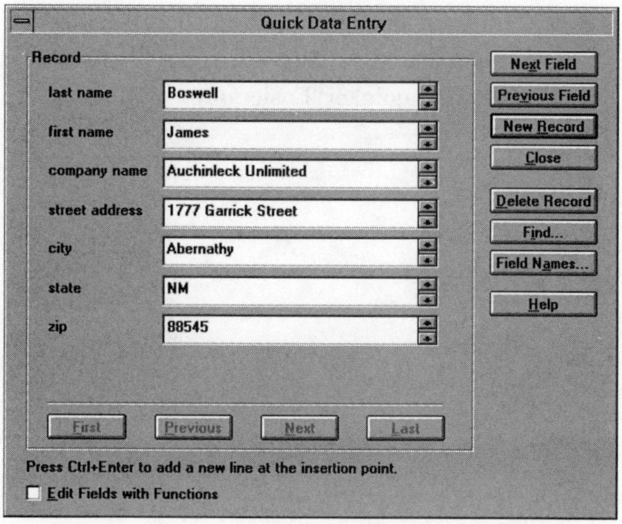

Fig. 13.4

Fill in the fields for each record, then press Enter to begin entering information for the next record.

7 When you complete the last field in the Quick Data Entry dialog box, press Enter or click New Record. The edit boxes in the dialog box clear, and the completed record is dumped into the data file, which you'll see taking shape behind the Quick Data Entry dialog box. Repeat the process for each of your records.

8 If you want to review your records, click the First, Previous, Next, and Last buttons in the Quick Data Entry dialog box to jump from record to record. Put the insertion point in any of the fields you want to edit, and type your changes.

If you want to make any changes to your field names while you're in the Quick Data Entry dialog box, click Field Names to display the Edit Field Names dialog box. Select a field name from the list, click Replace, click in the Field Name text box, and type your changes. Click OK when you're done.

9 Click Close when you've finished entering your last record. Select Yes to save changes to disk.

10 Name the data file in the Save Data File As dialog box that pops up. Don't type a file-name extension; WordPerfect supplies the .DAT extension for you. Click OK; your data file will look like the one in figure 13.5.

11 The Merge feature bar pops up automatically. If you want to add more records, click Quick Entry on the feature bar to display the Quick Data Entry dialog box. You can enter records directly in the document and manually insert the codes with the feature bar buttons, but Quick Data Entry is quicker. Easier, too.

These buttons enter data file codes if you want to enter records directly in the document.

Fig. 13.5
WordPerfect supplies the Endfield and Endrecord data file codes when you use the Quick Data Entry dialog box to enter records.

Each field ends with an Endfield code.

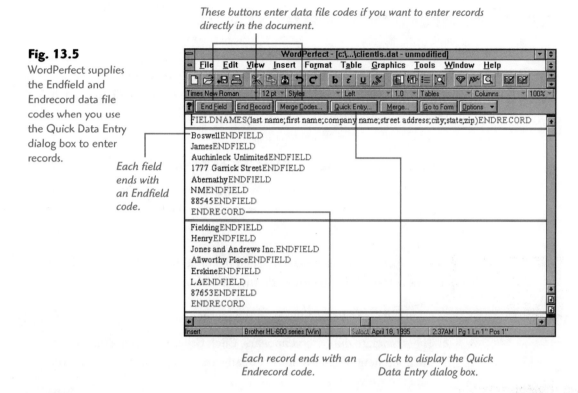

Each record ends with an Endrecord code.

Click to display the Quick Data Entry dialog box.

(Tip)

To print a more readable list of your data file records, click the Options button on the feature bar, and select Hide Codes. The Endfield and Endrecord codes will vanish from view (don't worry, they're still there). Click Options again; select Print, OK to Print with no page breaks. To redisplay the codes, click Options, Display Codes.

Your data file is created and saved. If you need to do any editing, you can make changes with the usual editing tools right in the document. Just be careful not to delete any codes.

Data files can be used and reused; most of the labor goes into creating them in the first place.

Form files are document shells

Building a data file is the biggest chore in a merge. Once that's done, creating a form file is a breeze. **Form files** contain the body text of your finished document, with merge codes that'll be replaced by the data file fields in a merge.

Creating a form file starts in a data file

Although the letter we're about to create will be written only once, after the merge we'll have individualized copies to send to each of the people in our data file.

Create the form file after you've finished the data file. With the data file document in the editing window, do the following:

1 Click the Go to Form button on the merge feature bar.

2 The Associate dialog box appears. Click Create to open a blank form file document, which is automatically associated, or linked, with the data file we've created.

3 Type the return address, just as you would in an ordinary letter, right at the top of the document.

> What? You missed that nifty header macro? See Chapter 12 for more information on creating macros.

4 Now we need the date. Press Enter two or three times to insert blank lines, and click the Date button on the feature bar. That sticks the DATE code at the insertion point. Whenever this generic letter is merged with the data file, the current date will appear where the DATE code is inserted.

If you have a macro for a document or letter header like the one we created in Chapter 12, this is a good opportunity to put it to use.

5 We want each recipient's address to appear at the top of the letter, followed by the salutation. Instead of typing each name and address, we'll insert the field names we created in the data file. The field names will act like blank lines in a form, waiting to be filled in with data from the data file. Press Enter a couple of times to move the insertion point below the date.

6 Click the Insert Field button on the merge feature bar. You see the Insert Field Name or Number dialog box, shown in figure 13.6.

Fig. 13.6
The Insert Field Name or Number dialog box lists all the field names in the associated data file.

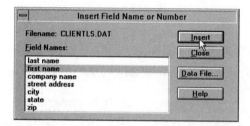

7 Select first name from the list of field names in the Insert Field Name or Number dialog box, and click Insert. The first name field is dumped into the form file at the insertion point, as shown in figure 13.7.

Fig. 13.7
The Insert Field Name or Number dialog box remains on the screen while you insert field names into the form file.

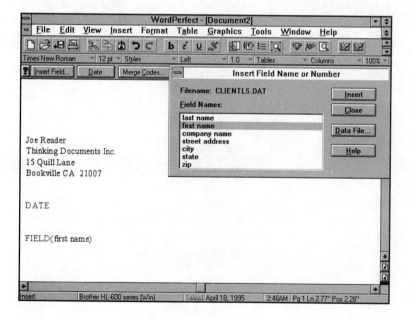

8 Insert a space with the space bar, select `last name` from the Insert Field Name or Number dialog box, and click <u>I</u>nsert. That puts the last name field one space over from the first name field, exactly where we want it.

9 Press Enter to skip to the next line, and insert the `company name` field. Do the same thing for the `street address`, and press Enter.

10 We want the letter to read "city comma state", so insert the `city` field name, type a comma and a space, then insert the `state` field name. Put two spaces after the `state` field name, and insert the `zip` field name.

11 Skip another couple or three lines with the Enter key and type **Dear**, followed by a space. Insert the `first name` field name on the same line, followed by a comma. So far, the form file looks like figure 13.8.

Fig. 13.8
As you set up a form file, visualizing the actual data in place of the merge codes can help with layout issues.

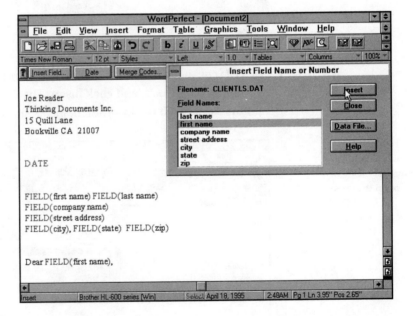

12 Skip a couple of lines below the salutation, and type the body of the letter and the closing. You can insert field names in the body of the letter anywhere you like, as seen in figure 13.9.

Fig. 13.9
Put field names
wherever appropriate
in the form file.

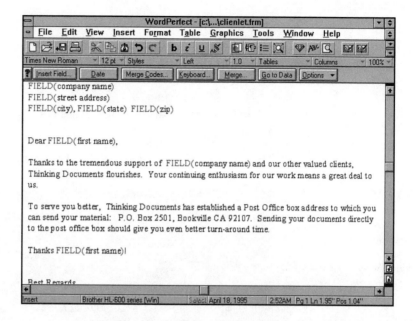

> FIELD(company name)
> FIELD(street address)
> FIELD(city), FIELD(state) FIELD(zip)
>
>
> Dear FIELD(first name),
>
> Thanks to the tremendous support of FIELD(company name) and our other valued clients,
> Thinking Documents flourishes. Your continuing enthusiasm for our work means a great deal to
> us.
>
> To serve you better, Thinking Documents has established a Post Office box address to which you
> can send your material: P.O. Box 2501, Bookville CA 92107. Sending your documents directly
> to the post office box should give you even better turn-around time.
>
> Thanks FIELD(first name)!
>
> Best Regards,

13 Close the Insert Field Name or Number dialog box, since you don't need it anymore.

14 Click File, Save for the Save As dialog box, and give your form file a name. Don't type an extension. WordPerfect supplies the .FRM extension for you.

We used all the field names we created in the data file in this form file, but that's not required. You might want to add a telephone number field to a data file, for example, which you wouldn't want to include in a letter, but that you might use in a phone list. A well-designed data file can be used with several different forms. Just ignore any inappropriate field names when you create your form files. WordPerfect will ignore them, too, when you perform the merge.

While we're at it, how about envelopes by the bushel too?

Since we're making the extra effort to send "personalized" letters to our clients, we don't want to ruin the effect with impersonal mailing labels. It's easy to create form envelopes to go with our form letter. Set up the field names, and we'll get a slew of perfectly addressed envelopes.

To add envelopes to the form file:

1 Click the Merge button on the feature bar, and select Merge in the Merge dialog box.

2 The Perform Merge dialog box, shown in figure 13.10, displays.

Fig. 13.10
Unless you have a good reason not to, use the default file selections in the Perform Merge dialog box.

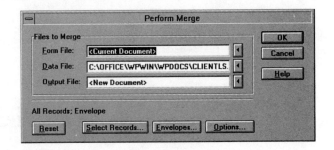

3 Select Envelopes for the Envelope dialog box. Type the Return address, if it's not already there.

4 Click the Mailing Address edit box, and select Field. That pops up the Insert Field Name or Number dialog box, as seen in figure 13.11.

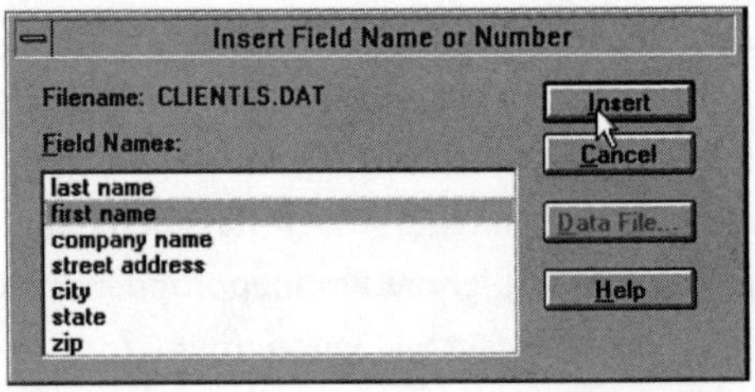

Fig. 13.11
Set up your envelope form by inserting fields from the Insert Field Name or Number dialog box.

5 Select field names, and click Insert to stick them in the right places in the Mailing Address edit box. Remember to use spaces, commas, and returns between the field names. The sample envelope window previews the final product as you work. When you're done, it'll look like figure 13.12.

Fig. 13.12
Putting field names
where you want them
is easy with a little
practice.

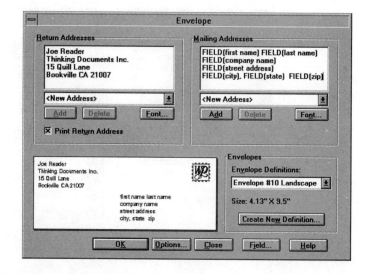

⊙(Tip)

Annoyingly, the Insert Field Name or Number dialog box doesn't stay up as
you insert field names in the envelope, but you can speed things up a little.
Double-click the field names instead of clicking the Insert button. It works just
as well, and it might shave a millisecond or two off your work day.

6 Click OK, and you're back at the Perform Merge dialog box, ready to
merge the data file into the form file and the envelope.

Bring it all together with a merge

As a few merger-mad companies discovered in the last decade, the best
mergers are seamless. That's hard to achieve in business, but it's a snap in
WordPerfect.

Once you've set up your data and form files, and added an envelope if you
want it, the real work is done. To finish the merge, click OK in the Perform
Merge dialog box.

WordPerfect's gears whirl for a moment, and you wind up with a multi-page
document of letters and (if you went through the exercise) envelopes. Each
letter is on a separate page; the envelopes are on separate pages at the end of
the document. Figure 13.13 gives you an idea of what happens in a merge.

Fig. 13.13

This two-page view shows the last page of letters and the first page of envelopes.

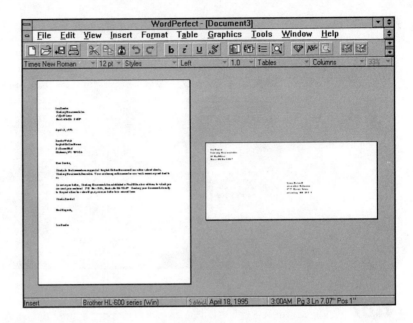

What do I do with this merge?

The idea behind this particular merge was to send out a mailing, so once the merge is completed, you'll want to print your letters and envelopes.

There's no need to save the merged document in this case. Since the data and form files are already saved, you can re-merge them any time. If your form file is something like an address book, you can save it with an ordinary WordPerfect file name. When you want to update the phone book, just add more records to the data file and perform another merge.

?Q&A

> ### With letters and envelopes in the same document, how do I print them separately?
>
> Just select File, Print, and print the letters and envelopes. If you have an envelope feeder on your printer, all you have to do is wait until everything is printed. If you don't have an envelope feeder, you'll have to manually feed envelopes to your printer, pushing the appropriate buttons (usually Continue or Form Feed) on your printer for each envelope.

I don't want to merge all my records

As your data files grow, you might want to merge only a few records at a time. You can select specific records to merge, or a range of records, with the Select Records dialog box.

In the form file, click the Merge button on the feature bar and select Merge in the Merge dialog box. Choose Select Records in the Perform Merge dialog box for the Select Records dialog box shown in figure 13.14.

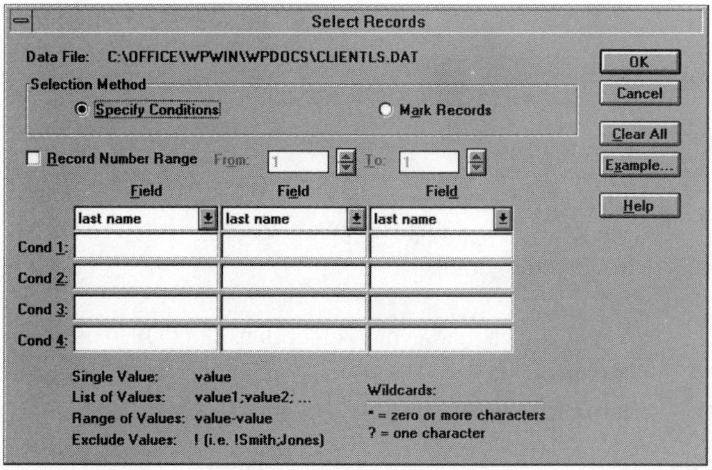

Fig. 13.14

The Select Records dialog box is a powerful database tool, but it's extremely easy to use.

For database wizards, the Select Records dialog box offers all the tools you need to pluck a few records out of large databases.

There's also a shortcut that makes choosing a few records a simple point and click affair. Click Mark Records to simplify the Select Records dialog box, as shown in figure 13.15.

Fig. 13.15
The Mark Records
option in the Select
Records dialog box is a
great simplifier.

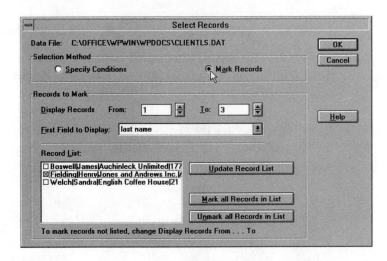

Browse the records in the Record List, and select the ones you want to merge. A little x appears beside each selected record, so you can see exactly what you're doing.

When you've made your selections, click OK. You return to the Perform Merge dialog box. Click OK—only the records you selected will be merged into the form file.

Merge bells and whistles

The sample merge we performed in this chapter was effective for what we wanted to accomplish. Most of the merges you're likely to want to do will be along similar lines.

There are also loads of sophisticated dialog boxestwists that you can introduce into a merge. Merge codes, inserted into your form or data files with the help of the feature bar, allow all sorts of merge tricks.

Click the Merge Codes button on the feature bar for the Insert Merge Codes dialog box shown in figure 13.16.

Fig. 13.16
WordPerfect's collection of merge codes is a sophisticated programming language.

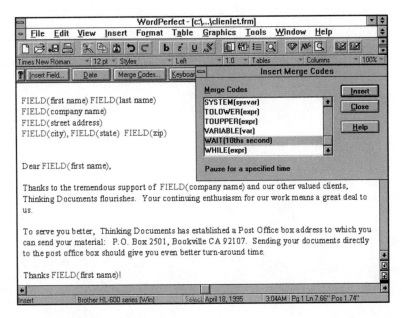

The Insert Merge Codes dialog box provides a brief explanation of each code when you select it from the list.

Here are a few other interesting ways to use WordPerfect's merge feature. Consult the on-line help or your reference manual for details on these procedures:

If you already have a database file from a genuine database program (such as Paradox), you can merge directly from that data file to your form file.

- You can create your data file in a table, which makes it much more readable than a traditional data file with all its merge codes. This works best, however, when you have only a few fields in your records.

- Labels are easy to merge to. See Chapter 9 for how to create a label, but use merge codes instead of typing data.

- Although this may be obvious, you can use the same data file with several form files (a letter, labels, a roster, envelopes, etc.) Design your data file with this in mind.

- You can manually customize each letter as it merges if you place the Keyboard merge code in your document (from the Merge feature bar). During the merge, WordPerfect stops at each record and prompts you to type the data before continuing.

14 When Only Columns Will Do

Endless wide pages of text are like boundless seas; impressive, but monotonous. Like islands that dot the waves, columns break up pages of text for visual variety.

In this chapter:

- Newspaper columns? Parallel columns? What's the difference?
- Newspaper columns are easy to work with
- How do I get quick columns?
- I need to adjust these columns
- I can't get these parallel columns to work!

Journalists chasing a few columns of newspaper space are a tough breed. One early reporter set the standard for toughness, back in the days when columns supported buildings instead of newspaper publishers.

An ancient Greek soldier named Phidippides ran all the way to Athens to report a historic Greek victory over the Persians. The twenty-two-mile run cost him his life, but that ultimate journalistic sacrifice hasn't been forgotten. Phidippides' exploit in reporting the battle of Marathon is celebrated every time a modern runner joins in one of those crazy marathon races.

WordPerfect columns won't confer that kind of immortality. On the other hand, setting up columns in WordPerfect is anything but a marathon job.

Why newspapers love newspaper columns

Imagine the morning paper without columns. You'd have long lines of text, marching from margin to margin across that wide page. It would be unreadable. As you read from left to right, your eyes take a quick breather at the right margin. Too much distance between margins, and your eyes start to feel like they've just completed a marathon of reading.

Columns shorten the distance to the right margin, giving your eyes a break. They're used on any pages of dense text—think of dictionaries and encyclopedias. Columns also give pages a lively, vigorous look, one of the reasons why they're used in magazines and newsletters.

There are three basic kinds of columns:

- **Newspaper columns** wrap text from one column to the next. When you reach the bottom of one column, text flows to the top of the next column, just like wrapped text at the end of a WordPerfect line. Newspaper columns are easy to set up, and easy to deal with while editing. Figure 14.1 shows newspaper columns. The first column is full, while the text only reaches partway down the second column.

Fig. 14.1

Newspaper columns wrap text from one column to the next.

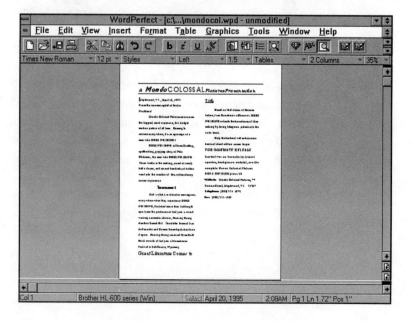

- **Balanced newspaper columns** are newspaper columns of even length. Figure 14.2 gives you an idea of what balanced newspaper columns look like. WordPerfect adjusts the text on the last page so that each column has an equal amount.

Fig. 14.2

If you plan to use balanced newspaper columns, type your text before applying the column formatting.

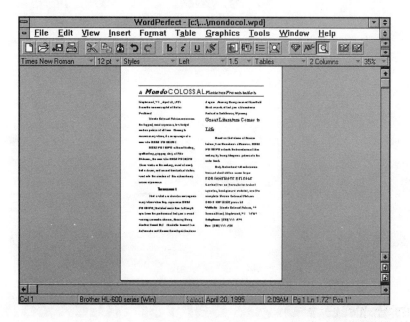

①(Tip)

The easiest way to use balanced newspaper columns: type your text with the ordinary left and right margin settings. When you've finished typing, move the insertion point to the beginning of the text, and click the Power Bar Columns button. Select Define, then click Balanced Newspaper, OK in the Column dialog box. Your text will be instantly formatted in balanced newspaper columns.

- **Parallel columns** place chunks of text in column rows across the page, just like in a table. In fact, tables are usually a much easier way to format parallel pieces of information. Parallel columns are often used to display related but different information side by side (dates and job descriptions in a resume, or a script with the actor's name, dialog, and stage directions, for example). Figure 14.3 shows parallel columns.

Fig. 14.3

Parallel columns are effective for specialized uses, but they can be tricky to deal with.

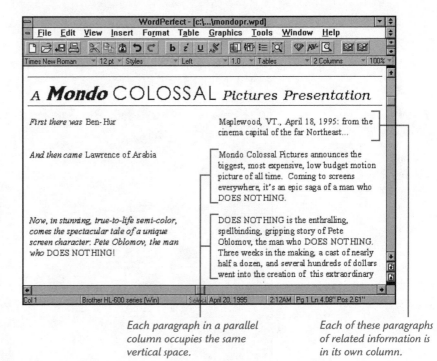

Each paragraph in a parallel column occupies the same vertical space.

Each of these paragraphs of related information is in its own column.

Use the Power Bar for quick columns

WordPerfect gives you control over the number of columns on the page, the width of each column, and the amount of space between columns. You can tinker until you're absolutely satisfied! But when all you want is columns, quickly, you can get them without fussing.

Put the insertion point at the spot where you want columns to begin and click the Columns button on the Power Bar. That gives you the menu of choices shown in figure 14.4.

Fig. 14.4

The Power Bar is the fastest way of getting at columns.

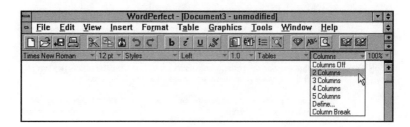

Click the number of columns you want, and start typing. Once you have enough text and you need to jump back and forth between columns for editing, move the mouse pointer where you want the insertion point, and click. To turn columns off again and return to ordinary lines of text, just click the Power Bar Columns button and select Columns Off.

The default columns you get with the Power Bar Columns button are newspaper columns. Despite the name, newspaper columns don't have to be used for newspapers or newsletters. They're fine for reports or any text for which you want column format.

> **I turned on three columns, but I only see text in the first column. What happened?**
>
> You probably don't have enough text to fill the second and third columns yet. If you aren't going to add more text, consider using balanced newspaper columns, so what text you do have is evenly distributed among the three columns.

How can I tell where column formatting begins and ends?

When you turn columns on, WordPerfect inserts a [Col Def] code into the text at the insertion point. Another [Col Def] code is inserted wherever you turn columns off. That makes it easy to put columns and regular text on the same page, as shown in figure 14.5. To see your column definition codes, open the reveal codes windows (View, Reveal Codes).

Fig. 14.5

Use the reveal codes window to move the insertion point before, after, or inside column formatting codes.

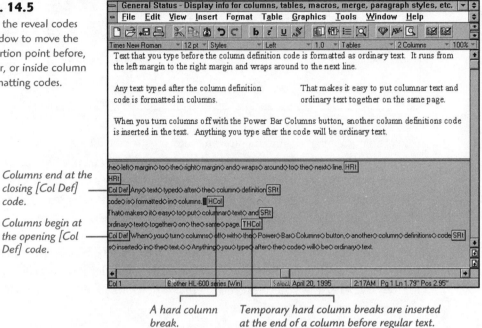

Columns end at the closing [Col Def] code.

Columns begin at the opening [Col Def] code.

A hard column break.

Temporary hard column breaks are inserted at the end of a column before regular text.

You might want a heading or an introduction before your columns begin, and maybe a conclusion below your columns. Just use the reveal codes window to see where the [Col Def] codes are, and put the insertion point before or after the codes.

To get rid of columns, delete the [Col Def] code in the reveal codes window.

(Tip)

If you get tired of maneuvering the insertion point to delete codes in the reveal codes window, just use the mouse to drag unwanted codes out of the window. That does the same thing as deleting the codes with Backspace or Delete. It's also more fun.

{Note}

Headers and footers (created with the Format, Header/Footer, Create command) are not affected by the column formatting in the body text of the page. If you want column formatting in headers and footers, turn on columns within the header or footer.

How do I end one column and start another one?

Since text wraps automatically from one newspaper column to another, you don't need to worry about where one column ends and the next one begins. But if you want to end a column at a particular spot in the text and start another column, you can insert a **hard column break**.

There are two ways to end one column and force the text to begin in another:

- Press Ctrl+Enter. That inserts a [HCol], or hard column break code (refer to fig. 14.5) to snap off one column at the insertion point and start another one.

- Select Column Break from the Power Bar Columns button list.

 Pressing Ctrl+Enter within ordinary, non-columnar text inserts a hard page break, ending the current page and putting the insertion point at the top of the new page.

Default columns settings are usually fine...

The columns you get with the Power Bar Columns button are regular newspaper columns with 1/2 inch of space between them. The width of the columns depends on how many columns you choose, your margins, and the paper size you are using. WordPerfect automatically calculates column width for you: the more columns you select, the skinnier they get.

Figure 14.6 shows the default settings for two pages with the same text. Page one has two 3-inch columns, and page two has four 1 1/2-inch columns. Each is what you get with the WordPerfect defaults.

Fig. 14.6
The WordPerfect
default column settings
work, but if you're not
satisfied, it's easy to
make changes.

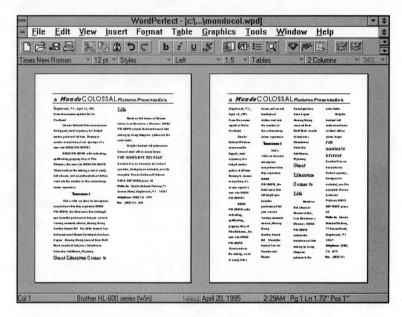

 (Tip)

When using columns, you can usually decrease outside margin space (1/2 inch, for example), thus increasing the amount of text you can fit on one page.

These columns need adjustment

The default settings work well for most uses. But if you don't like the way the page looks with the defaults, you can change the settings. Add more or less space between columns, change the width of your columns, or even create columns of unequal width.

 Plain English, please!

In page layout jargon, the space between columns is called the **gutter**. WordPerfect calls it **spacing between columns**. 99

It's easy to make changes to any column setting. Click the Columns button on the Power Bar, and select Define to get the Columns dialog box shown in figure 14.7.

Fig. 14.7
The handy preview window in the Columns dialog box models your adjustments.

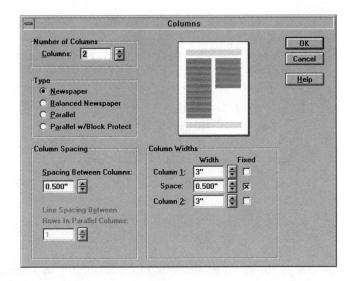

How do I fine-tune my columns?

Columns don't have to be evenly spaced. In fact, changing the pattern of the text on the page with columns might help keep your readers from falling asleep.

The Columns dialog box is the column control panel

Let's use the Columns dialog box to format a press release.

Click the Power Bar Columns button, and select Define to get the Columns dialog box, as shown in figure 14.7. To use the Columns dialog box to change column settings, follow these steps:

1 Click the arrows next to the Columns edit box to pick the number of columns. You can have as many as 24 and as few as two. We'll click the up arrow for three columns.

2 The values in the Column Widths edit boxes change from 3" to 1.83", and Column 3 is added to the Column Widths section of the dialog box. WordPerfect calculates the change in column widths for us, narrowing the columns to accommodate the third one.

3 We'll select <u>N</u>ewspaper for column type. Newspaper columns are the easiest type to work with, and they work well for most uses.

4 The first column from the left, Column <u>1</u>, is going to be for the name, address, and phone number of the release's sender. To set it off from the rest of the page, we'll widen Column <u>1</u> to 2.33". WordPerfect will automatically adjust the widths of Columns <u>2</u> and <u>3</u> to accommodate the wider column.

(!) (Tip)

Clicking the arrows for Column Widths changes widths in increments of .1". For a different value, just type it in the edit boxes. You can type fractions, such as 2 1/3, which WordPerfect automatically converts to 2.33.

(*) {Note}

If you don't want WordPerfect to automatically adjust column widths, click the Fixed check boxes for any of the columns. That "fixes" the width at its current value, and the gutter widths, or space between the columns, will adjust to accommodate the changes, but only if these aren't also checked for fixed width.

5 The default setting for gutters or <u>S</u>pacing Between Columns is .5". We'll stick with the default setting, but you don't have to. You can adjust the gutters between all the columns with the <u>S</u>pacing Between Columns arrows, and for each individual gutter in the Space edit boxes under Column Widths.

(*) {Note}

When you adjust column widths and gutter spacing between columns, remember that the total width of the columns and the spaces between them is fixed by the page margin settings. WordPerfect adjusts each width and space when you make changes. No matter what adjustments you make, the total of the widths can't exceed the total space between margins.

If you want wider columns, wider gutters, or both, you can give yourself more room by reducing the size of the margins before you display the Columns dialog box. Click Format, Margins for the Margins dialog box, and enter new values for the left and right margins.

With the new settings, the Columns dialog box looks like figure 14.8.

Fig. 14.8
Width adjustments in the Columns dialog box are limited by the amount of space between the page margins.

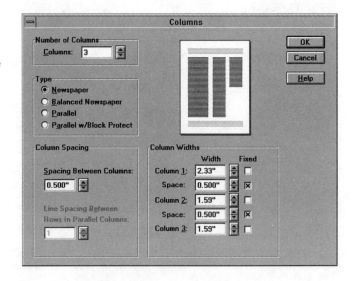

Click OK, and we're ready to type the text.

How do I move around in these columns?

Typing and editing text in columns is the same as typing and editing in an ordinary page, with one difference: the keyboard commands for moving the insertion point change.

To move the insertion point from column to column, press Alt+arrow key. Alt+Home moves the insertion point to the top of the current column; Alt+End puts the insertion point at the bottom of the current column.

Is there an easier way to adjust column spacing?

Figure 14.9 shows the results of our column formatting, with text and a header added.

Fig. 14.9
Among the question-able qualities of this press release is the spacing between columns.

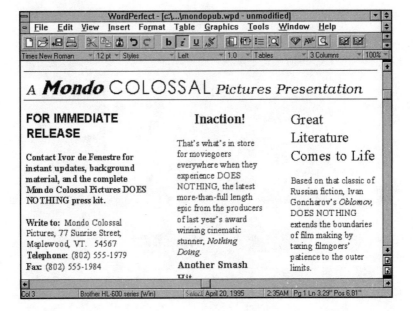

The column settings in this press release are not completely normal, but not nearly as abnormal as the film itself. This press release has a few problems, including the spacing between columns. We used the default setting of .5", which is fine for the default two-column layout. For three columns, however, 1/2-inch gutters look too wide, especially when using normal left justification which often leaves more than .5" white space between columns.

Instead of trying to make the adjustments in the Columns dialog box, we'll use the ruler bar. Click View, Ruler Bar. Now drag the column width markers to make the adjustments, as shown in figure 14.10.

Drag these column width markers left or right to adjust column width.

Fig. 14.10
Dragging the ruler bar column width markers is easier than adjusting column width in the Columns dialog box.

Page margins can be adjusted by dragging the margin markers.

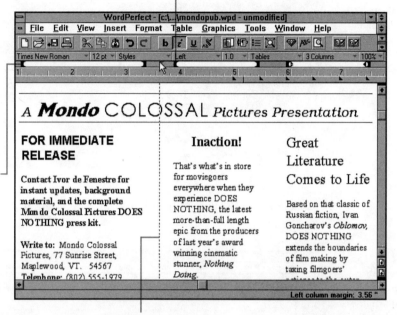

The broken line indicates the new column margin while dragging.

These columns need borders

Putting borders between columns is a fast way to dress up a columnar page. WordPerfect has special border styles for columns. To get at column borders:

1 With the insertion point anywhere within your columns, click Format, Columns, Border/Fill for the Column Border dialog box.

2 Click the Border Style button and select Column Between from the border palette, as shown in figure 14.11.

Fig. 14.11

The other column border style is Column All, which is available only from the Border Styles drop-down list.

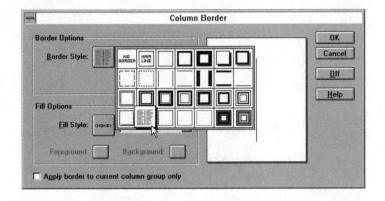

3 Click OK. Borders appear between each column, as shown in figure 14.12.

Fig. 14.12

Borders between columns add a decorative touch; the *New York Times* uses very skinny ones.

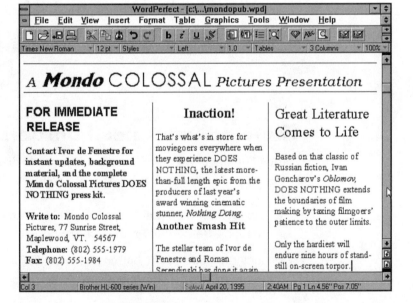

Q&A

How come I only get horizontal lines when I select Column Between borders from the Paragraph Border box?

You're in the wrong dialog box. If you select Format, Paragraph, Border/Fill, you'll see the Column Between style, but the line is horizontal. For vertical column borders, you have to choose Format, Columns, Border/Fill.

How do I get these parallel columns to work?

Parallel columns can be difficult to work with. Also, it's virtually impossible to apply them to existing text. There is one surefire method of making sure your parallel columns work:

1 Before you start typing text, click the Power Bar Columns button, and select Define.

2 Choose the number of columns you want, and select Parallel.

3 Click OK to return to the document, and type the first block of text in column 1 (first column from the left margin).

4 Press Ctrl+Enter to insert a hard column break after the text in column 1.

5 Type the first block of text in column 2. Press Ctrl+Enter to insert another hard column break after the text in column 2.

6 If you're using three columns, that puts the insertion point in column 3; if you've got two columns, you go back to column 1. Either way, keep typing blocks of text and inserting hard column breaks after each block until you're done.

Figure 14.13 shows the hard column breaks after each block of text in two parallel columns.

Fig. 14.13
Parallel columns are doable, provided you insert hard column breaks after each block of text.

Insert hard column breaks after each block of text.

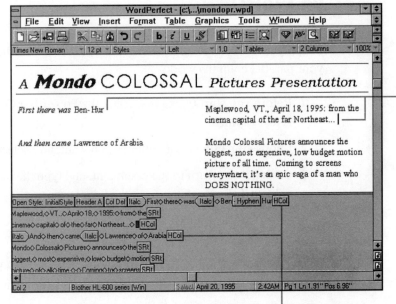

The hard column break codes show up in the reveal codes window.

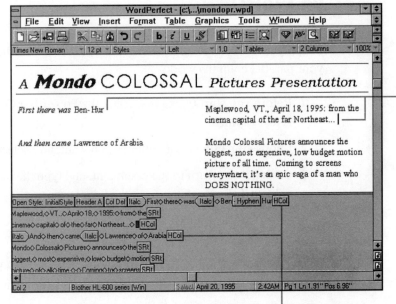**Q&A**

These parallel columns are so hard to use. Isn't there an easier way?

Text formatted in parallel columns looks good and is functionally useful, but tables accomplish exactly the same thing with a lot less work. Entering text in a table is a snap, and if you want, you can turn off table lines so that the text looks just like parallel columns.

15

Dressing Up Your Text

In this chapter:

- With WordPerfect, you're the typographer
- TextArt gives text an artistic bent
- What's a watermark?
- How can I produce a typeset-quality document?
- I need to use foreign characters

From eye-catching special effects to typeset precision, WordPerfect has a bag of tricks to help you produce publication-quality documents.

Why do we sit through bad movies, only to wonder "Why on earth didn't I walk out?" Probably because in even the worst movie, something hooks us. It might be scenic settings or brilliant camera work. Sometimes the hook is more subtle, like the lighting or the atmosphere.

Pages of text have atmosphere and qualities of light, too. Those medieval illuminated manuscripts are so called because the gold leaf and artwork lit up the pages.

You don't get gold leaf in WordPerfect, but there are some nifty tools to bring your pages to life. Like those hard-to-pin-down qualities in movies, formatting and decorative touches on the page can help to hook a reader and keep him reading to the end.

Call in the typographer? No need. It's you!

The typographer's job is to take charge of the appearance of the page. How bright or dark the page looks, the impression it makes—brash or subtle, friendly or sophisticated—that's all in the typographer's hands.

It's a highly skilled craft, but with WordPerfect, there's absolutely no need to learn it. You can be your own typographer with no special training or skill.

I want to see what this font looks like before I use it

Like any good typographer, your first decision is the one that will have the biggest impact on the look of your pages: what font to choose? Previewing how your font will look is helpful in making a decision, and you can do that without even opening your document. That's useful if you want to sample different fonts without actually changing a document's formatting.

 **{Note}**

> You can easily change fonts in an open document by clicking the Power Bar Font Face button and selecting a font from the list. The text from the insertion point on gets the new font. Or select text first, and use the Power Bar Font Face button to change the font for the selection.

To preview different fonts:

1 Choose For̲mat, F̲ont to open the Font dialog box, as shown in figure 15.1.

Fig. 15.1
Use the Font dialog
box to preview fonts
and their attributes
before deciding on
which font to use in
your document.

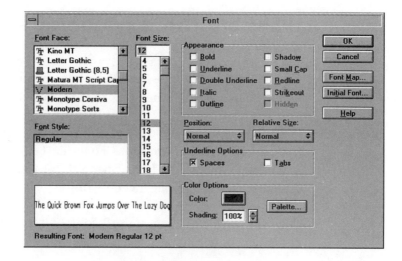

2 Select any font from the Font Face list.

3 Note that the selected fonts now display with sample text in the preview box at the lower-left corner of the dialog box. WordPerfect calls this the "WYSBYGI" ("wizz-biggy") box: "What You See Before You Get It."

4 Select other fonts to see what they look like. You can also select different point sizes and other attributes to see how they will affect the font you have chosen.

5 When you are through previewing your fonts, choose Cancel to return to your document without choosing a font.

 (Tip)

One way to see what a font looks like with more than one line of text is to change fonts in the file viewer. Choose File, Open, click any file, and then choose View. Click the Viewer window with the right mouse button, and from the QuickMenu, choose Font. Choose any font to see what it will look like. Be sure to set the original font again before closing the Open File dialog box.

What are those symbols by the font names?

Click For̲mat, F̲ont for the Font dialog box. As you browse the list of font faces, you'll notice the symbols by the font names (refer to fig. 15.1).

Fonts such as Kino MT and Letter Gothic are preceded by a double "T"— these are called **TrueType fonts**. Fonts like Letter Gothic (8.5) are preceded by a printer symbol—these are called **Printer fonts**. And fonts like Modern, preceded by a "V," are called **Vector fonts**.

TrueType and Vector fonts are **soft fonts**. All the information needed to display and print soft fonts is kept in files on your hard disk.

TrueType fonts were designed to work with Windows. They're the most common soft fonts. TrueType fonts are **scaleable**, meaning that you can change their size. They also appear the same whether printed or displayed on the screen. WordPerfect and Windows both come with a slew of TrueType fonts, and any fonts installed in Windows are automatically installed in WordPerfect.

Ever wonder why fonts have those odd names?

The invention of moveable type—letters carved in blocks of wood or engraved on bars of metal, arranged to form words, then inked and pressed against paper—revolutionized the world. Moveable type led to the printing press, which made the mass production of books and newspapers inexpensive and practical.

It all began with handwriting. The early font faces imitated written characters. Roman faces like Times New Roman, the WordPerfect default font face, are patterned on the writing style of the ancient Romans. Gothic or Black Letter faces like Braggadocio, with their upright, thick lines, recall the handwriting of medieval monks. Innovative designers such as 18th-century William Caslon gave font faces a more modern look by basing designs on shapes created with engravers' tools. Another WordPerfect face, Caslon Openface, derives from Caslon's designs.

The real advantage of TrueType fonts is that you get the same results, regardless of the printer you print to—laser, dot matrix, or even fax. If you have a choice, TrueType fonts are generally better than Vector or even Printer fonts.

⊛ {Note}_____| Vector fonts are like TrueType fonts; they can be sized, and they display and print with the same look. But where TrueType fonts are composed of zillions of little dots, Vector fonts are outlines or "suggested shapes" for characters that WordPerfect fills in on the fly.

⊛ {Note}_____| Printer fonts are built in to your printer. The Printer font you see listed in figure 15.1 is in my printer, but not necessarily yours. This only matters because, unlike TrueType fonts, WordPerfect may not display a selected printer font. It'll print, but you may see something different on the screen. If I select Brougham, for example, WordPerfect displays Courier. Although printer fonts look good and print quickly, if you send the document to someone else, he may have trouble getting the same results with his printer.

How do I add more fonts?

If you're not happy with the choices of fonts you get with Windows and WordPerfect, you can add more. Buy them on floppy disk or CD-ROM, or download them from an on-line information service.

When you add fonts, you install them in Windows. Once installed in Windows, they're automatically installed in WordPerfect.

To install new TrueType fonts:

1 In Windows Program Manager, double-click the Main program group icon.

2 Double-click the Control Panel icon, then double-click the Fonts icon in the Control Panel window.

3 Click Add in the Fonts dialog box for the Add Fonts dialog box, shown in figure 15.2.

Fig. 15.2
Adding TrueType fonts to WordPerfect is a one-step job; just add them to Windows first.

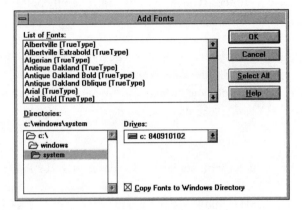

4 Select the location of your new fonts in the Directories and Drives boxes in the Add Fonts dialog box.

5 Windows builds a list of the fonts it finds in the location you specified. Select individual fonts from the List of Fonts (select several by holding down Ctrl and clicking different fonts with the mouse), or click the Select All button, then click OK. The fonts will be added to your WINDOWS\SYSTEM subdirectory (if you have checked Copy Fonts to Windows Directory). The next time you run WordPerfect, you'll see them on the font list.

✱{Note} If you have no use for fonts like WP Cyrillic B, select the unwanted font in the Control Panel Fonts dialog box in Program Manager, and click Remove. This also saves precious memory, and can help improve Windows performance. Once removed, you won't see the font on the WordPerfect list. It's only deleted from your hard disk if you select the Delete File From Disk check box, so you can add it back again with the steps outlined previously.

(Tip) To see a sample of the fonts in the Control Panel Fonts dialog box in Program Manager, click the font face name.

TextArt, for text with an artistic bent

Giambattista Bodoni was an 18th-century typographical genius, whose beautiful designs are still in use today. Pick up a copy of the *Washington Post*, and you'll see Bodoni's font in the newspaper's headlines. Bodoni compiled an *Inventory of Types* that covered all types of fonts. Farseeing as he was, however, Bodoni couldn't have imagined TextArt.

TextArt turns fonts into silly putty. It lets you stretch, squeeze, and bend fonts into shapes like the one shown in figure 15.3.

Fig. 15.3
With TextArt, fonts assume mind-bending shapes.

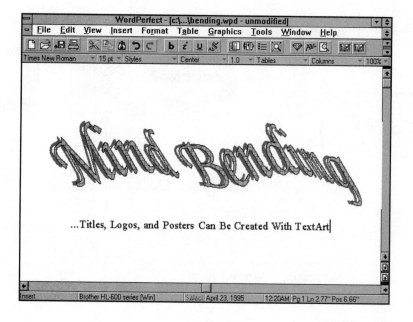

Put text through bend-and-stretch exercises with TextArt

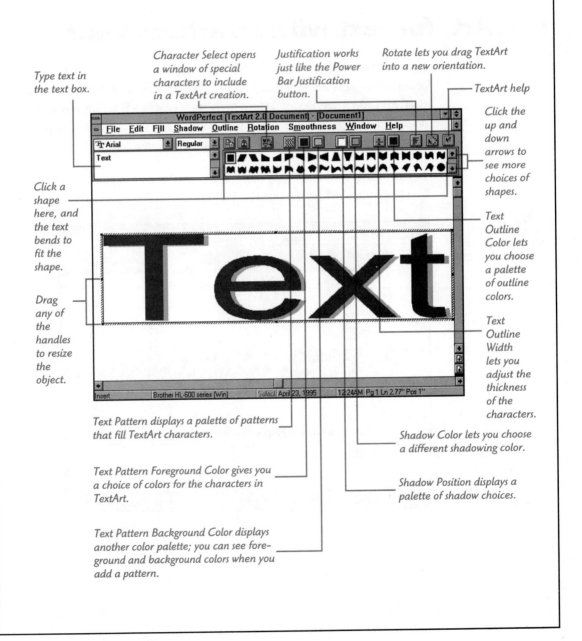

Type text in the text box.

Character Select opens a window of special characters to include in a TextArt creation.

Justification works just like the Power Bar Justification button.

Rotate lets you drag TextArt into a new orientation.

TextArt help

Click the up and down arrows to see more choices of shapes.

Click a shape here, and the text bends to fit the shape.

Drag any of the handles to resize the object.

Text Outline Color lets you choose a palette of outline colors.

Text Outline Width lets you adjust the thickness of the characters.

Text Pattern displays a palette of patterns that fill TextArt characters.

Text Pattern Foreground Color gives you a choice of colors for the characters in TextArt.

Text Pattern Background Color displays another color palette; you can see foreground and background colors when you add a pattern.

Shadow Color lets you choose a different shadowing color.

Shadow Position displays a palette of shadow choices.

Bending TextArt to your will

TextArt gives you an electronic crayon box to play with. Use TextArt to create banners, titles, and logos. Need to whip up a quick poster for the company picnic? Here's what you do:

1 Click the TextArt button on the Toolbar. Stand by for a moment or two; because TextArt uses OLE 2.0, things slow down considerably, even on a fast computer. Eventually, you'll see the editing window fill with the TextArt Toolbar and editing display. Everything should return once again to normal speed.

2 The insertion point should be in the text box in the upper-left of the TextArt window. If not, just click the text box.

3 Type your text, but try to keep it short. The longer the text, the more distorted it gets, as you can see in figure 15.4.

4 Click a shape, and watch as the text you typed bends and stretches. Trial-and-error is the way to proceed here. Besides, it's fun to play around with.

5 Click any of the Toolbar buttons to add patterns or to change colors, character thickness, shadow effects, or fonts. Experiment until you come up with something you like. Figure 15.4 shows some of the effects you can create.

Fig. 15.4
You can achieve some eye–arresting effects with TextArt.

| Those TextArt characters are actually outlines of characters. When you first pop up TextArt, the outlines are filled in, so they look solid. Click the Text Patterns button on the Toolbar, and choose No Fill to see the outlines more clearly.

6 Click the Rotate button, and drag any of the rotation handles shown in figure 15.5 to change the orientation of the characters. Click the Rotate button again to make the rotation handles disappear.

Fig. 15.5

Rotating the characters is nifty, but distorts the image.

Rotation handles

7 When you're satisfied with your creation, click anywhere outside the broken-line border to plop the image into a document. The editing window returns to normal, and the Standard Toolbar pops back.

❝ **Plain English, please!**

Objects in WordPerfect are any sort of graphic image—TextArt, Charts, or artwork—inside a document. ❞

Editing Text Art

Once you've stuck TextArt into a document, you can save the document for a stand-alone TextArt object. You can reuse saved TextArt; copy and paste it into other documents; or add text above, below, or around it.

To move TextArt on the page, move the pointer over the TextArt object and click. That pops up black square **sizing handles** around the object and the pointer turns into a four-headed arrow, as shown in figure 15.6.

Fig. 15.6

Use the mouse to drag the TextArt object anywhere you like, or to size it to fit your needs.

Now drag the object anywhere you like. Click anywhere outside the object to make the handles disappear and fix your TextArt in place.

To edit the object, point at it and right-click for the QuickMenu shown in figure 15.7. Choose TextArt 2.0 Document Object, Edit, to get the TextArt Toolbar back.

Fig. 15.7

The QuickMenu gives you a choice of editing and positioning options.

When you're finished editing, click anywhere outside the object to return to the normal editing window.

> Double-clicking a TextArt object also pops up the TextArt editing window and Toolbar. I find the QuickMenu handier because it gives you more choices, but either way is fine.

Create fancy stationery with watermarks

Take a sheet of good-quality stationery and hold it up to the light. That faint image you see is a **watermark**. It's usually the paper manufacturer's name, but sometimes you'll find a design, or both. Paper makers have distinguished their work with watermarks for the past three hundred or so years.

Manufacturers impress the watermark directly on to the sheet; WordPerfect lets you do the same thing with your printer. WordPerfect watermarks are faint designs or characters on the background of the page. You can use a WordPerfect image for a watermark, or use any document file to create your own.

WordPerfect images make great watermarks

As with headers and footers, watermarks repeat on every page until you turn them off, and you can put up to two watermarks on a page. Start from a blank document, or stick a watermark directly into your current document.

To create a watermark in the current document:

1 Click Format, Watermark for the Watermark dialog box.

2 In the Watermark dialog box, select Watermark A, and click Create.

3 That switches to full-page view and displays the watermark feature bar, shown in figure 15.8.

Fig. 15.8
Your document is still active, but you don't see it as you create a watermark.

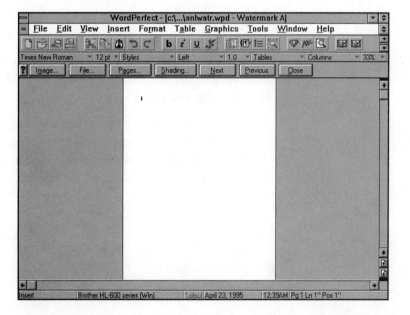

4 Click the Image button on the feature bar for the Insert Image dialog box. The Filename box displays a list of WordPerfect images, found in the graphics directory created when you installed WordPerfect.

5 Select a file name, and click View to preview the image. Figure 15.9 shows the Insert Image dialog box with the file viewer popped up.

Fig. 15.9
Image files are stored
in the WordPerfect
graphics subdirectory.

> Don't close the viewer after selecting a file to preview. Keep the viewer
> popped up, and you can view one file after another by selecting them from
> the list. If the viewer is in the way of the Filename list, click its title bar and
> drag it out of the way.

6 Once you find an image you like, click OK in the Insert Image dialog
box. No need to close the viewer first. Your selected image is displayed,
faintly, in the watermark editing window.

7 Point at the image itself, and you see the four-headed arrow. Drag to
move the image around on the page. Point at any of the little handles.
The pointer turns into a double arrow; drag to resize the image, as
shown in figure 15.10.

Fig. 15.10
Moving and resizing graphics in Word-Perfect is easy with the mouse.

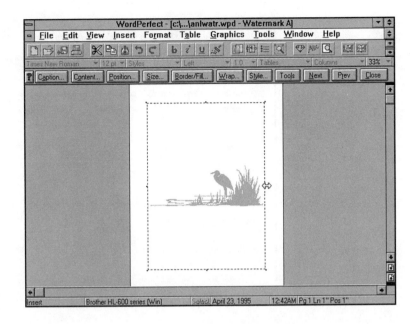

 *{Note}*

Notice that in figure 15.10, the graphics feature bar has replaced the water-mark feature bar. To get the watermark feature bar back, click <u>C</u>lose on the graphics feature bar.

8 For a fainter or darker image, click the <u>S</u>hading button on the feature bar, and enter a higher or lower value in the <u>I</u>mage Shading box. (See the preceding Note if you don't have the <u>S</u>hading button on your screen.)

9 Click <u>C</u>lose when you're finished adjusting the image. That returns you to your document, where you'll see the watermark behind the text. Figure 15.11 shows a document with a watermark behind the text.

Fig. 15.11
The default shading value of 25% gives you a smooth image like this; reduce it too far and the image looks grainy.

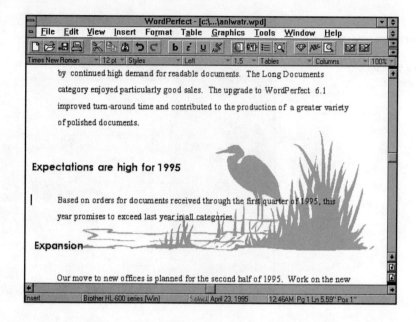

If you need to tinker with the watermark further, click Fo_r_mat, _W_atermark, _E_dit.

> You can also point at a watermark and right-click for the QuickMenu. Select _W_atermark to edit the watermark.

To get rid of a watermark, open the reveal codes window, and drag the watermark code out the window. If you merely want to discontinue it (to resume the watermark later), choose Fo_r_mat, _W_atermark, choose the watermark you want to discontinue, and click _D_iscontinue.

How do I create my own watermark?

You can turn any text or graphics file into a watermark. For example, you can create a company logo with TextArt and save it as a document file.

Switch to the document in which you want the watermark. Select Fo_r_mat, _W_atermark, _C_reate for the watermark editing window. Click the Fi_l_e button on the watermark feature bar, and double-click the file containing your TextArt logo. Click _Y_es to insert the file into the watermark.

Make any adjustments you want in the watermark editing window, click Close on the watermark feature bar, and you might wind up with something like that shown in figure 15.12.

Fig. 15.12

Combining features like watermarks and TextArt can save you a trip to the printer.

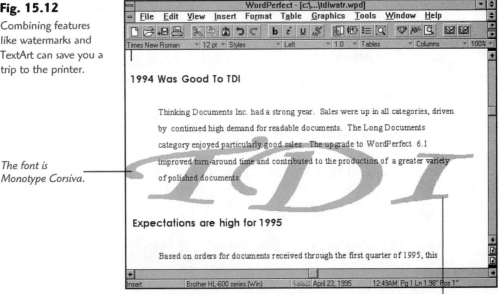

The font is Monotype Corsiva.

Light gray was selected as the color for foreground, background, and outline in TextArt.

 **{Note}**

Windows printer drivers often print the outline of graphics, such as TextArt, in solid black, which makes it difficult to read the document text. To avoid this, turn off the graphic outline altogether when creating the TextArt image. The WordPerfect printer drivers don't have this problem.

WordPerfect puts a typesetter at your desk

Documents created in WordPerfect and printed on a laser printer look almost like pages set and printed by a professional printer. The "almost" is partly because the spacing between letters in a typeset document is perfect. In

WordPerfect, certain pairs of letters, which vary from font to font, look as though they have minor variations in the amount of space between them.

It's subtle, but enough to give a perfectionist pause. Spacing variations are due to the shape of certain characters, and they're especially obvious in larger point sizes (see fig. 15.13).

Fig. 15.13

Lowercase e's and n's are especially prone to the appearance of having extra space.

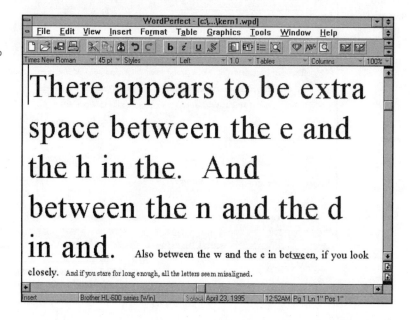

That's *kerning*, not kernel, Colonel

That minor problem illustrated in figure 15.13 can be fixed. **Kerning** is the typesetter's term for adjusting the spacing between pairs of letters. If you've created titles with large-sized letters and run into odd-looking spacing, you'll be pleased to hear that WordPerfect does kerning automatically.

Plain English, please!

Kerning is so called because the projecting parts of letters like "J" in metal type are called **kerns**. Computers often allow too much space between letters for kerns, especially where there are complementary projections that could be placed closer together. "A" and "V" are good examples, showing that the kerns could overlap a bit.

To turn on automatic kerning to fix spacing problems between letter pairs:

1 Select the text you want adjusted, or just put the insertion point at the beginning of the document.

2 Click Fo**r**mat, **T**ypesetting, **W**ord/Letter Spacing for the Word Spacing and Letterspacing dialog box shown in figure 15.14.

Fig. 15.14
Kerning is usually needed only with very large point sizes, and you may never need it at all.

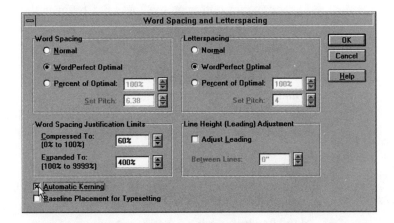

3 Select **A**utomatic Kerning, and click OK.

Automatic kerning has one big drawback: it only works for certain pairs of letters. Worse, the letter pairs vary from font to font, so you can't know if automatic kerning will do the job for you until you try it.

If automatic kerning doesn't fix the problem, try manual kerning. Put the insertion point between the two characters you want to kern and select Fo**r**mat, **T**ypesetting, **M**anual Kerning. That pops up the Manual Kerning dialog box. Click the **A**mount arrows to adjust spacing between the two letters, and observe the effect.

 Q&A

*How come the **Manual Kerning** choice on the Fo**r**mat, **T**ypesetting menu is grayed out?*

You've selected text. Manual kerning only works for two characters. Simply position the insertion point between the two characters, and try again.

Line spacing? Leading? What's that all about?

Adjusting the spacing between lines in WordPerfect is a snap—provided you want your lines to be single, one and a half, or double-spaced. Click the Power Bar Line Spacing button and take your pick.

 (Tip)

> You can specify fractions of a line-for-line spacing by choosing Other from the Line Spacing button on the Power Bar, typing in the fraction you want (for example, **1 1/3** (1 and 1/3 lines of space between each line of text), and clicking OK.

Finer adjustments in line spacing can be made in increments of .001". To do that, select Format, Typesetting, Word/Letter Spacing for the Word Spacing and Letterspacing dialog box (refer to fig. 15.14).

Look under Line Height (Leading) Adjustment and click Adjust Leading. Then click the Between Lines arrows to enter a value of between .01" and 27.3" (really) of space between lines. You can even reduce the spacing to less than a full line by entering negative values.

 Plain English, please!

Leading (pronounced *LED-ding*, like pencil lead) is the typesetter's term for the space between lines. Typesetters working with metal type used thin strips of metal, often made of lead, to divide lines of type. The strips are called leads, and the more you added, the more space between lines you got. Hence, leading.

How about letterspacing?

Full justification is used in the body text of books to give the page a formal, balanced look. If you've tried full justification, you'll have noticed something right away: in order to make a fully justified line flush with both the left and right margins, WordPerfect inserts a lot of space between words and letters.

Letterspacing and **word spacing** combat these unsightly spaces in justified text. Select Fo<u>r</u>mat, <u>T</u>ypesetting, <u>W</u>ord/Letter Spacing for the Word Spacing and Letterspacing dialog box (refer to fig. 15.14). Select any of the following in the dialog box:

- Word Spacing <u>N</u>ormal and Letterspacing Nor<u>m</u>al set the amount of space between words and letters to the font manufacturer's specifications. <u>W</u>ordPerfect Optimal, the default setting, uses the program's values for word and letter spacing for a particular font.

- P<u>e</u>rcent of Optimal for word and letter spacing lets you fiddle with the values. Values less than 100% reduce the spaces between words and letters; values greater than 100% increase the spacing. Trial-and-error is the way to proceed here.

- **Pitch** is the number of characters per inch. When you select <u>S</u>et Pitch and click the arrows to enter new values, you're directly controlling the number of characters per inch that are displayed and printed.

- Word Spacing Justification Limits is like a vise for lines of text. If the words in a fully justified line are too close together, set a higher value than the default in the <u>C</u>ompressed To box. To reduce the spacing between the words, enter a lower value in the E<u>x</u>panded To box.

Pardon my French: inserting special characters

Suppose you have to write a letter in French (or Spanish or German). You haul out those old high school and college language texts, keep the dictionary handy, and laboriously churn out your letter. You're finally done, but there's one problem: how do you type all those accented characters?

WordPerfect solves the problem. Select <u>I</u>nsert, <u>C</u>haracter to pop up the WordPerfect Characters dialog box shown in figure 15.15.

Fig. 15.15

Click the Character Set button to choose from a variety of different character sets; Japanese or Cyrillic, for example.

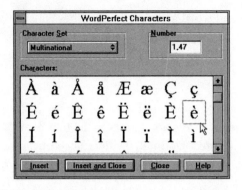

Click any of the special characters, select Insert or Insert and Close, and the character is inserted at the insertion point.

⊛ **{Note}**

The Number in the WordPerfect Characters dialog box identifies each character. There are fifteen sets of characters, for everything from ASCII to Japanese, numbered 1 through 15. Each character in each set is also numbered. So 1,71 is character set 1 (Multinational), character number 71, which happens to be ü.

How can I use the Characters dialog box more efficiently?

Lifting your fingers from the keyboard to click characters in the WordPerfect Characters dialog box is a nuisance. Here's a shortcut: press Ctrl+W, type a character and punctuation mark combination, then press Enter.

For example, press Ctrl+W, type **a'**, press Enter, and á is inserted at the insertion point. Table 15.1 shows keyboard shortcuts for some common accented characters, with a couple of other special characters thrown in for good measure.

Table 15.1   Keyboard shortcuts for common accented characters

Press Ctrl+W, then type...	Then press Enter to get
a`	à
a´	á
e^	ê
u"	ü
c,	ç
AE	Æ
n~	ñ
co	©
/2	½
/c	¢

Substitute any character for the letters in the first column of table 15.1 to get that character in the second column.

16

Jazz Up a Document with Graphics

In this chapter:

- How do I add a line to this document?
- My next text could use a picture pick-me-up
- This graphic looks great, but it doesn't fit in my text!
- Can I move and resize a graphic?
- What's a text box?

Even the strongest words benefit from the visual impact of graphics. And, inserting graphics in WordPerfect documents is always easy!

A cliché is something we think all the time, but as right-thinking people, we don't dare utter. Here's one: a picture is worth…. You get the picture.

But no picture is worth even a handful of the right words—think of Life, Liberty, and the Pursuit of Happiness. Try expressing that in a picture. Nathaniel Hawthorne was right when he wrote "One picture in ten thousand…ought to live in the applause of mankind."

Pictures, and graphics generally, can enhance (but not replace) words. Especially if the words themselves don't scintillate. WordPerfect doesn't include any of Hawthorne's one-in-ten-thousand pictures, but it does have a handy collection of text-enhancing graphics.

Here's your line: graphic lines

You can do a lot with a line or two. Call attention to your text, break up a page, add a little visual interest—one well-placed line can be more effective than a more complex image.

WordPerfect makes inserting, moving, and editing lines a breeze. You also get a choice of vertical or horizontal lines in different weights and styles. And if you don't like any of the choices offered, you can create your own line.

How do I get a line on lines?

To insert a line at the insertion point, click Graphics, Vertical Line for a vertical line that runs from the top margin to the bottom margin of the page. Click Graphics, Horizontal Line for a horizontal line that goes from the left to the right margin. Figure 16.1 shows the Graphics menu and a full-page view of a vertical line.

 Plain English, please!

What WordPerfect calls a graphics line—like the vertical and horizontal lines described here—is called a rule by typesetters. Here's a straightforward bit of typesetting jargon: how do you add straight lines to a page? With a ruler. **99**

  If you have a lot of lines to insert in a page, you might find the Graphics Toolbar handy. Right-click the Toolbar for the QuickMenu, and select Graphics. Clicking the Horizontal Line or Vertical Line buttons inserts either kind of line, just like the Graphics menu's Horizontal and Vertical Line commands.

Fig. 16.1
The default lines run from margin to margin. This text has 1.5" left and right margins to show the vertical line.

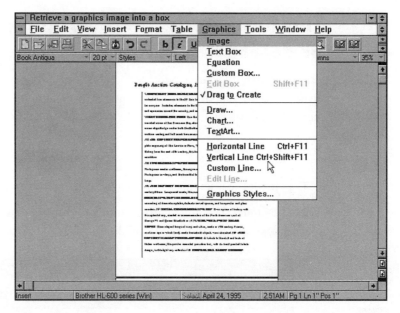

Q&A

I just inserted a horizontal line; now I've lost the flashing insertion point!

The insertion point is still there, but it takes the shape of the line you inserted. It's hidden by the line, but if you look closely at the very beginning of the line, you'll see it faintly ticking away. When you start typing or when you press Enter, the insertion point comes out from hiding.

{Note}

A vertical line inserted at the left margin might be out of sight because it's offset from the text margin by .125". Just scroll the editing screen to the left to view your line.

This line needs some work: move, resize, or delete it

Once inserted, lines are easily moved, deleted, and formatted. You might divide your document with a vertical line, for example, and then want to move it to another spot on the page.

To move a line:

1 Point at the line; the pointer changes from I-beam to white arrow.

2 Click once. The pointer turns into a four-headed arrow, and handles appear, as shown in figure 16.2.

Fig. 16.2
The pointer remains a four-headed arrow as long as it points at the line.

Drag with the four-headed arrow to move a line. ———

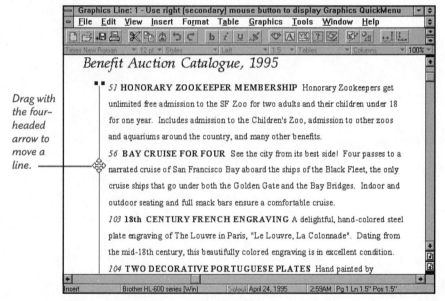

3 With the pointer anywhere along the line, just drag it to a new position. A broken outline of the line follows the pointer around; release the mouse button and the line snaps into place.

You can also use the mouse to change the width of a line. If you put the pointer directly over one of the handles, it turns into a double-headed arrow. Drag the double-headed arrow to thicken the line, as shown in figure 16.3.

Fig. 16.3

Click a line once, and you can move it or resize it.

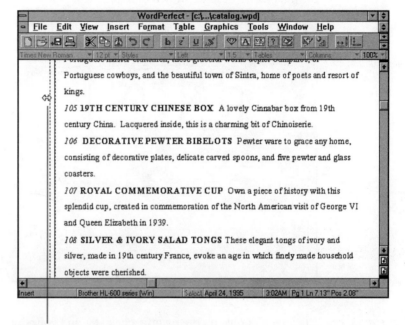

Dragging a handle with the double-headed arrow makes the line thicker or thinner.

To get rid of the handles, click anywhere outside the line.

How do I get rid of this line?

To delete the line, point at it, and click for the handles. Press Delete—the line is gone.

I want a fancier line

Lines make page dividers, and they can also decorate a document. WordPerfect gives you a whole palette of line styles.

For fancier lines, right-click an existing line for the QuickMenu, and select Edit Horizontal Line (or Edit Vertical Line, depending on what you've got). That pops up the Edit Graphics Line dialog box. Click the Line Style button for the palette of lines shown in figure 16.4.

Fig. 16.4
These line styles look like wedges, but you get either vertical or horizontal lines.

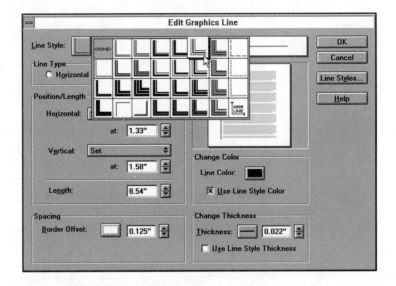

Click your choice on the palette, click OK, and your line is transformed into the selected style. Figure 16.5 gives you an idea of how to use a decorative line.

Fig. 16.5
Used sparingly, lines make a great adjunct to text.

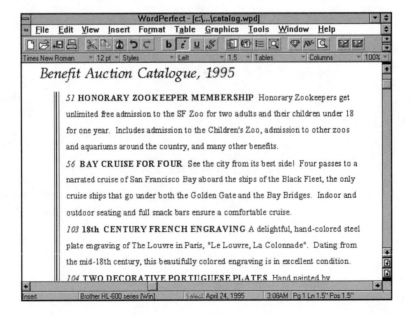

Use the Edit Graphics Line dialog box to adjust the length and position of your lines if you like. (I find the mouse easier for most line maneuvers.)

(Tip)

> You can also double-click a line to pop up the Edit Graphics Line dialog box.

I know my line, and this isn't it

If you don't like any of the line styles available in the Edit Graphics Line dialog box, create your own. Click the Line St**y**les button in the dialog box (not the **L**ine Style button; that gives you the palette of existing styles in figure 16.4).

In the Line Styles dialog box that pops up, click C**r**eate for the Create Line Style dialog box shown in figure 16.6.

Fig. 16.6
Customizing a line is easy to do, and once you name your custom line, you can use it over and over again.

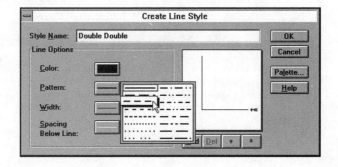

Select a **C**olor, **P**attern, or **W**idth, type a name for your custom style in the Style **N**ame edit box, and click OK when you're done.

Your custom style will appear on the St**y**les list in the Line Styles dialog box.

When text needs a pick-me-up... Add a picture

WordPerfect comes with an assortment of pictures, graphical messages like `Top Secret`, and decorative borders and images that can add a little punch to your pages.

To stick a graphic into your document at the insertion point:

1 Look your document over and decide where the graphic ought to go. It's easy to move graphics around, but deciding on a position in advance will save you a little work.

2 Click Graphics, Drag to Create, then click OK. That lets you pop graphics into your documents by dragging with the mouse.

3 Click the Image button on the Toolbar, then move the pointer into the editing window. The pointer turns into a little hand clutching a picture frame (but only when the pointer is actually *in* the editing window).

4 Position the pointer at the upper left corner of the area where you want the graphic, and drag toward the lower right corner. That picture frame the hand was clutching expands, as seen in figure 16.7.

Fig. 16.7
The broken-line box indicates the position and dimensions of the graphic.

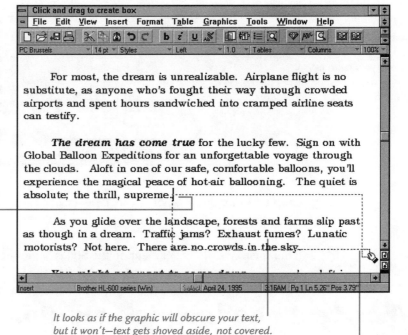

The point at which you start to drag is the upper left corner of the graphic.

It looks as if the graphic will obscure your text, but it won't—text gets shoved aside, not covered.

The lower right corner of the graphic is wherever you release the mouse button.

5 Don't worry about exactly placing the graphic—it'll be easy to move it later on. Release the mouse button at the lower right hand corner of where you want your graphic, and the Insert Image dialog box pops up.

6 If you know which graphics file you want, just double-click it on the Filename list. If you're browsing, click View to pop up the file viewer. As you select graphics file names, they appear in the viewer, as seen in figure 16.8.

Fig. 16.8
Click a file, and it appears in the viewer. As you select files, leave the viewer on to see each one in turn.

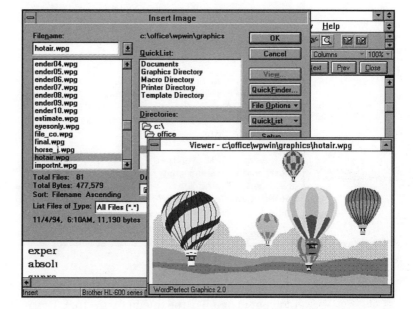

7 When you find a graphic you like, click OK in the Insert Image dialog box. The graphic image pops into place in your document, and the Graphics Feature bar appears at the top of the editing window.

8 If everything is perfect, click Close on the feature bar. If you need to make some adjustments (and you probably will), read on.

How do I fit this graphic on the page?

Popping a graphic into a document is easy. Once popped, you'll almost always have to tinker with the graphic to properly fit it on the page. Tinkering is easy too.

This graphic pushed my text aside!

Like anything inserted in a WordPerfect document, whatever's already in place gets shoved aside to make room for the graphic. As you can see in figure 16.9, that isn't exactly what we want.

Fig. 16.9

Graphics (and any other inserted objects) unceremoniously shove existing text around to make room.

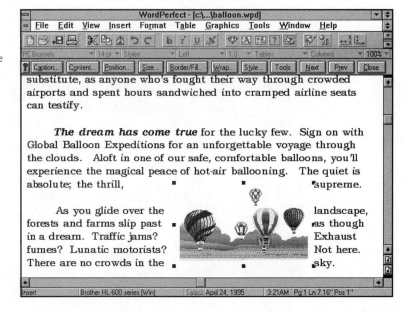

We want the text to snake around the graphic, instead of having our paragraph cut in half like the one in figure 16.9. That's called **wrapping**, and it's easily done.

To wrap text around a graphic:

1 Click the <u>W</u>rap button on the feature bar. That pops up the Wrap Text dialog box, shown in figure 16.10.

Fig. 16.10

For paragraphs severed by graphics, text wrap is a quick fix.

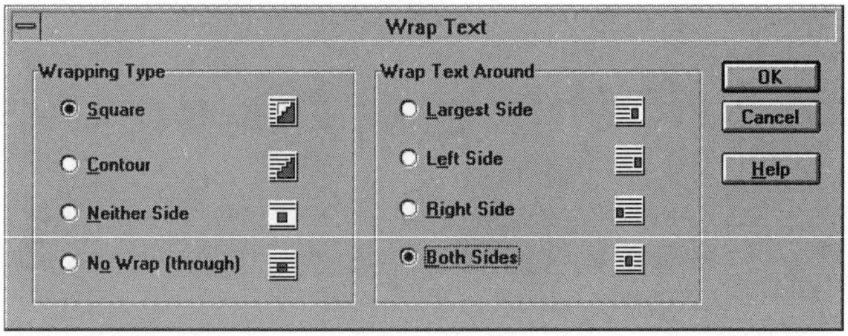

2 The illustrations next to each choice in the Wrap Text dialog box are pretty self-explanatory. Trial and error is fine here too; you can always come back and change wrapping options. We'll choose S̲quare for Wrapping Type, and L̲eft Side for our Wrap Text Around option.

⊛ *{Note}*

Wrapping text around the left side of a graphic is usually a safe choice. Since the eye reads from left to right, text wrapped around the right side can be difficult to read. The default choice is B̲oth Sides, which is what gave us our original problem result in figure 16.9.

3 Click OK. See a big improvement (refer to fig. 16.11).

Fig. 16.11
Wrapping text around a graphic is a good way of integrating the text with the picture.

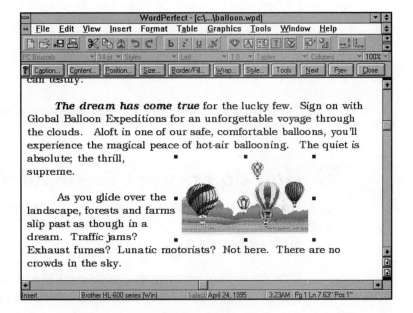

If you don't like the squared-off look, try the C̲ontour option in the Wrap Text dialog box (refer to fig. 16.10). Selecting C̲ontour, L̲eft Side in the Wrap Text dialog box gives you the effect shown in figure 16.12.

Fig. 16.12
Contouring text around a graphic is a good way of knitting your text and image together.

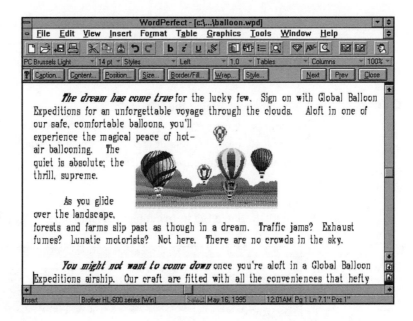

Text wrap has improved the way our graphic looks on the page, but we can still do better.

How do I resize this graphic?

Figures 16.11 and 16.12 show a graphic with text neatly wrapped around the left side of the image. We've also got a large blob of white space to the right of the graphic that doesn't look quite right.

We'll simply expand the graphic toward the right margin to fill in the space. Point at the middle handle on the right border of the graphic. The pointer becomes a double-arrow; drag to the right margin to expand the image, as shown in figure 16.13.

If you've lost your graphic's handles, just click the graphic to make them reappear.

Fig. 16.13
Drag any of the graphic's handles to stretch the image in any direction.

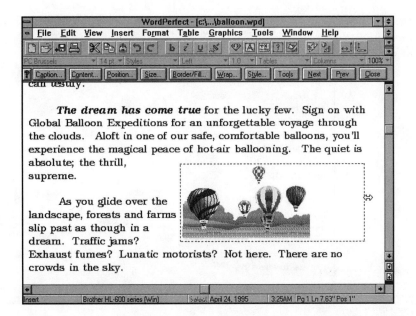

This graphic looks like a reflection in a funhouse mirror

Resizing graphics is easy to do, but when you stretch anything, you distort it. It's like those balloons with pictures on them; the picture looks fine, until you blow up the balloon.

Figure 16.14 shows what happens to our image when we stretch it to the right margin.

Fig. 16.14
Remember those
concave and convex
mirrors at the fun fair?

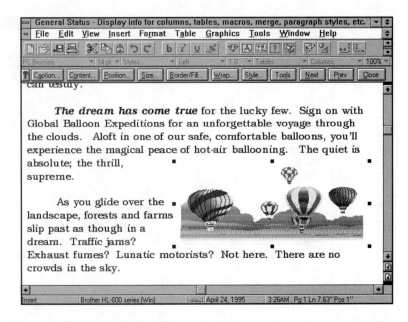

If you yank an image in one direction, you can tug it in the other direction to eliminate the distortion. That, with a little trial-and-error work, should take care of the problem.

I can't get this image quite right

If the yanking and tugging approach doesn't seem to work, WordPerfect provides another way of dealing with the resized image distortion.

Click the Content button on the feature bar for the Box Content dialog box (see fig. 16.15).

Fig. 16.15
The Box Content
dialog box helps you
adjust your image.

Click Preserve Image Width/Height Ratio, and WordPerfect automatically adjusts the image to prevent distortion as you resize it. Click OK, and you lose the funhouse effect. WordPerfect maintains the image's original width-to-height ratio, no matter how high and wide you drag your graphic.

X<Caution> Clicking the Reset button in the Box Content dialog box will delete your image if you've made any changes, such as resizing it. You get a warning from WordPerfect first; if you've experimented with Reset, click Cancel when the warning message pops up.

Retaining the original Height/Width ratio may still leave you with too much white space around the image. If so, deselect Preserve Image Width/Height Ratio in the Box Content dialog box, and go back to yanking and tugging.

How do I move a graphic around?

Moving graphics is straightforward. Click the graphic to select it, and slide the pointer over the image until you get the four-headed arrow. Now just drag to move the graphic anywhere you like.

What about a caption?

If your graphic needs further explanation, add a caption. Click Caption on the feature bar to pop up the Box Caption dialog box shown in figure 16.16.

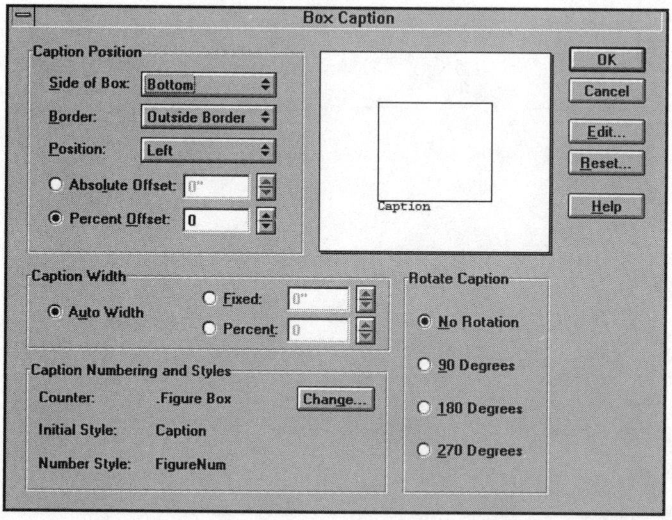

Fig. 16.16
Choose the Caption Position in the Box Caption dialog box; the preview window reflects your choices.

Put the caption below, above, or to one side of the image with your choice in the Side of Box edit box. With a caption above or below the graphics box, you can also center, left-, or right-justify the caption text by clicking the Position button.

When you've settled on the caption's position, click Edit. Type the caption, and click Close on the feature bar for something like figure 16.17.

Fig. 16.17
A caption describes images that aren't self-explanatory, or conveys information that doesn't fit in the body text.

 (Tip)

If you lose the feature bar during any of these maneuvers, right-click the graphic for the QuickMenu, and select Feature Bar to get it back.

Just what is a graphics box?

WordPerfect puts graphics inside a box. When you move or resize an image, you're actually moving and resizing the box that contains the image. It's as if you were stretching or compressing a canvas by changing the size of the picture frame around it.

There are different styles of boxes for images, text, and tables; and a particularly nifty style for buttons.

Click Style on the graphics feature bar, and click your choice in the Box Style dialog box to instantly restyle your graphic.

I need to make this text stand out

A **text box** is just what you'd expect: a graphics box containing text instead of an image. Text boxes make important information jump out at the reader.

To create a text box:

1 Right-click the Toolbar, and select Graphics on the QuickMenu to pop up the Graphics Toolbar.

 2 Click the Text Box button, and your pointer turns into the hand-clutching-frame shape. Position the frame wherever you want the text box, just as we did with the image box.

3 When you release the mouse button, you get two thick black lines with the insertion point between them.

4 Type your text.

5 Change the font, click the <u>B</u>order/Fill button on the feature bar to add fill, and move the text box if necessary. Click <u>C</u>lose on the feature bar, and you'll wind up with something like figure 16.18.

Fig. 16.18
Text boxes call attention to an important message.

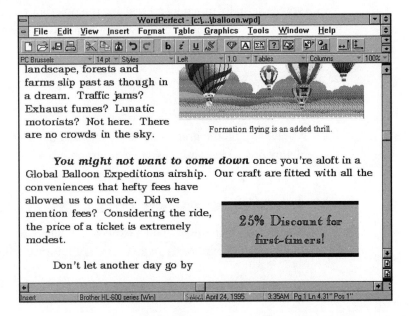

⊛ *{Note}*

The default Text Box Style gives you the two heavy black lines shown in figure 16.18. To choose a different style, right-click the text box and select <u>F</u>eature Bar from the QuickMenu. Click the St<u>y</u>le button on the feature bar for the Box Style dialog box, and double-click your choice of box <u>S</u>tyle. Double-clicking Image, for example, gets rid of the black lines.

Editing text in a text box is a snap. Just double-click the box—that puts the insertion point in the box for easy editing. Click anywhere outside the box when you're done.

 **{Note}** Double-clicking an image has a dramatically different effect. You'll think your system has ground to a halt, but actually it's WordPerfect's gears whirring as it loads WP Draw. That's WordPerfect's built-in drawing program, which we look at in Chapter 19. You can use the WP Draw tools to edit your image, but you might find they're more than you want. To exit WP Draw and return to your document, click anywhere outside the graphics box. And to avoid WP Draw, right-click (don't double-click) an image when you want to make changes.

How do I get rid of graphics boxes?

Deleting any kind of graphics box, image, text, whatever, is the easiest part of inserting graphics. Just click the graphics box, then press Delete.

And if you decide that you didn't want to delete your graphic after all, click the Undo button on the toolbar to get it back.

17

Tables Turn Documents into Spreadsheets

WordPerfect tables help bring order and precision to your documents. They'll even figure your mortgage payment for you!

When officials in Washington "table" legislation, they're delaying (if not killing) it. "Shelved" would be a better word, but it wouldn't do to say so to constituents expecting action.

Those constituents would be better served with a WordPerfect table. In WordPerfect, tables are tools for action. You use tables to quickly organize and analyze information. Any kind of information, in large amounts or small. You might say that tables put data on the table.

What exactly is a table?

How many busy days have you started by grabbing a scrap of paper and jotting down something like this?

To-dos:	Calls:
Pick up dry cleaning	Joe, re: contract
Return library books	Plumber!!
Finish Jones project	...

That's a table. We use them all the time to organize information. Tables are handy because they make entering data easy. Tables also make data easy to read at a glance.

> Like parallel columns, tables arrange text and numbers side-by-side in orderly rows. Unlike parallel columns, tables are very easy to work with.

Create a quick table

WordPerfect tables make managing data especially easy. Using columns or tabs to organize written information works okay, but as you add and delete items, keeping a neat columnar structure can be a real chore.

Suppose you have several clients to meet, and you need to note your expenses for the accounts department. Create a table to quickly enter, organize, and even calculate your data. To build a table:

1 First, think about how many rows and columns you need. We want headings for Client, Item, and Amount, so that gives us three columns. And we've got three client meetings planned, with each client on a separate row. Add a row for the column headings, and we've got four rows in all.

> A rough idea of a table's structure, especially the number of columns needed, is important in WordPerfect, but don't worry if it changes. You can always add rows and columns later.

2 Click the Tables button on the Power bar, hold the mouse button down, and drag across three columns and four rows. 3×4 appears at the top of the button's display, as seen in figure 17.1.

Fig. 17.1

Keep pressing the mouse button as you select columns and rows with the Power Bar Tables button.

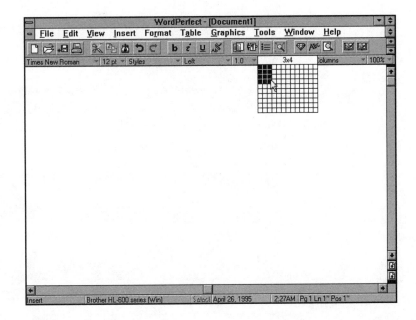

Q&A

I keep clicking the Power Bar Tables button, and that little display disappears on me!

You have to click and hold the Power Bar Tables button. Don't release the mouse button until you've selected the desired number of columns and rows.

{Note}

If you move the mouse pointer to the top of the Table QuickCreate grid, you get No Table. If you mistakenly select the wrong number of rows or columns, just click Undo and try again.

3 When you release the mouse button, a grid of three columns and four rows snaps into place on the document, with the insertion point in the first box of the grid. The boxes are called **cells**. Type the heading for the first column in the first cell.

{Note}

The tables Toolbar pops up when you create a table. Put the insertion point outside the table, and the standard Toolbar reappears. Click anywhere inside the table to get the tables Toolbar back.

4 When you've finished with the first heading, press Tab to move the insertion point into the second cell on the top row. Type in the second heading, and do the same thing for the third.

5 We want those headings to stand out from the rest of the information on the table, so we'll put them in boldface. Drag across all of the cells in the top row to select them, then click the Bold button on the Toolbar. Figure 17.2 shows the table so far.

Fig. 17.2
Drag across whole rows, columns, or single cells to select them. QuickSelect—double-, triple-, or quadruple-clicking—doesn't work in tables.

When the pointer points left or up, click to select the cell.

These boxes at the intersection of rows and columns are cells.

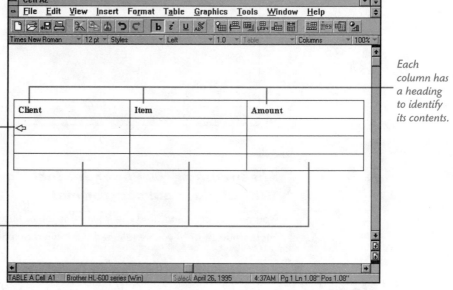

Each column has a heading to identify its contents.

{Note}

As you drag across cells in a table, the pointer points left. The same thing happens if you point very carefully at vertical lines in a table. And if you point with equal care at the horizontal lines, the pointer points up. When the pointer changes direction like that, click to select the cell the pointer is in.

6 Now, type the rest of the information in the table: client names, expense items, and amounts. Don't bother typing dollar signs for the amounts; we'll take care of that in the next step. Use Tab, Back Tab, or the arrow keys to move the insertion point from cell to cell.

(Tip)

If you reach the end of your table and need another row, just press Tab; WordPerfect adds a row to the end of your table.

7 When you enter numbers in a table, you can format them all at once with commas, dollar signs, whatever. Just type the plain digits, select all the cells you want to format, and click the Number Type button on the Toolbar. That pops up the Number Type dialog box shown in figure 17.3.

Fig. 17.3
The Preview window displays the various number formatting options, but the number shown (–1234) has nothing to do with your data.

```
┌─────────────────────────────────────────────┐
│ ▭            Number Type                     │
│ ┌─Select Type For──────────┐   ┌──────────┐  │
│ │ ⦿ Cell   ○ Column  ○ Table│  │    OK    │  │
│ │ Reference: C2:C4          │  └──────────┘  │
│ └───────────────────────────┘  ┌──────────┐  │
│                                 │  Cancel  │  │
│ □ Use Column Type               └──────────┘  │
│ ┌─Available Types───────────┐  ┌──────────┐  │
│ │ ○ Accounting  ○ General   │  │ Custom...│  │
│ │ ○ Commas      ○ Integer   │  └──────────┘  │
│ │ ⦿ Currency    ○ Percent   │  ┌──────────┐  │
│ │ ○ Date/Time   ○ Scientific│  │Initial Type│ │
│ │ ○ Fixed       ○ Text      │  └──────────┘  │
│ └───────────────────────────┘  ┌──────────┐  │
│                                 │   Help   │  │
│ ┌─Preview───────────────────┐  └──────────┘  │
│ │  [($1,234.00)]            │                │
│ └───────────────────────────┘                │
└─────────────────────────────────────────────┘
```

8 In the Number Type dialog box, select Currency and click OK. The selected cells are formatted with dollar signs and two decimal places.

9 Position the cursor above the table, and add a centered title. The finished table looks like figure 17.4.

Fig. 17.4
Tables display data in an organized way.

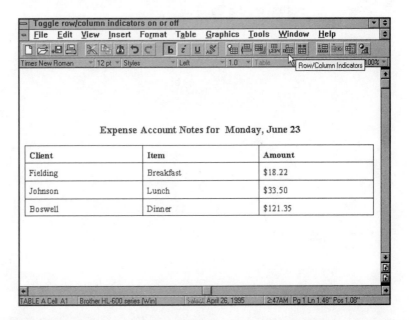

Expense Account Notes for Monday, June 23

Client	Item	Amount
Fielding	Breakfast	$18.22
Johnson	Lunch	$33.50
Boswell	Dinner	$121.35

How do I edit this table?

Tables give you a lot of control over your data. By breaking up data into cells on a grid, tables let you operate on a single item, several items, or all your data at once.

Think of a street map. It's a mass of data that's saved from being a mess of data by its grid structure. Any decent map has letters and numbers around the perimeter that help you locate particular streets. Looking for Jones Street? The map's index tells you Jones is in C3, so you locate 3 on the map's perimeter and run your eye over to the area where 3 intersects with C.

Tables have the same setup:

- Columns are identified by letters.
- Rows are identified by numbers.
- Each cell, the intersection of a column and a row, is identified by the corresponding column letter and row number. Cell C3 in a table is the cell in column C, row 3. A cell's identifying column letter and row number is called the **cell reference** or **cell address**.

 Those numbers and letters that identify rows and columns are called row and column **indicators**. To display them, click the Row/Column Indicators button on the Toolbar.

Anatomy of a WordPerfect table

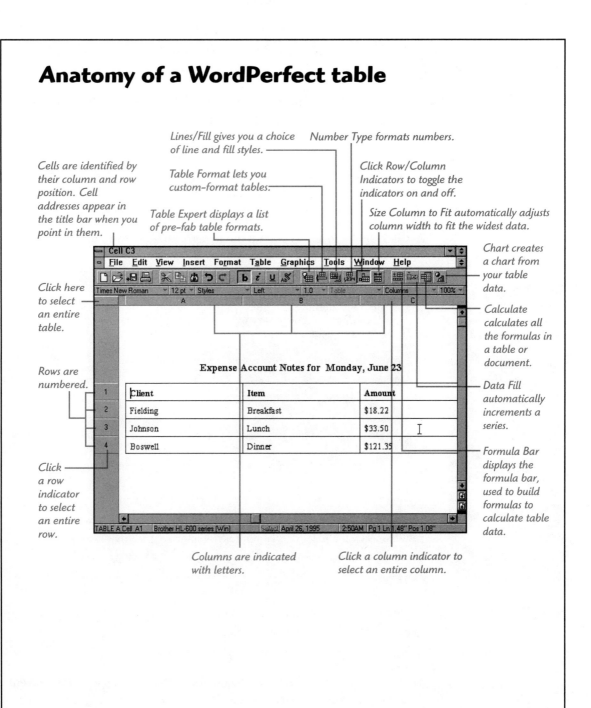

Lines/Fill gives you a choice of line and fill styles.

Number Type formats numbers.

Cells are identified by their column and row position. Cell addresses appear in the title bar when you point in them.

Table Format lets you custom-format tables.

Click Row/Column Indicators to toggle the indicators on and off.

Table Expert displays a list of pre-fab table formats.

Size Column to Fit automatically adjusts column width to fit the widest data.

Click here to select an entire table.

Chart creates a chart from your table data.

Rows are numbered.

Calculate calculates all the formulas in a table or document.

Data Fill automatically increments a series.

Click a row indicator to select an entire row.

Formula Bar displays the formula bar, used to build formulas to calculate table data.

Columns are indicated with letters.

Click a column indicator to select an entire column.

How do I add rows and columns to this table?

Suppose we need to fit another client meeting in the already heavy day we're tracking in the table shown in figure 17.4. We'll just add another row to the table:

1 We met this client over drinks, so we need to squeeze a new row in between Lunch and Dinner (refer to fig. 17.4). Click anywhere in row 4 to put the insertion point in the row.

2 Click Table, Insert to pop up the Insert Columns/Rows dialog box shown in figure 17.5.

Fig. 17.5
Use the Insert Columns/Rows dialog box to add rows and columns, and to control their placement in the table.

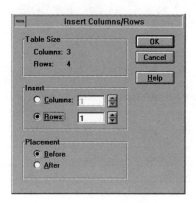

(Tip) The default placement choice is Before; when you squeeze in new rows and columns, click the row or column *after* the inserted one. That saves you the bother of selecting After in the dialog box.

(Tip) A quick way to insert a row at the insertion point: press Alt+Ins. To delete a row at the insertion point, press Alt+Del.

3 In the Insert Columns/Rows dialog box, Table Size displays the current size of the table. We're inserting 1 Row, with Placement Before row 4, the selected row. Click OK, and the new row pops into place, as shown in figure 17.6.

Fig. 17.6

Inserting columns works the same way as inserting rows.

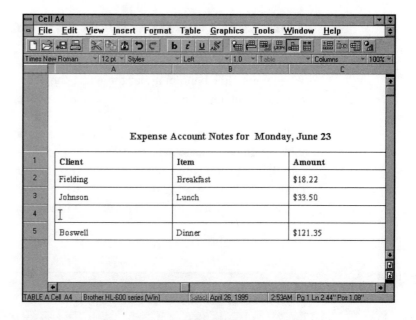

4 Now, just type the data into the newly inserted row.

Deleting rows and columns is equally easy. Click a row or column indicator to select the row or column, and press Delete. That pops up the Delete dialog box shown in figure 17.7.

Fig. 17.7

The Delete dialog box offers the choice of getting rid of just the data or the entire row or column.

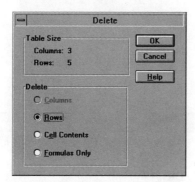

Select Rows or Columns to delete the whole row or column. Click OK, and the cells and all they hold vanish. If you want to leave blank cells in place but delete their contents, select Cell Contents, and click OK.

This cell doesn't look big enough for my data...

When you hold a balloon under the water tap, it swells as you fill it. Empty the water out, and the balloon shrinks back to its original size.

Cells work the same way, except they won't burst if you overfill them. They look small, but cells expand vertically to accommodate whatever you type into them. As you type, lines wrap with soft returns, just like they do in the editing window. Pressing the Enter key works like it does in the editing window, too—you start a new paragraph in the same cell.

Figure 17.8 shows cells stretched to hold additional lines of text.

Fig. 17.8
I pressed Enter after the client name, and typed the firm name on a new line.

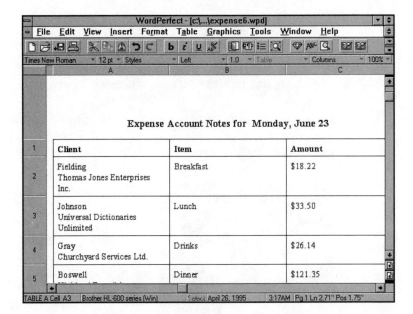

I want wider cells

Text typed in cells wraps at the right cell border line. That's handy for fast data entry, but your table might wind up looking too long and skinny if you've got a lot of cells with several lines in them.

You can fix that problem by widening the column. Click anywhere in the column you want to widen, then click the Size Column to Fit button on the Toolbar.

The selected column instantly stretches to the width of the longest line in the column, as shown in figure 17.9. If you select more than one column, all selected columns adjust at once.

> When sizing columns to fit existing text, it's a good idea to start with the columns on the left first. By the time you get to the columns on the right, there may not be enough room to widen them any further.

Fig. 17.9
Adjusting column widths is easily done, and can make for a more readable table.

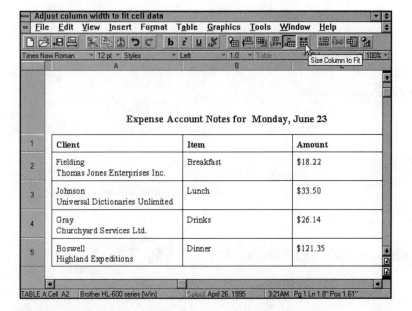

Adjusting column widths is a drag

If you have one cell with a very long line in it, you might not want the Size Column to Fit button to stretch all the cells in the column to the length of that one line. You want *most* of the entries to fit on one line, but it's okay if a few of them wrap.

In that case, just point at the right border line of the column you want to widen. The pointer turns into a black double-arrow; now drag to widen the column, as shown in figure 17.10.

Fig. 17.10
The broken line follows the pointer around as you drag the double arrow.

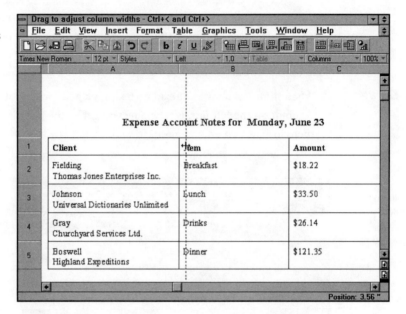

When you're satisfied with the new column width, release the mouse button. The column border line snaps into the new position.

Tables are spreadsheets, too

With a calculator, a scrap of paper, and a pencil, we can get through a lot of arithmetic in little time. A spreadsheet takes care of arithmetical chores even faster. **Spreadsheets** combine the easy editing features of a word processor with the calculating might of the most powerful scientific and financial calculators. WordPerfect has a built-in spreadsheet, and it's a dandy.

We've used tables so far in this chapter to organize text. Let's use WordPerfect's spreadsheet features to turn our table into an electronic calculator.

The formula bar turns tables into calculating machines

To make a spreadsheet out of your table, click the Formula Bar button on the Toolbar. That puts the formula bar at the top of the editing window, as shown in figure 17.11.

Click to reject changes to formulas, and to turn off formula editing.

The current cell is displayed here, handy to see where the formula is going to wind up.

Click to accept a formula, insert it into the current cell, and turn off formula editing mode.

Click in here, then type to build formulas.

Fig. 17.11
The formula bar turns WordPerfect into a powerful calculator.

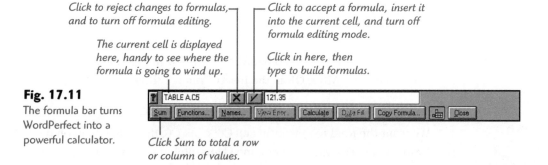

Click Sum to total a row or column of values.

You use **formulas** and **functions** to calculate data in WordPerfect:

- A **formula** is like a recipe; a series of steps that operate on ingredients to produce a final result. Formulas use **values** as ingredients. 8 and 12 are examples of values; 8+12=20 is a formula.

- **Operators** are the instructions in the formula recipe. They determine what happens to the values in a formula. + is an operator; so are – and *.

- **Functions** are ready-made formulas, a bit like buying your soup in a can instead of making it yourself. The ingredients in a function are called **arguments**. For example, AVE(A1:A3) tells WordPerfect to give us the average of all the values in cells A1 through A3.

How do I add up a column of numbers?

Of all the gadgets in WordPerfect, the SUM function is one of the handiest. One click of the <u>S</u>um button on the formula bar adds all the values in a row or column. We'll use SUM to add up the values in column C of our table (refer to fig. 17.11).

1 We need to add another row to the table in figure 17.9 for our total. Click anywhere in row 5 to put the insertion point in the row. Right-click for the QuickMenu, and select Insert to pop up the Insert Columns/Rows dialog box.

(Tip)

> Earlier in the chapter, we used the Tables, Insert command to get the Insert Columns/Rows dialog box. Use either the menu bar or the QuickMenu to access this or any table command, your choice.

2 We want the new row to go below the last row in the table. Select 1 Rows and click After, OK in the Insert Columns/Rows dialog box.

3 In cell B6 in the new row, type **Total:**.

4 We want the total to appear in cell C6; click C6, then click Sum on the formula bar. The values in column C are totaled with a SUM function, and the result appears in C6, as shown in figure 17.12.

❌ \<Caution\>

> It's a good idea to double-check your work when you use WordPerfect's functions. For example, the SUM function needs values in the cells to sum. If there are blank cells in the range you're adding up, SUM may not work at all, or the sum you get may not be correct.

You'll have noticed that the function uses cell references instead of the actual values as its arguments. That's true of all WordPerfect functions and formulas. That way, you can change the values in the cells referenced by the function, without having to change the function itself.

Plain English, please!

> The reference C2:C5 refers to all the cells from C2 through C5. That's called a **range**. Ranges are groups of two or more cells. **Range references** consist of the first and last cell addresses in the range, separated by a colon.

The function is displayed in the formula bar when the cell containing it is clicked. The function's arguments are in parentheses.

Fig. 17.12
When you click the Sum button, all the values in a column or row are totaled, and text is ignored.

Clicking the Sum button puts a SUM function in the active cell.

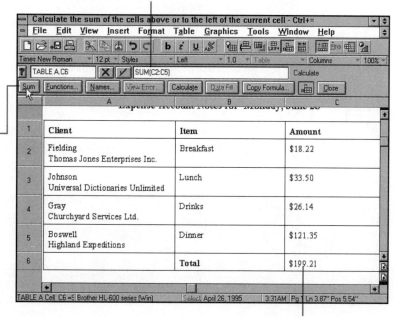

Only the result of a formula or function is displayed in the cell.

How do I write my own formula?

We used one of WordPerfect's canned formulas—the SUM function—to total our amounts in figure 17.12. Writing your own formula is equally easy.

Suppose that we get reimbursed for only 80 percent of our total expenses. We'll add another column to show our reimbursement for each item, and write a formula to calculate 80 percent of each amount.

To write your own formula in a WordPerfect table:

1 First, we need to add another column: click column C, right-click for the QuickMenu, and select Insert.

2 In the Insert Columns/Rows dialog box, select 1 Columns and click After to add a new column D.

3 Type **Reimburse** in D1 for a column heading.

4 Click cell D2 to make it the active cell.

5 Click the formula bar editing window to activate formula editing mode.

6 Click cell C2. That puts the cell reference C2 in the formula bar editing window. Our formula will use whatever value happens to be in C2.

7 Type ***.8** in the formula bar editing window. That multiplies the value in C2 by .8, or 80%.

8 Click the check mark button on the formula bar. That completes the formula and puts it in cell D2. Only the result is displayed in D2; the formula is displayed in the formula bar when D2 is the active cell. It looks like figure 17.13.

Fig. 17.13
Formula building is mostly a process of clicking cells and typing operators.

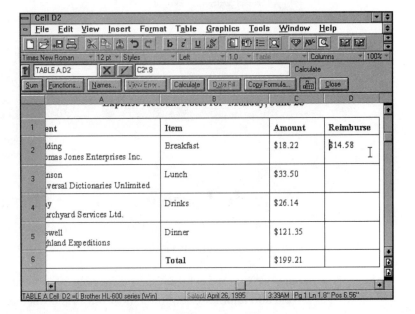

Can I copy this formula?

Write a formula in a table once, and you can use it again and again by copying it to other cells. It's not only a big time-saver; copying formulas helps to avoid spreadsheet errors too.

To copy the formula in D2 to the other cells in column D:

1 Click cell D2 to make it the active cell, and click the Copy Formula button on the formula bar.

2 The Copy Formula dialog box shown in figure 17.14 displays.

Fig. 17.14
The Copy Formula dialog box lets you copy formulas to rows or columns.

3 Select Down and enter **3** in the Times edit box to copy the formula to the three cells below D2.

4 The formula is copied to the other three cells, with the results displayed in the cells, as seen in figure 17.15.

Some references are relative

We can copy the formula to the other cells in column D, and the cell reference automatically changes to reflect the new rows. C2 in our formula is a **relative** reference; it changes relative to where you place the formula. For example, if you copy the formula in D2 to D3, the formula automatically changes to multiply 0.8 times cell C3.

Think of the formula as a marksman and the cell reference as his target. A relative reference is just like a moving target, tracked by the marksman wherever it goes. That lets us copy the formula and get the correct result wherever the formula is copied.

The cell reference in the formula changes
to the correct cell in each row.

Fig. 17.15
Copying formulas saves
you a lot of typing.

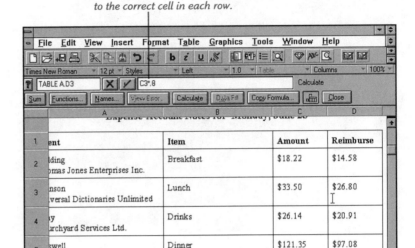

To total the amounts in column D, click cell D6, and then click the <u>S</u>um
button on the formula bar.

SUM is just the beginning

WordPerfect is a serious spreadsheet. SUM is just one of many functions that
you can use to calculate data in tables. To browse the selection of functions
in WordPerfect, click the <u>F</u>unctions button on the formula bar for the Table
Functions dialog box shown in figure 17.16.

Fig. 17.16
The PMT function is a
handy mortgage
calculator.

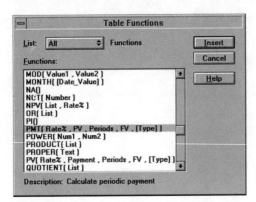

There are functions to analyze investments and to calculate the number of days between two dates, just to mention two of many.

Can I put this table in another document?

You can create a table in an existing document or in a new document, as we've done in this chapter. You'll probably also want to import tables into other documents too. Our expenses table, for example, might well have to be justified with a supporting memo. Tables work well in reports and letters, too.

You can import a table as a regular file or as text in a graphics box. Importing the table to a graphics box lets you wrap text around it, add a caption, and manipulate it like any other graphics object.

To import a table into another document as a graphics box:

1 Save the table just as you'd save any other document.

2 Open the document in which you want the table, and click Graphics, Custom box.

3 In the Custom Box dialog box, select Table, from the Style Name list, and click OK.

4 Position the graphics box frame at the upper left corner of where you want the table, drag to the lower right corner, and release.

5 Click the Content button on the graphics feature bar for the Box Content dialog box.

6 Enter the table's file name in the Filename edit box, and click OK.

7 The table pops into the graphics box. Use the graphics feature bar to wrap the text, add a caption, or change the box style.

8 Click Close on the graphics feature when you're through. Figure 17.17 shows a full-page view of what you might end up with.

Fig. 17.17
This graphic was
resized. I also changed
the font size to
squeeze the table into
the graphics box.

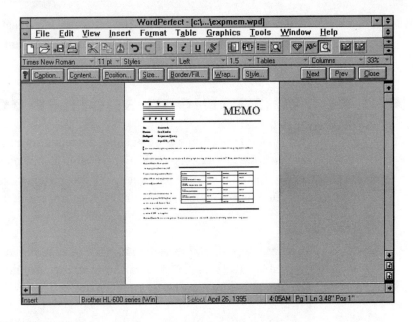

 {Note}_____ | Chapter 16 covers editing graphics in detail. Chances are, you will have to
make some minor adjustments to your table to squeeze it into your document.

This table could use a facelift

Tables can be used to create custom forms, invoices, and any other document that lends itself to tabular form. To create tables like that, all the
WordPerfect formatting and editing tools and features are at your disposal.

But when your table is only in need of a quick change of clothes, click the
Table Expert button on the Toolbar. That pops up the Table Expert dialog
box shown in figure 17.18.

Click a style on the A̲vailable Styles list, then click A̲pply. Your table is
instantly transformed, as seen in figure 17.19.

Fig. 17.18

The Table Expert has a wardrobe of formats for tables, including some startling effects!

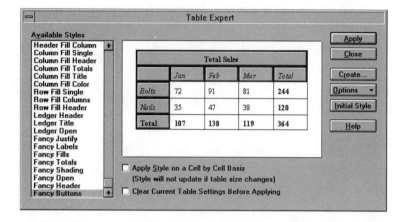

Fig. 17.19

In the case of these expenses, the conservative look might be the best choice of formats.

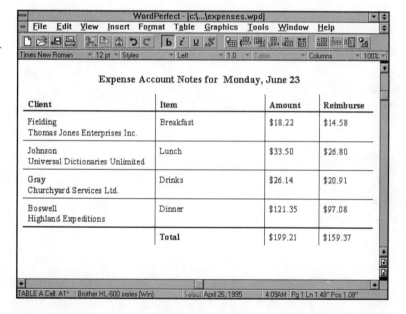

If you don't like any of the table styles you see in the Table Expert dialog box, create your own style. Experiment with Format and Lines/Fill from the Table menu until you come up with something that works.

If you like your creation, save it as a Table Expert style, and use it again.

18

Documents Big and Small, Few and Many

WordPerfect helps take the sting out of writing jobs big and small. And when you've done many such jobs, WordPerfect makes all your hard-won files easy to get at.

Novelists and publishers like to provide value for money. That's why our beach reading is so bulky. But when a publisher is his own novelist, the large economy size in books comes into its own. Samuel Richardson was an 18th-century publisher whose novel *Clarissa* ran to seven big volumes. Not a page-turner by modern standards, but its sheer bulk commands respect.

We're unlikely to match Richardson's output (or his profits), but when our documents grow in size and number, WordPerfect is up to the job. There's a powerful file manager to cope with large numbers of documents, and a battery of features to help deal with big documents.

Outlining organizes documents

When an office building goes up, a skeleton of girders gets fleshed out, step by step, with wiring, plumbing, outer walls, and so on. An outline is like a skeleton of girders in a document; you lay out the document's topics and headings, then flesh them out with text.

Any document that can be broken down into topics and subtopics is a good candidate for an outline. Finished outlining? WordPerfect converts your outline to the actual headings and subheadings in the document.

Outlines help you present the information in a document logically, and WordPerfect makes using outlines very convenient.

How do I create an outline?

Say we're a film studio preparing a report for our bankers on the subject of our most recent releases. This report needs to be carefully written, so we want to outline it first. Each release, and the introduction and conclusion, might be our main topics, with relevant subtopics beneath them.

To create an outline:

1 Click Tools, Outline. We get the outline feature bar, the numbered line for our first outline item, and a stylized numeral one in the left margin.

2 Type **Introduction** on the numbered first line and press Enter. That skips to the next line, automatically numbered with a 2. So far, our outline looks like figure 18.1.

?Q&A

How come I don't see my level icons?

Drag the horizontal scroll button to the left to display the left margin. If you still don't see the level icons, click Options on the feature bar and select Show Level Icons.

Fig. 18.1
Once you turn on
outlining, just type
your first heading and
press Enter.

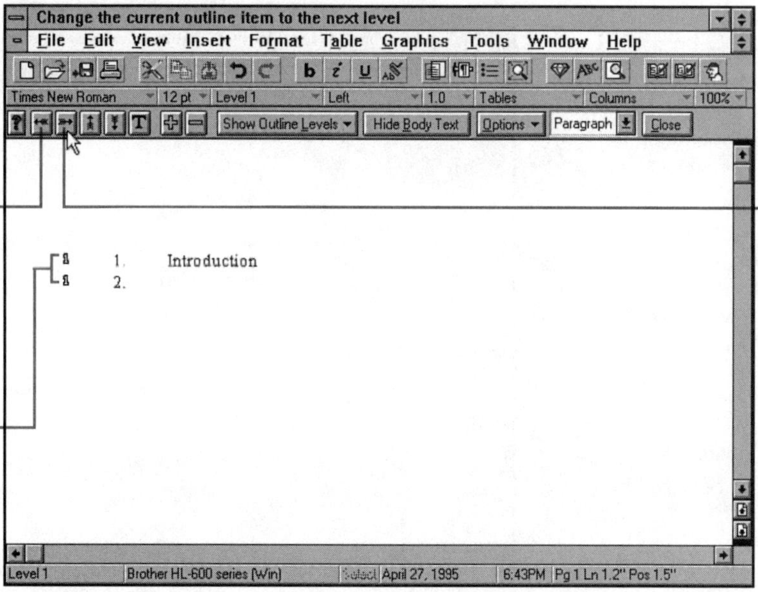

Click the left arrow
to promote the
current line to the
next higher outline
level.

Level icons indicate
the outline level; 1
is the highest level,
for major topic
headings.

Click
the right
arrow to
demote
the
current
line to
the next
lower

Change the current outline item to the next level

File   Edit   View   Insert   Format   Table   Graphics   Tools   Window   Help

Times New Roman   12 pt   Level 1   Left   1.0   Tables   Columns   100%

Show Outline Levels ▼   Hide Body Text   Options ▼   Paragraph ▲   Close

1.   Introduction
2.

Level 1   Brother HL-600 series (Win)   Select   April 27, 1995   6:43PM   Pg 1 Ln 1.2" Pos 1.5"

> ❝ *Plain English, please!*
>
> Outline **levels** refer to the relative importance of items in the outline. Level 1
> is for the most important items, like chapter titles; level 2 is for major topics in
> the chapter; and so on, all the way down to level 8. In practice, using the
> outline style, these levels correspond to I, A, 1, a, (1), and so on—just like you
> learned in 8th-grade English class. Each level also aligns at a tab stop. ❞

3 The introduction is a major heading, making it a level 1 item. We want a
subtopic or two under that major heading, so we'll demote the second
line to a level 2 item. Click line 2 and click the right arrow on the
feature bar (refer to fig. 18.1).

4 That indents the line, the 2. turns into an a., and the level icon changes
to a stylized 2 to indicate that it's a level 2 line. Type the subtopic
heading and press Enter. The result looks like figure 18.2.

Fig. 18.2

Click the right feature bar arrow to demote outline items; the left arrow to promote them.

The original level icon acquires a – sign, indicating that there are displayed subordinate items.

The level icon indicates a level 2 item.

Pressing Enter begins a new level 2 line for a second subtopic.

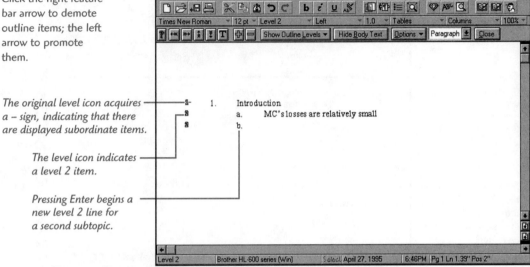

5 Type the second subtopic heading and press Enter at the end of the line for an additional subtopic.

6 For level 3 subtopics under a level 2 subtopic, click the right arrow on the feature bar and type the headings, pressing Enter after each one.

7 When you're ready for a new level 1 item, click the left arrow on the feature bar on a new line, repeatedly if necessary, until you get a number 2. and a level 1 icon in the left margin.

8 Continue to press Enter at the end of each line. Click the left and right arrows on the feature bar to promote and demote items, and type your headings. Add a title, and as the outline takes shape, it looks like figure 18.3.

As you build up your outline, a sea of subtopics can become confusing to look at. Position the insertion point next to a higher-level item and click the + and – buttons on the feature bar to hide or display subordinate items within outline families (see fig. 18.3).

Fig. 18.3
Building an outline gets faster with practice. The more you use the feature, the more indispensable you'll find it.

Click to display all the subordinate items in the current family.

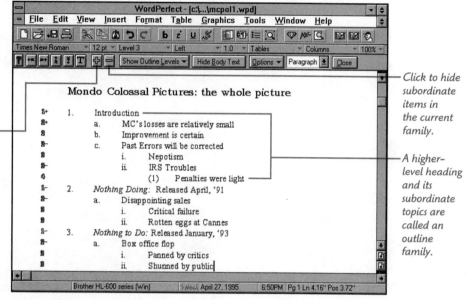

Click to hide subordinate items in the current family.

A higher-level heading and its subordinate topics are called an outline family.

66 ***Plain English, please!***

An **outline family** is an outline item and its subordinate items; for example, a level 1 item and all the level 2, 3, etc. items below it. Or it can be a level 2 item and its subordinate items—the parent item in an outline family can be an item of any level. 99

(Tip)

Double-click a level icon to toggle on and off the display of subordinate items in the outline family.

Figure 18.4 shows the same outline with only the level 1 outline items in the first two topics displayed.

Fig. 18.4

Outlines are less
confusing to look
at when you hide
subordinate items,
especially as you
work on new items.

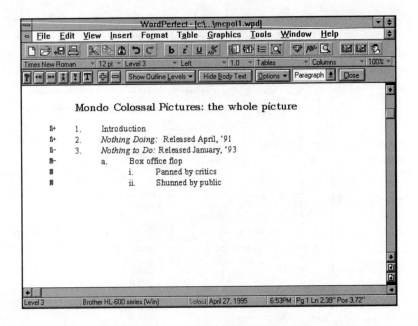

Got the outline finished? Add body text

The idea behind an outline is to help you organize a document. Once you've
finished the outline, you've got a few options for adding body text:

- Turn off outlining by clicking Options on the feature bar and selecting
  End Outline. Type your body text at the end of the outline if you want it
  in the same document.

- Or save your outline and open a new document for body text. You can
  print the outline and refer to the printout as you write.

The third choice is to add body text within the outline. This has several
advantages. You can refer to the outline easily, because it's in front of you
all the time, and you can convert all your outline items to headings in the
document.

Adding text within the outline saves you from having to retype the outline items as headings, and it gives you a ready-made structure for your
document.

To add body text to an outline, first save your document, then:

1 Press Enter at the end of the line with the outline item under which you want to add text.

2 Click the T button on the feature bar. That converts the line to body text.

3 Type your text. Repeat steps 1 and 2 for any other outline items under which you want to add text. Figure 18.5 shows an outline with body text.

Fig. 18.5
You might find it less distracting to hide subordinate outline items as you add body text.

Click this button to toggle between outline mode and body text on the current line.

The level icon indicates body text.

Click here to hide or display body text.

> Printer - Show name and type of printer. Double-click for Select Printer dialog.
>
> **File Edit View Insert Format Table Graphics Tools Window Help**
>
> Times New Roman   12 pt   Level 3   Left   1.0   Tables   Columns   100%
>
> Show Outline Levels   Hide Body Text   Options   Paragraph   Close
>
> 1.   Introduction
>   Mondo Colossal continues to strive for quality, quantity, and profit. Although our series of *Nothing* movies has proven less than successful, we have great hopes for our new series. Tentatively called *Something*, titles in the prospective series will include *Something for Nothing* and, *Something for Everyone.* We are especially hopeful about the latter.
>   a.   MC's losses are relatively small
>   Although this was an undeniably disappointing year for Mondo Colossal, it was less disappointing than last year, which in turn had been slightly less disappointing than the year before. Losses were large, although not ruinous.
>   b.   Improvement is certain
>   c.   Past Errors will be corrected
>   i.   Nepotism
>   ii.   IRS Troubles
>   (1)   Penalties were light
> 2.   *Nothing Doing:* Released April, '91
>   a.   Disappointing sales
>   i.   Critical failure
>   ii.   Rotten eggs at Cannes
>
> Level 3   Brother HL-600 series [Win]   Select April 27, 1995   6:59PM Pg 1 Ln 4.75" Pos 3.99"

To toggle the display of body text, click the Show [or Hide] Body Text button.

How do I get rid of these outline numbers and letters?

We've got our body text lined up where we want it, under the appropriate outline items. To complete the document, convert all the outline items to headings.

Click the drop-down arrow on the outline definitions list on the feature bar, and select Headings. Figure 18.6 shows you what happens.

Fig. 18.6
Two clicks turns an
outline into a report.

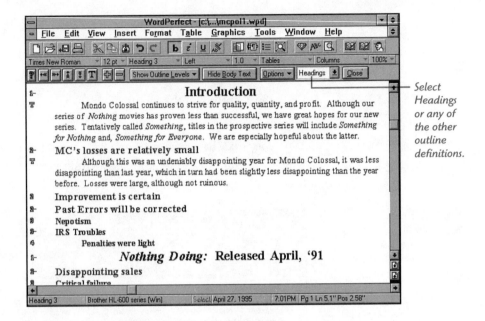

Select
Headings
or any of
the other
outline
definitions.

To display the outline again, select Paragraph or any of the other outline
definitions from the drop-down list on the outline definitions button.

Figure 18.7 shows a different outline style.

Fig. 18.7
Choose whatever
outline style you like;
you can switch back
and forth between the
definitions anytime.

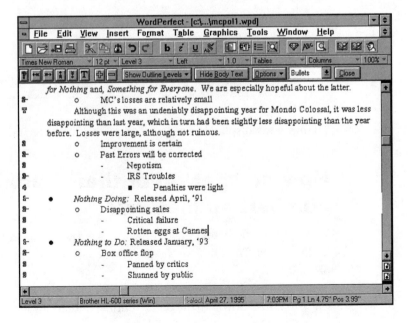

I need to move this outline item

Outlines change. You'll want to move items up or down, and back again, as your thinking about the final document changes.

  To move a single outline item, put the insertion point anywhere within the item and click the up or down arrow on the feature bar.

To move an outline family up or down:

1 Point at the outline level icon. The pointer turns into a two-headed white arrow.

2 Click once to select the entire family.

3 Drag the two-headed arrow up or down. A solid line moves with the pointer, indicating where the selected text is going to wind up. Figure 18.8 shows an outline family on the move.

Fig. 18.8

Moving an outline family is much easier than moving your real family!

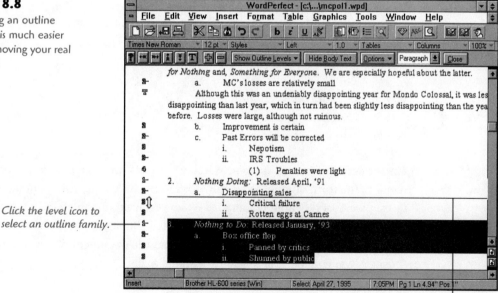

Click the level icon to select an outline family.

As you drag, the solid line indicates where the family's moving.

⊛ *{Note}* You can also convert an existing document to outline form. If you're working on a report with a confusing number of topics, for example, click Tools, Outline to turn on outline mode. Then use the feature bar to convert body text to outline items and to promote or demote items you've converted. In outline form, you'll see your document a lot more clearly.

❶ *(Tip)* You can use the keyboard to quickly create and modify an outline. Press Ctrl+H to turn on outlining. After pressing Enter and adding a new outline number, press the Tab key to move one level to the right. To move one level to the left, press Shift+Tab. To turn off outlining, press Ctrl+H again.

This big document is cumbersome

If you work with large documents in WordPerfect, you'll notice that the program slows down quite a bit when those documents are open. Editing chores like Find and Replace seem to proceed in slow motion when you're working with large files.

It would be more convenient to break up that big file into smaller files, provided you could put them back together again when you want to. That's exactly what a **master document** does.

Master documents hold the pieces, called **subdocuments**, of a large document, in the form of icons. You can work in the individual subdocuments, those pieces of the large document. When you want all the pieces assembled again, you expand the master document. That's handy if you want to print the whole thing, or Find and Replace throughout the document. When you're finished, you collapse the master document again.

How do I create a master document?

Setting up a master document is easy. Suppose we have four chapters of a novel on our hands, in four different files. The files are named CHAP1.WPD, CHAP2.WPD, and so on. The novel's title is *North Wind*. We'll create a master document called NORWND.WPD that will hold our individual chapters as subdocuments.

To create a master document:

1 Click the New Blank Document button on the Toolbar to open a new document.

You can turn an existing document into a master document; just open it and go through the steps we're about to take.

2 Click File, Master Document, Subdocument to pop up the Include Subdocument dialog box.

3 Select the first file you want as a subdocument from the Filename list in the Include Subdocument dialog box. In the example, it's the file CHAP1.WPD, as shown in figure 18.9.

Fig. 18.9
Regrettably, you can't select more than one file at once.

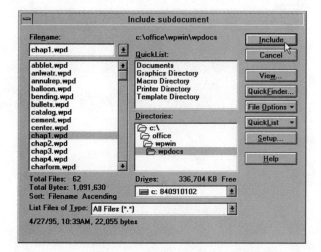

4 Once you've made your selection, click Include. The dialog box disappears, and what happens next depends on what view mode you're in. In draft view mode, you see a shaded comment bar across the editing window, as shown in figure 18.10.

5 In page view, you get a tiny document icon in the left margin. Click the icon, and a balloon pops up with the subdocument's file name in it, as shown in figure 18.11.

Fig. 18.10
The subdocument's file name is displayed in draft view.

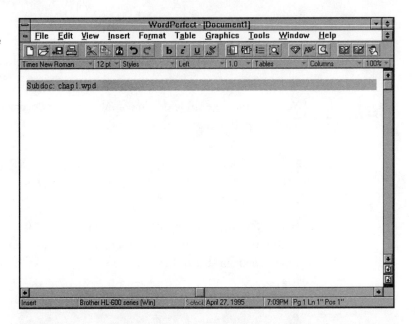

Fig. 18.11
Subdocuments look like this in page view when you click the subdocument icon.

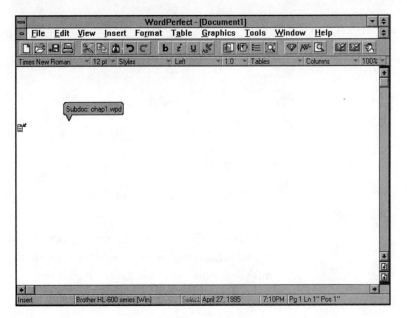

I don't see that subdocument icon!

It's tiny, and it's also parked on the extreme left of the editing window. Drag the horizontal scroll button all the way to the left and you'll see it.

---

6 Press Enter to skip to the next line. Click File, Master Document, Subdocument for the Include Subdocument dialog box, and select the next file from the list. Click Include (or double-click the file name), and repeat for all the files you want as subdocuments.

You can also right-click the subdocument icon and select Subdocument from the QuickMenu for the Include Subdocument dialog box.

---

7 Add a header or any text (an introduction, for example) that you want in the master document. Click the Save button on the Toolbar to save the master document. It might look like figure 18.12.

Fig. 18.12
The master document is a good place for a title page or a table of contents.

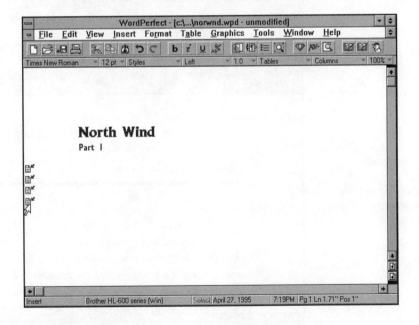

I want my document in one piece!

Our one-page master document, shown in figure 18.12, is like a collapsed telescope—it's small, but there's more to it than meets the eye.

To snap it open and combine the four subdocuments into one file, click <u>F</u>ile, Master <u>D</u>ocument, <u>E</u>xpand Master for the Expand Master Document dialog box shown in figure 18.13.

Fig. 18.13
Click Mark to select all or none of your subdocuments.

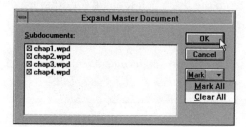

Select any or all of your subdocuments, and click OK. WordPerfect tells you it's expanding subdocuments, and after a moment or two your selected subdocuments appear on the screen, as shown in figure 18.14.

Fig. 18.14
Subdocuments are strung one after the other when expanded.

Shows end of one subdocument

Shows the beginning of the next subdocument

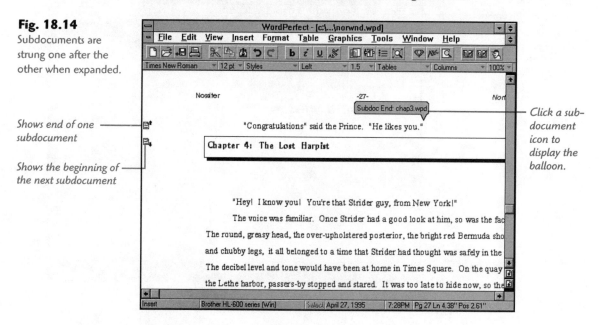

Click a subdocument icon to display the balloon.

 **{Note}** | If you want your subdocuments to begin on a new page, press Ctrl+Enter to insert a hard page break at the end of each subdocument.

What can I do with this expanded document?

Expanded master documents are especially useful for Find and Replace operations. If you've got a word change to make, and the word occurs in all your chapters, you don't have to open each chapter file to make the change; just perform the Find and Replace in the expanded master document.

Here are a couple of other things to keep in mind when you expand subdocuments:

- If your subdocuments include page number codes, pages will be numbered consecutively from the first page of the first subdocument to the last page of the last subdocument. Printing an expanded master document prints all of your subdocuments with the correct pagination. Don't put new page number codes in your subdocuments, though; those change the pagination from the code to the end of the document.

- In expanded master documents, formatting changes from the point at which any new format codes are encountered. If subdocument 1 has 1" margins, for example, subdocuments 2, 3, and 4 will get 1" margins as well. But if one of those subdocuments has a different margin setting, the margins will change from that point on.

Put the expanded document away again

Once you've printed or edited in an expanded master document, there's no need to save the expanded master document—that just takes up disk space. Instead, condense the master document into subdocuments again. You get the option of saving any changes in each subdocument when you do that.

To condense an expanded master document, either double-click one of the subdocument icons or select File, Master Document, Condense Master for the Condense/Save Subdocuments dialog box shown in figure 18.15.

Fig. 18.15
If you've made editing changes in the expanded master document, save them in the subdocuments.

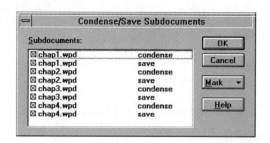

Each subdocument is listed twice; choose to save and/or condense any or all of the subdocuments. Click OK when you've made your selections, and the subdocuments shrink back to icons.

Viewing a condensed master document

If your subdocuments have hard page breaks to begin or end them, the subdocument icons will appear on separate pages in a condensed master document in page view.

You might find it handier to view condensed master documents in draft mode instead. This lets you view all the subdocument comment bars in one window, as shown in figure 18.16.

Fig. 18.16
Viewing a condensed master document in draft mode is handy if your subdocuments are divided with hard page breaks.

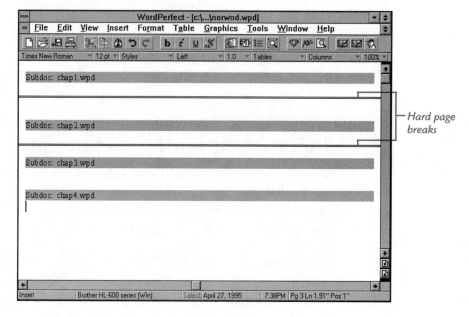

I need a table of contents

A table of contents is like a road map to your document. It's a good organizational tool for the document's author and a convenience for the reader. That's especially true in a large document with many sections.

To create a table of contents:

1 Click Tools, Table of Contents. That pops up the table of contents feature bar shown in figure 18.17.

Fig. 18.17
Tables of contents have heading levels like outlines.

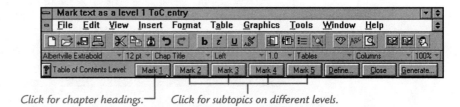

Click for chapter headings. ⎯   *Click for subtopics on different levels.*

2 Like outlines, tables of contents have different levels of headings, labeled 1 through 5. Level 1 is for the most important headings, like chapter titles; levels 4 and 5 are for subtopics in the chapters. Select the text you want to appear in the table of contents for your level 1 heading and click the Mark 1 button on the feature bar.

3 Move the insertion point to the next heading you want to appear in the table of contents. Figure 18.18 shows a level 2 heading in Chapter One. Select the text and click the Mark 2 button on the feature bar.

4 Go through the entire document. Mark the text for table of contents headings and click the appropriate Mark button on the feature bar.

✳ {Note}

Find and Replace is handy for marking table of contents text. If your heading text is formatted in a different font, for example, click Edit, Find and Replace to pop up the Find and Replace Text dialog box. Select Match, Font and select the font in the Match Font dialog box. Click OK, and select Type in the Find and Replace Text dialog box. Click Specific Codes and select Font in the Specific Codes dialog box. Click OK. Now when you click Find Next in the Find and Replace Text dialog box, you'll go straight to text formatted in that font.

Fig. 18.18

Mark text for level 2 headings you want in the table of contents and click the Mark 2 button.

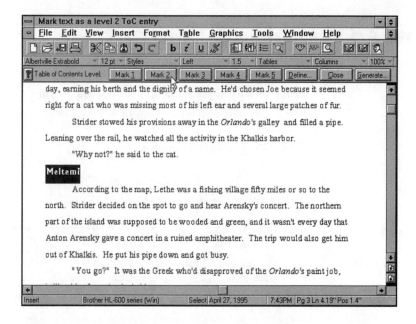

5 When you're finished marking text, click Close on the table of contents feature bar.

6 Move the insertion point to the page where you want the table of contents. That'll be the first or last page in the document.

7 Click Tools, Table of Contents and click the Define button on the feature bar. That pops up the Define Table of Contents dialog box shown in figure 18.19.

Fig. 18.19

You can tinker with styles and page numbering options, but all you really need here is to set the number of levels.

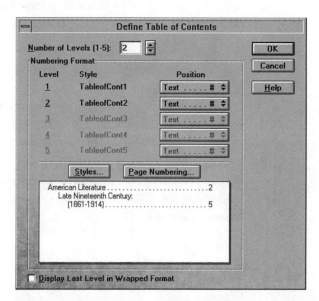

8 Click the arrows to set the Number of Levels you want in your table of contents. In the figure, that's 2.

9 Click OK. Now click Generate on the table of contents feature bar. WordPerfect's gears whirl for a moment, and your table of contents appears, as shown in figure 18.20.

Fig. 18.20

This is the default table of contents. Serviceable, but if you want a different look, tinker with the settings in the Define Table of Contents dialog box.

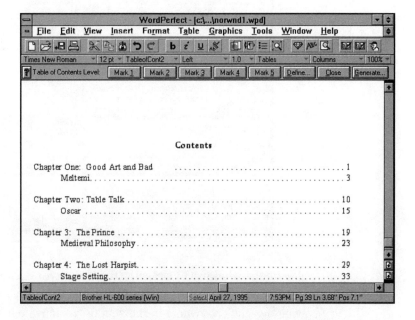

I want to see lots of files at the same time

When you're working in several different files, it's helpful to display them together. That's especially true if you're working on subdocuments and master documents. Comparing subdocuments side by side before you expand them helps you spot inconsistent formatting from document to document.

To view multiple files:

1 Click the Open File button on the Toolbar and select the files you want from the Filename list. Click the first file, then Ctrl+click the other files to select them all.

2 Click OK in the Open File dialog box and the files open one after the other in separate full-screen windows.

3 Click <u>W</u>indow, <u>T</u>ile Horizontal for the screen arrangement shown in figure 18.21.

Fig. 18.21
With four files open, you don't see too much of the file.

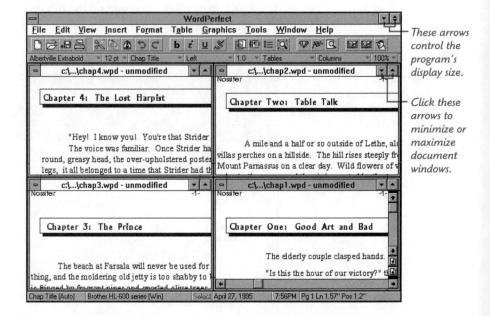

These arrows control the program's display size.

Click these arrows to minimize or maximize document windows.

Resize the windows by dragging the borders or clicking the minimize and maximize arrows in the upper-right of each window. To scroll in a document window, click anywhere in the window to activate it, then use the scroll bar.

And if you want to get windows out of sight fast, click the minimize button. That reduces a document window to an icon at the bottom of the screen. Double-click the icon to restore the document.

> Double-click a document window title bar to quickly maximize it. To shrink it back to a smaller window again, click the restore double-arrow in the upper-right corner of the document window.

How do I manage all these files?

Computers are wonderful because they remember everything you tell them. The curse of the computer is that it *does* remember everything. It doesn't take long before you accumulate more files than you know what to do with.

Here's a strategy you might try to manage large file collections:

- Create a new subdirectory to hold all your documents of a particular type—letters, for example.

- Use QuickFinder (see Chapter 2) to locate all your letter files and to move them into the new directory.

With all your correspondence in one directory, it'll be much easier to find any one letter. That comes in handy when the boss demands to see a letter you wrote a year ago.

Create a new subdirectory for files of one type

The WordPerfect directories dialog box pops up under different names depending on what you're doing. But by any name, it's a powerful file manager.

Use the directories dialog box in its Open File guise to create a new subdirectory:

1 Click the Open File button on the Toolbar to pop up the Open File dialog box, one of the directories dialog box's many aliases.

2 In the Directories list, double-click WPWIN. That'll make the new directory a subdirectory of the main WordPerfect directory.

3 Click the File Options button and select Create Directory.

4 Click Create Directory to pop up the Create Directory dialog box. (See fig. 18.22). Type the directory name in the New Directory edit box. We'll call the new directory "letters." No need to type the path, and lowercase letters are fine.

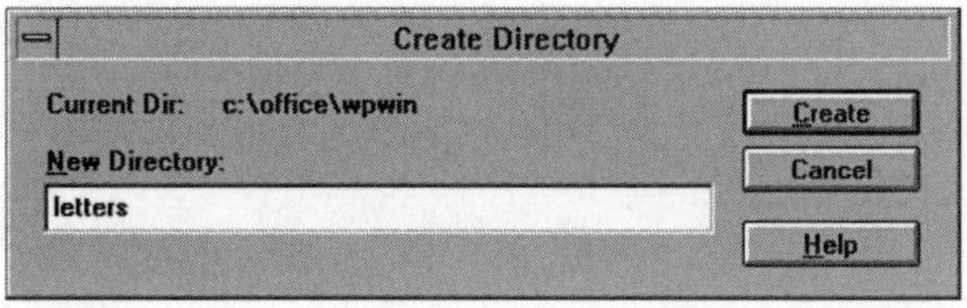

Fig. 18.22

You can do all your file chores from the directories dialog boxes without leaving WordPerfect.

Create Directory
Current Dir: c:\office\wpwin
New Directory:
letters

Create
Cancel
Help

5 Click Create in the Create Directory box. You'll see the new letter directory in the Directories list in the Open File dialog box.

For now, the letter directory is empty. We'll use QuickFinder to fill it up.

Let QuickFinder gather your files together

Most of us create a document, name and save it in a hurry, and then promptly forget all about it. Which is fine until you want the document again. If your file names are like mine, remembering what you called the file might not be so easy. QuickFinder can help you out.

Let's use QuickFinder to find all the letters we've stored in WordPerfect. Those letters might not have obvious names, but QuickFinder will search through the text in the files to find text that might only be found in a letter. To put QuickFinder to work:

1 Click the Open File button on the Toolbar to pop up the Open File dialog box.

2 Click the QuickFinder button in the Open File dialog box to pop up the QuickFinder dialog box.

3 We're interested in finding all our letters, and the one thing that they'll have in common is the salutation ("Dear…"). Type **Dear** in the Search For edit box.

4 Trouble is, the word "dear" is likely to crop up in a lot of documents that aren't letters. We want "Dear" with a capital D. Position the insertion point before the "D" in "Dear" in the Search For edit box and click the Operators button. That pops up the Search Operators dialog box, as shown in figure 18.23.

Fig. 18.23
Search operators allow you to refine QuickFinder searches.

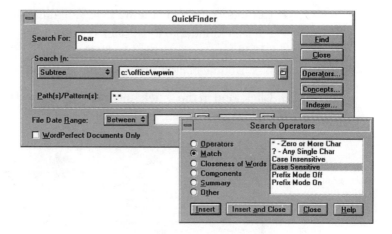

5 Select Match in the Search Operators dialog box and then click Case Sensitive.

66 *Plain English, please!*

Search operators act on text the way mathematical operators like + and − act on numbers. The search operator AND, for example, is just like a + sign for text. Search for Jerry&Jones, and you'll find every file in which the words "Jerry Jones" occur. 99

6 Click Insert and Close and the matching operator Case is inserted in the Search For edit box in the QuickFinder dialog box (see fig. 18.24).

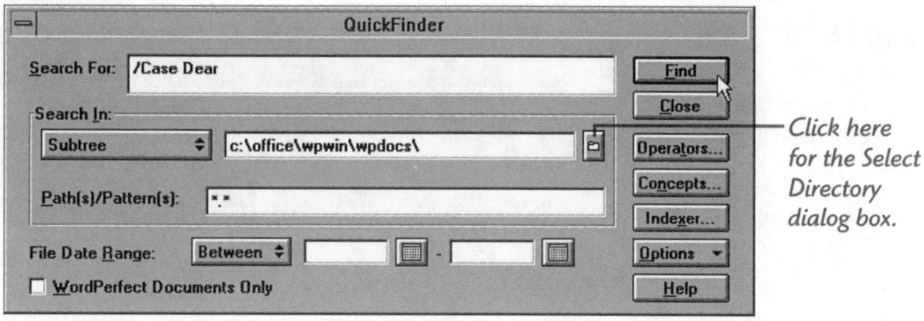

Fig. 18.24
The matching operator Case searches for only upper- or lowercase letters, depending on the letter that follows the operator.

Click here for the Select Directory dialog box.

7 Our letters are all in the WPDOCS subdirectory, so that's where we'll tell QuickFinder to look. Click the directories button next to the Search In edit box (refer to fig. 18.24). That pops up the Select Directory dialog box. Double-click WPDOCS in the Directories list and click OK.

8 Click Find in the QuickFinder dialog box and the Search Results List dialog box appears, as shown in figure 18.25.

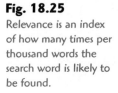

Fig. 18.25

Relevance is an index of how many times per thousand words the search word is likely to be found.

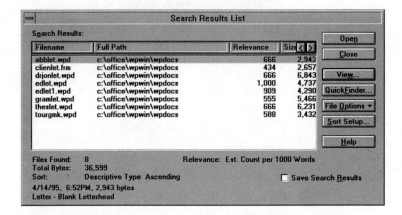

9 QuickFinder seems to have found all our letters. Select a file and click View to examine it.

10 To move the letters to the letters directory we created earlier, Ctrl+drag through the list of files to select them all.

11 Click File Options and select Move. That gets us the Move Files dialog box shown in figure 18.26.

Fig. 18.26

You can move files to and from any directory in the Move Files dialog box.

12 Click the directories button (refer to fig. 18.24) next to the Move Selected Files <u>T</u>o edit box to pop up the Select Directory dialog box. Double-click the letters directory in the Select Directory dialog box, then click OK.

13 Back in the Move Files dialog box, click <u>M</u>ove. That moves all our letters to the letters directory.

The next time we need to look at an old letter, we can cut down on search time by flipping right to the letters directory in any of the directories dialog boxes. And when we write new letters, we can save them right to the letters directory.

A bit of a chore, but after you've accumulated a few hundred letters, you'll be glad you did it!

19

WP Draw, for Instant Artists

WordPerfect's drawing and charting programs turn words, ideas, facts, and figures into just the right pictures and charts.

Leonardo da Vinci filled thousands of pages with notes on everything from helicopters to human anatomy. The text is obscure—it's written backwards. The drawings, which cover every page, are sharper than photos. When Leonardo wanted clarity, he drew a picture.

WordPerfect gives you two ways to make your point with pictures. Charts describe numbers in colorful images, and there's an easy-to-use charting feature built into the program.

WordPerfect's drawing feature, WP Draw, is an electronic drawing board. Use it to draw anything—diagrams, sketches, even a copy of Leonardo's Mona Lisa.

What can I do with a drawing program?

"Words fail me." "I was speechless." Artists know what to do in situations like that: they draw a picture. Even non-artists can be called on to make a drawing of some kind. We might have to diagram new office assignments, or sketch a map for directions.

WP Draw comes in handy for chores like those. Instead of crude hand-drawn sketches, you can turn out slick drawings. And when you've finished drawing, it's easy to pop your WP Draw art into a document.

WP Draw is the ultimate doodling tool

There are plenty of practical things you can do with WP Draw, including using it for the fine art of doodling. Doodling is actually the best way of getting to know the WP Draw tools and techniques.

To doodle around with WP Draw:

1 Click <u>G</u>raphics, <u>D</u>raw, and twiddle your thumbs for a moment or two while WordPerfect loads WP Draw. Eventually you'll see the WP Draw window and toolbars. Click and hold the line tool on the left of the window, and you get a choice of lines, as shown in figure 19.1.

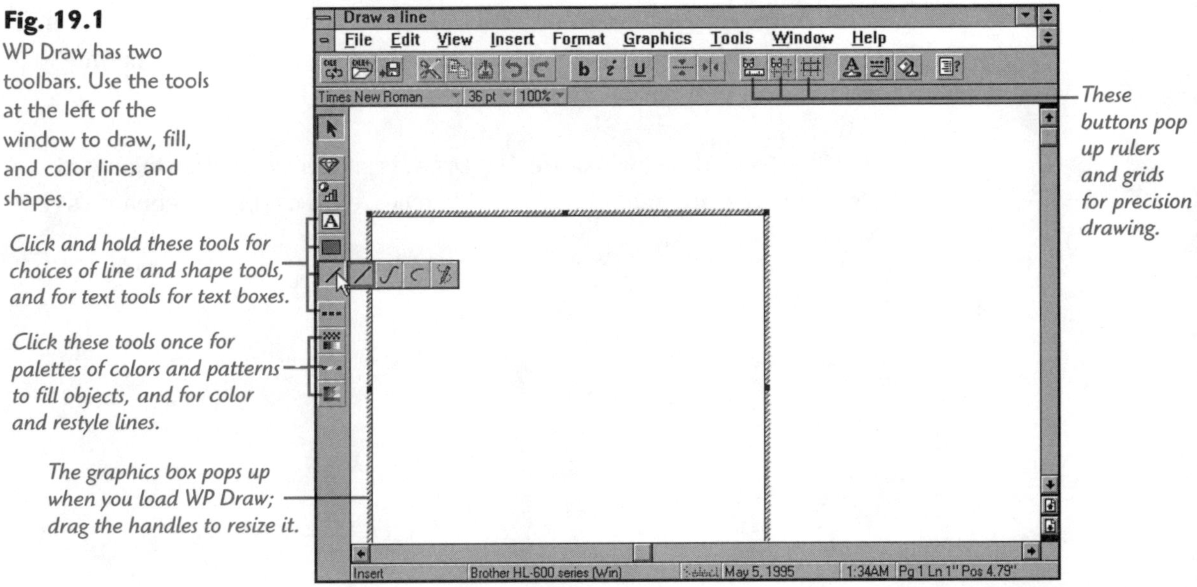

Fig. 19.1
WP Draw has two toolbars. Use the tools at the left of the window to draw, fill, and color lines and shapes.

Click and hold these tools for choices of line and shape tools, and for text tools for text boxes.

Click these tools once for palettes of colors and patterns to fill objects, and for color and restyle lines.

The graphics box pops up when you load WP Draw; drag the handles to resize it.

These buttons pop up rulers and grids for precision drawing.

 **<Caution>** OLE taxes your computer's processing power and memory. When you create and embed OLE objects, it's a good idea to constantly save your work. My computer has a bad habit of gagging on OLE; if yours does too, save often to avoid losing your work.

2 That little pencil icon (refer to fig. 19.1) among the line tools is for freehand drawing; use the other tools for ellipse sections, straight lines, and curved lines. Try a curved line—click the curved line tool, and as the pointer moves into the graphics box, it turns into a cross-hair.

66 *Plain English, please!*

An **ellipse** is a flattened circle, or an oval. If the flattened circle is open, it's an ellipse section (think of the St. Louis arch, for example). 99

3 Click with the cross-hair to anchor one end of the line. Now drag, click at each curve, and drag again. Double-click at the end of the line. The result looks like figure 19.2.

Three cheers for OLE

OLE (pronounced just like the bullfighter's cheer, *oh–lay*, and short for **Object Linking and Embedding**) is an amazing feature of Windows programs. It allows you to create an object in one program and embed it in another. An object can be anything: a drawing, clip–art image, chart, even a document.

Embedding an object is like pulling a grape from the bunch and dropping it into a bowl of jello. With one big difference: an embedded OLE object is linked to the original. Create a chart in Quattro Pro, embed it in WordPerfect, and any editing you do in the Quattro Pro chart also changes the chart you embedded in WordPerfect. That would be like peeling another grape in the bunch and having the embedded grape lose its skin, too. Mind–boggling, but it really does work. Slowly. To perform these OLE tricks, your computer has to work as hard as though you were running two programs simultaneously. Which, when you use OLE, is more or less what you're doing.

Click the pointer button to get rid of the cross-hair pointer and get the regular black pointer back.

Double-click the cross-hair pointer here to anchor the other end of the object.

Fig. 19.2

Your first click anchors the object. Drag to draw, then double-click when you're finished.

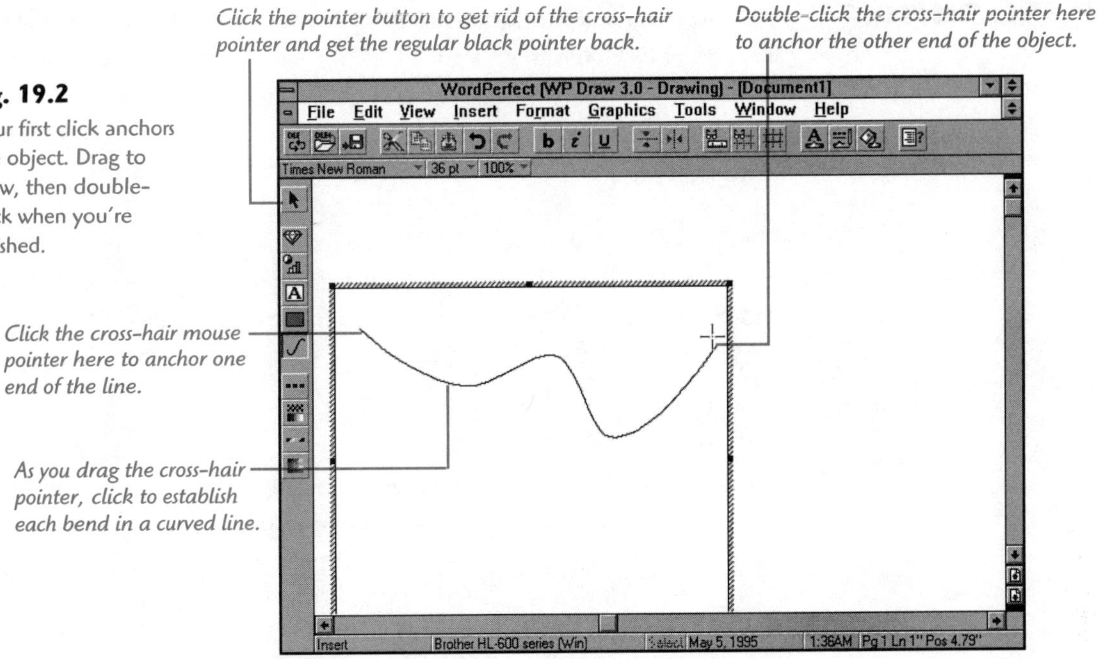

Click the cross-hair mouse pointer here to anchor one end of the line.

As you drag the cross-hair pointer, click to establish each bend in a curved line.

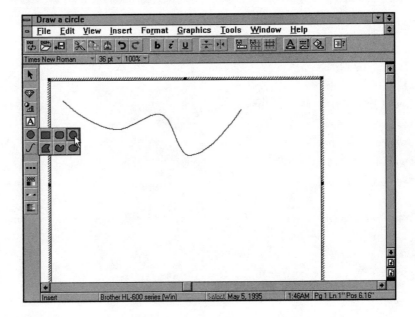

4 Drag the graphics box sizing handles to expand your workspace. To pick another tool, just click it. For a circle, click and hold the closed object button and select the circle tool, as shown in figure 19.3.

Fig. 19.3

You'll never need a compass as long as you use WP Draw.

5 Position the cross-hair wherever you want the center of the circle, drag to draw the circle, then release when you've got the diameter you want.

6 The circle fills in automatically. To change the fill color, or to use no fill at all, click the black arrow button to get rid of the cross-hair.

7 With the black pointer, click the circle to pop up the object handles. Now click the Fill Color button at the bottom of the Drawing Toolbar, as shown in figure 19.4.

Fig. 19.4
For no fill, choose white from the palette of colors.

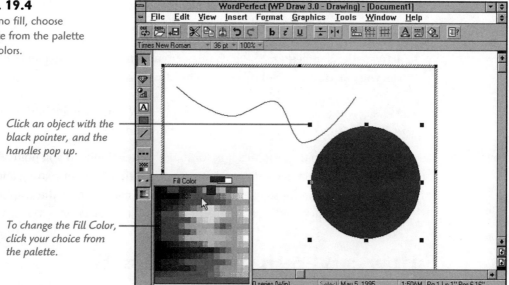

Click an object with the black pointer, and the handles pop up.

To change the Fill Color, click your choice from the palette.

8 Click your choice on the palette, and the fill color changes instantly. For an unfilled circle, click white on the palette.

9 To get rid of the handles, click anywhere outside the object.

Selecting white as the fill color doesn't really make the object unfilled. To do that, you have to choose Format, Fill Attributes, and choose None as the Fill Type.

If you select a fill color before you draw a filled object, the object is filled with the selected color.

How do I get rid of this object?

To delete an object, click it with the black pointer to pop up the handles. Then press Delete.

This drawing needs some work

Doodling is the least of what you can do with WP Draw. But if your doodle begins to look like art, you can help it along with some artistic editing.

Point with the black arrow at any object in the graphics box, and click once to activate the handles. Once the handles are activated, there are plenty of things you can do with the bits and pieces of your drawing:

- Drag a handle to resize the object in any direction. Or point at the edge of an active object and drag to move it around the page.

- Right-click in the graphics box for handy QuickMenus. If you point inside an object and right-click, the QuickMenu offers formatting and editing choices for the selected object. Point elsewhere in the graphics box and right-click for a QuickMenu with object selection options.

How can I reshape this object?

If you look closely at an active object, you'll notice that in addition to the black sizing handles, there's a smaller, unfilled handle at the corner of a rectangle or near the curve of an oval. That's an editing handle, shown in figure 19.5.

Fig. 19.5
Use the editing handles to reshape an object.

Editing handle

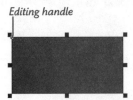

Double-click the editing handle, and more editing handles pop up along the perimeter of curved objects, or at the corners of pointed objects. Drag any of the editing handles to reshape the object, as shown in figure 19.6.

Fig. 19.6
Drag the editing
handles to create eye-
catching shapes.

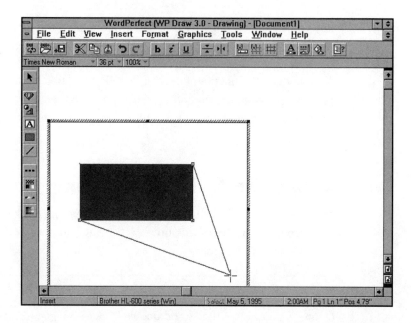

You can also use editing handles to twist curved lines into knots.

I keep pointing at the editing handle, but I don't get a cross-hair to drag it with!

Double-click the editing handle first, then drag with the cross-hair. Or point at the editing handle, right-click for the QuickMenu, and select Edit Points to pop up the other editing handles.

For perfectly straight horizontal and vertical lines, press the Shift key as you drag with the cross-hair.

I'm not much of an artist, but I need a green cheetah!

Creating original artwork from scratch can be more than many of us can handle. However, WordPerfect's draw program also makes it easy to modify existing graphic images.

Say you've placed the CHEETAH.WPG graphic in your document and now decide you want a green cheetah with no tail. No problem!

Double-click the cheetah graphic; WordPerfect takes you to the WP Draw program. Change the fill color from yellow to green, then select and delete the tail. The cheetah may look a bit weird, but at least it's the cheetah *you* want!

Okay, I'm finished drawing

When you're satisfied with your WP Draw creation, click anywhere outside the graphics box. This shuts down WP Draw and pops your drawing into a WordPerfect document.

⓵ (Tip)

> If you want to edit your graphic image in a full screen, access WP Draw by holding down the Alt key and double-clicking the graphic. To return to your document, choose File, Exit and Return to Document.

✱ {Note} For more on graphics objects in documents, see Chapter 16.

Can I make charts in WordPerfect?

Numbers tell stories, just as words do. Annual reports, marketing studies, and similar documents rely on numbers to make their point. To a trained eye, numbers might speak with the eloquence of words; but for the rest of us, there isn't a lot of poetry and drama in tables of numerical data.

Charts make those numbers come alive. Just as a photo enlivens a dry description, a chart both summarizes and dramatizes a table of numbers. Since WordPerfect makes creating charts a snap, you can use a chart whenever your document includes numerical data. Charts can supplement your data, or even replace it.

Use WordPerfect's built-in chart for fast results

WordPerfect has a ready-made sample chart built right into the program. Just enter your own numbers and labels, and you've got an instant chart.

Suppose you're preparing a billing report for a small accounting practice. You want a chart that shows the billings generated by each of the four partners for each quarter of 1994.

To put WordPerfect's sample chart to work on your own data:

1 Click Graphics, Chart to pop up the WP Draw Chart window shown in figure 19.7.

Fig. 19.7

You can change WordPerfect's sample chart to several different layouts using your own data.

The data in each row is a data series.

The Y axis shows the values in the rows of the Datasheet.

The X axis shows the categories in the Datasheet columns.

The chart legend is the key to the chart.

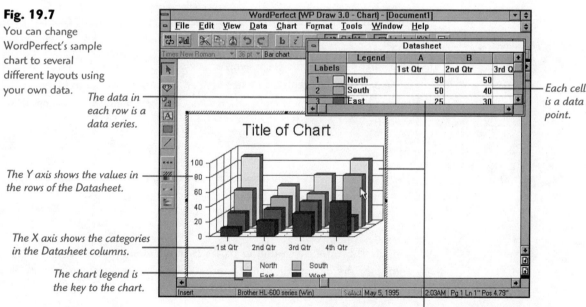

Each cell is a data point.

The labels and numbers in the Datasheet produce this chart; change the Datasheet, and the chart changes, too.

2 The sample chart reflects the data and the labels in the sample Datasheet. All we need to do is enter our own data in the rows and columns of the Datasheet, as shown in figure 19.8.

Fig. 19.8

Enter your own labels and values in the Datasheet to create your own chart.

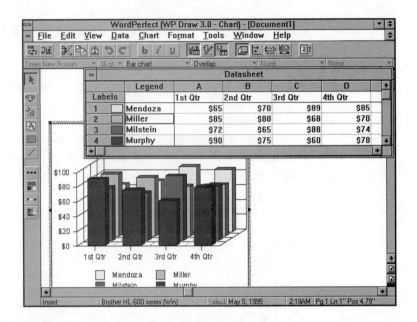

⊛ *{Note}*_____ To format numbers with dollar signs, or any other way, select the cells, right-click for the QuickMenu, and select Format. Make your selections in the Format dialog box that pops up, then click OK. For details on formatting data in tables, see Chapter 17.

⊛ *{Note}*_____ The Datasheet is easier to work with if you expand it, as shown in figure 19.8. Just drag the borders of the Datasheet window to see more of it.

3 The chart now shows the four partners' names and their billings for the four quarters, but it still needs some work. Double-click the Title of Chart label to pop up the Titles dialog box shown in figure 19.9.

4 Enter titles for the X and Y axes if you want them, and a title for the chart. Click OK in the Titles dialog box when you're done. Figure 19.10 shows the result of adding a chart title, subtitle, and Y-axis title.

Fig. 19.9
Chart titles, and all
the labels in a chart,
should tell the reader
everything he needs to
know about the chart.

Click any object inside
the chart to pop up
these handles.

The Y-axis title goes here.

The X-axis label goes here.

The chart
title goes
here.

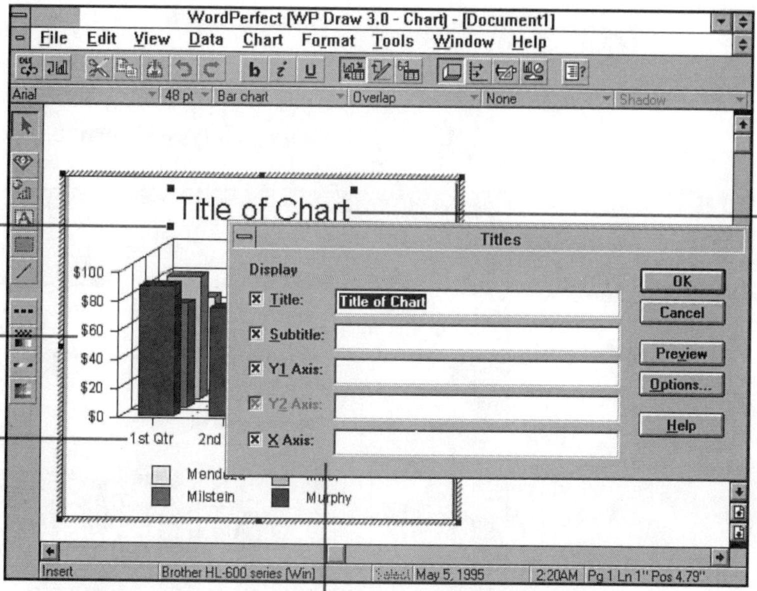

Double-click any object to pop up the
Titles dialog box to edit the object.

The Auto Redraw button is activated by
default. It automatically redraws the
chart when you change the Datasheet.

Click the View Datasheet button
to hide or display the Datasheet.

Fig. 19.10
With informative titles
and labels, the reader
knows at a glance what
the chart is meant to
convey.

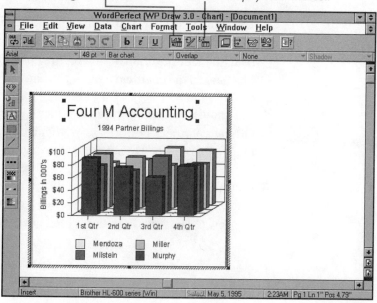

5 The chart shown in figure 19.10 is a 3D chart. These charts generally look fine, but depending on the data, some columns may obscure others. Click the 3D Chart button on the Toolbar to transform the chart into the more readable 2D type shown in figure 19.11.

Fig. 19.11

The difference between 2D and 3D charts is largely aesthetic; click the 3D Chart button to toggle between them.

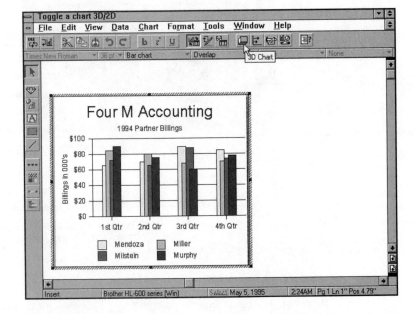

6 The bars in the chart shown in figure 19.11 overlap one another. That, too, is a neat visual effect, but in this case, it makes the chart harder to read. Click the Overlap button on the Power Bar and select Cluster. That makes the chart clearer, as you can see in figure 19.12.

7 Our chart is just about finished. Wider bars might better convey the different partners' performances, though. Click the Layout button on the Toolbar for the Layout dialog box shown in figure 19.13.

8 Click the arrows in the Width edit box until you achieve the effect you want. Widening the bars to 70 gives us a more readable chart. Click Preview to see your alterations, then click OK when you're satisfied.

Fig. 19.12
WordPerfect has plenty of eye–catching ways to format charts, but sometimes simpler is clearer.

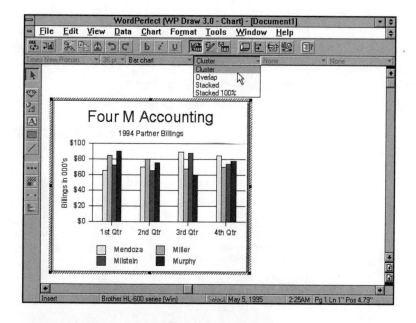

Fig. 19.13
Every detail of your charts can be edited until the chart says exactly what you want it to say.

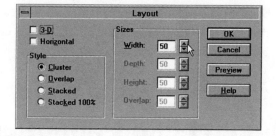

When you're happy with your chart, click anywhere outside the graphics box to pop the chart into a document. You can add text or save the chart as a stand-alone file. As with any other graphic object in a document, charts can be resized by dragging the handles, or moved around the page by dragging with the four-headed arrow.

To edit the chart further, just double-click it to return to the chart editing window. Figure 19.14 shows the chart we've created in a document with added text.

Fig. 19.14
Once the chart was placed in a document by clicking outside the graphics box, I just added some text and a header.

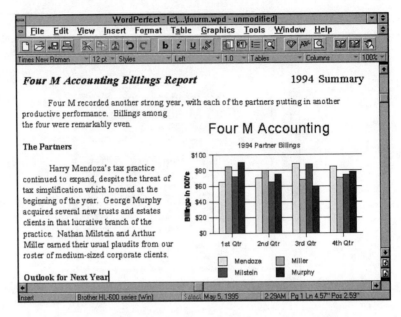

⊛ *{Note}* Use the QuickMenu to alter the chart once it's in a document. Just point at the chart and right-click to resize (as I did), add a caption, change the fonts, or to do any other editing chores.

What else should I know about charts?

WordPerfect has dozens of chart formats to choose from. Click Graphics, Chart for the WP Draw Chart window, then click the Data Chart Types button on the Power Bar and select Gallery to pop up the Data Chart dialog box shown in figure 19.15.

Click a selection on the Chart Type list to view the gallery of subtypes. Double-click any one of them to instantly transform your chart. The best choice of chart depends on your data:

- **Bar charts** like the ones in figure 19.15 show comparisons among different items in one period of time, or changes in different items over several periods (annual sales and expenses for one year or several, for example).

Fig. 19.15

WordPerfect has a chart for every type of data, and each chart type has several subtypes to choose from.

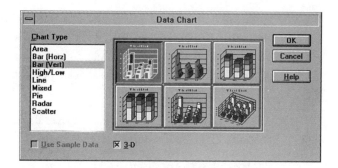

- **Pie charts** are used to show the relationship between the parts and the whole. Pie charts only show one data series (different budget items as parts of the total budget, for example). Figure 19.16 shows WordPerfect's selection of pie chart choices.

Fig. 19.16

Use pie charts to illustrate the parts and the whole.

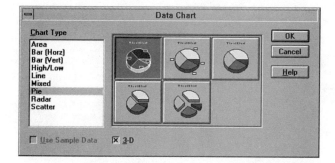

- **Line charts** show changes over time for one item or several (your stock's performance over the past six months against the Dow, for example). Figure 19.17 shows the selection of line charts.

Fig. 19.17

Line charts dramatize changing values over time.

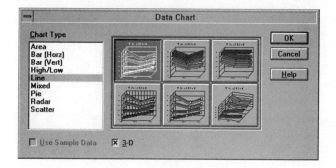

- **High/Low charts** are like line charts, with the addition of high/low bars along the data series. They show high and low values in a single time period as well as changing values over many periods. One common use of high/low charts is to show a stock's performance in one day, and over the course of many days.

- **Area charts** show changing values over time, like line charts, and proportional relationships, like pie charts.

- **Scatter charts** are often used in statistics to show the strength of the relationship between single values and a mean value.

- **Radar charts** illustrate differences between each data series, and between many data series simultaneously. They're sometimes used in complex project management applications.

20

Customizing WordPerfect

Scrambled eggs, or fried? Brown shoes with blue suits, or black? A range of custom options gives us the same control over WordPerfect.

In this chapter:

- I want to see more of my document and fewer gadgets
- How can I work more efficiently?
- I'm tired of the same old buttons
- How do I add my own Toolbar button?
- What is the Equation Editor?

When you buy a shirt in a hurry, you tend to grab whatever's handy. Then you get home and find that it doesn't quite fit. I hate it when that happens.

Buy your shirts from a Jermyn Street tailor in London, and they'll be custom-made exactly the way you want them. Just be prepared to take out a second mortgage to pay the bill.

As you use WordPerfect, you may find that aspects of the program don't quite suit your style. Like a shirt that doesn't quite fit, sometimes a WordPerfect feature works fine, but just doesn't feel quite right. That's no problem—there are plenty of ways to customize WordPerfect for a perfect fit, and none of them will cost you a cent.

I want to see more words and fewer gadgets

Some people like to keep all their papers and office supplies within reach on the desk. Others can't work unless their desk is spotless and bare. Word-Perfect adapts to both styles. There are two quick ways to change what you see in the document window:

- Click View, and select any checked item, such as Toolbar, Power Bar, or Status Bar, to hide any of those features. To get them back, select the item from the View menu again.

- For a completely austere look, click View, Hide Bars. That gives you the Hide Bars Information dialog box shown in figure 20.1.

Fig. 20.1
You can even hide the dialog box by clicking the Disable This Message Permanently checkbox.

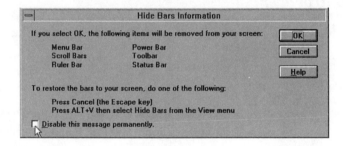

Click OK in the Hide Bars Information dialog box, and you'll get the document window shown in figure 20.2.

To get it everything back again, press the Esc key.

(!) (Tip)

> Documents with graphics can slow down WordPerfect's performance. To bring the program back up to speed, click View, and make sure Graphics is not checked. (If it is checked, just click it.) That hides the document's graphics, but leaves the outline of the graphics boxes so you can still see their placement on the page.

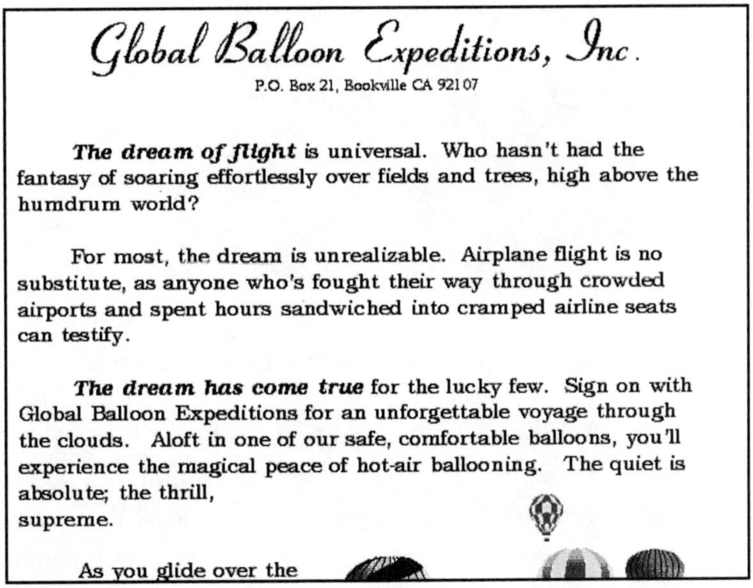

Fig. 20.2

For a look of stark simplicity, hide all the WordPerfect bars.

Global Balloon Expeditions, Inc.

P.O. Box 21, Bookville CA 92107

The dream of flight is universal. Who hasn't had the fantasy of soaring effortlessly over fields and trees, high above the humdrum world?

For most, the dream is unrealizable. Airplane flight is no substitute, as anyone who's fought their way through crowded airports and spent hours sandwiched into cramped airline seats can testify.

The dream has come true for the lucky few. Sign on with Global Balloon Expeditions for an unforgettable voyage through the clouds. Aloft in one of our safe, comfortable balloons, you'll experience the magical peace of hot-air ballooning. The quiet is absolute; the thrill,
supreme.

As you glide over the

Can I save my document window's custom look?

The View menu offers quick adjustments to the look of the document window, but you have to make your adjustments every time you run WordPerfect.

To see your custom look whenever you run the program, click Edit, Preferences for the Preferences dialog box shown in figure 20.3.

Double-click any of the icons in the Preferences dialog box. That pops up further dialog boxes that allow you to customize all kinds of WordPerfect features.

For example, you may find yourself using the vertical and horizontal scroll bars less the more you use WordPerfect, relying on the keyboard movement controls instead. You can easily banish the scroll bars from the screen; that gets rid of an unused feature, and frees up more window space in which to view your document.

Fig. 20.3
Customize Word-
Perfect's operations
from the Preferences
dialog box.

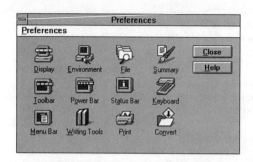

To remove the scroll bars from the default document display:

1 Click Edit, Preferences to pop up the Preferences dialog box, and
double-click the Display icon.

2 That gets you the Display Preferences dialog box. When you click the
options buttons at the top of the Display Preferences dialog box, the
choices in the rest of the dialog box change. Document is selected as
the default, with the choices shown in figure 20.4.

Fig. 20.4
The options in the
Display Preferences
dialog box change
when you select the
choices at the top of
the dialog box.

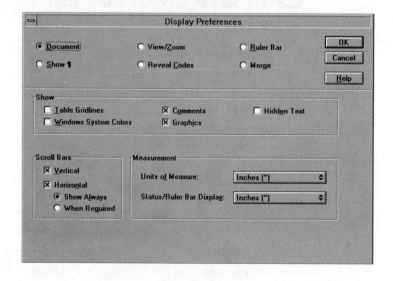

3 If you never want to see the scroll bars, deselect Vertical and Horizontal
under the Scroll Bars choices. If you tend to create wide documents
that run past the right margin, deselect Vertical scroll bars and click the
When Required option under Horizontal. That displays the horizontal
scroll bar only when your document goes past the right margin.

4 Once you make your choice, click OK in the Display Preferences dialog box, then click <u>C</u>lose in the Preferences dialog box.

The selections made in the Preferences dialog box are in effect whenever you run WordPerfect. All choices are changeable; just reverse the steps outlined above to restore the scroll bars to the display.

Speed up your work: keep your most-used features in reach

Between the Toolbar and the Power Bar, there are a lot of WordPerfect features a mouse click or two away. You might find that you hardly ever use some of those features, while other features that you do want are not on the default bars.

WordPerfect lets you create your own Toolbar, with only the features you want on it. When you name and save the Toolbar, it'll appear on the Toolbar menu along with the other Toolbar choices. It's like buying a toolbox from the hardware store, removing the tools you don't use, and adding ones that you do.

How to create a custom Toolbar

The idea behind a custom Toolbar is to put the tools *you* want within reach. I'm going to create a Toolbar I'll call Useful, with the features I use most often on it. You can make your own choices for your own useful Toolbar.

To create the Useful Toolbar:

1 Click <u>E</u>dit, Pr<u>e</u>ferences for the Preferences dialog box and double-click the <u>T</u>oolbar icon. That pops up the Toolbar Preferences dialog box shown in figure 20.5.

2 Click C<u>r</u>eate in the Toolbar Preferences dialog box for the Create Toolbar dialog box (see fig. 20.6). Type a name in the <u>N</u>ew Toolbar Name edit box.

Fig. 20.5

Click a choice on the
Available Toolbars list,
and the specialized
Toolbar buttons pop
up on the Toolbar.

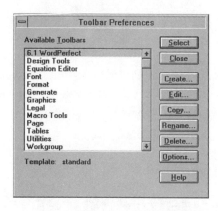

Fig. 20.6

If you want the
Toolbar assigned to a
particular template,
click the Template
button and make your
choice; otherwise, it
goes in the standard
template.

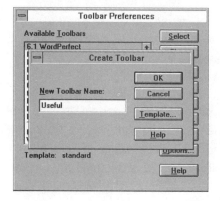

3 Click OK in the Create Toolbar dialog box. That pops up the Toolbar
Editor dialog box, as shown in figure 20.7. By default, the Add a Button
To Activate a Feature option is selected. Click the Feature Categories
drop-down arrow.

4 Select Edit from the Feature Categories drop-down list, and a list of
editing features appears in the Features drop-down list. Select a feature,
click Add Button, and the button for the feature appears in the blank
Toolbar at the top of the editing window, as shown in figure 20.7.

5 Continue to select feature categories and features and add them to the
Toolbar. If you change your mind about a button you've added, just
drag it off the Toolbar. The pointer becomes a little trash basket, as
shown in figure 20.8. When you release the mouse button, the dragged
Toolbar button gets thrown out.

Fig. 20.7

When you select a feature, a picture of the corresponding button and its description appear in the dialog box.

The button appears here.

Select a feature from the list and click Add Button.

Read the description of the selected button here.

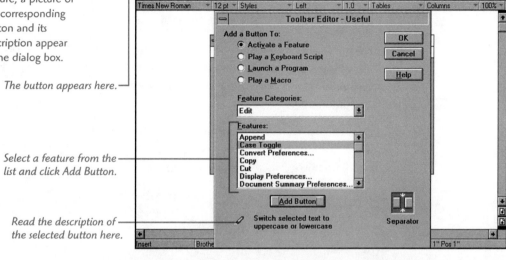

Fig. 20.8

Throw a button in the trash if you want to; you can always add it back if you change your mind.

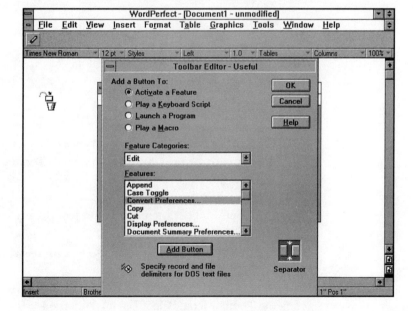

6 To add a space between buttons, click the Separator button and drag a separator onto the Toolbar.

7 To change the location of a button, just drag it where you want it to go.

(Tip) If you're sure of the button you want, double-click a feature from the main menu to add the button to the Toolbar.

8 Explore the list of features. If you work with many documents at once, for example, consider File features such as Close All, which closes all open documents at the same time (it prompts you to save modified documents first).

9 When you've added all the buttons you want, click OK. Your new Toolbar is added to the list of Available Toolbars in the Toolbar Preferences dialog box, as shown in figure 20.9.

Fig. 20.9
The Useful Toolbar fills the entire Toolbar space, but you can have more or fewer buttons on your own creation.

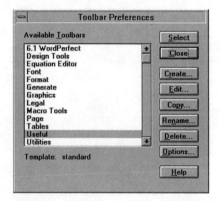

10 Click Close in the Toolbar Preferences dialog box and in the Preferences dialog box to return to the default Toolbar and the editing window.

Whenever you want the Useful Toolbar, just right-click the current Toolbar and select it from the QuickMenu. All the buttons are fully functional; they even have their own QuickTips in case you forget what any button does.

If you want to add or remove buttons, click Edit, Preferences, and double-click the Toolbar icon. Select Useful from the Available Toolbars list in the Toolbar Preferences dialog box, then click Edit.

 **{Note}** If you add more buttons than there's room for on a Toolbar, a second row of buttons is created automatically. Scroll arrows appear on the right of the Toolbar so you can quickly flip from row to row.

Tired of the same old buttons? Change 'em!

Some people take the same route to work every day, others like to vary the trip. Whatever your tastes, WordPerfect accommodates you. If you prefer text to little pictures, you can change the Toolbar to text, or to both text and pictures.

To change the Toolbar's appearance:

1 Right-click the Toolbar for the QuickMenu and select <u>P</u>references to pop up the Toolbar Preferences dialog box.

2 Click <u>O</u>ptions for the Toolbar Options dialog box. To change the Toolbar to text buttons, like the Power Bar, select <u>T</u>ext. For a completely different look, change the font as well. You'll wind up with something like what's shown in figure 20.10.

Fig. 20.10
Altering the appearance of the WordPerfect editing window is like moving furniture around in the house—not strictly necessary, but it makes for a change of scenery.

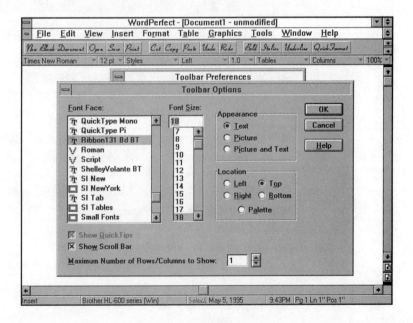

3 Click the arrows for <u>M</u>aximum Number of Rows/Columns to Show to display more buttons at the same time.

4 If you like the icons and the text, select P̲icture and Text for the effect shown in figure 20.11. Since the changes are immediate, if you don't like the result you can try something different before choosing OK.

Fig. 20.11
Depending on how much of the editing window you're willing to give up, your remodeling choices are limitless.

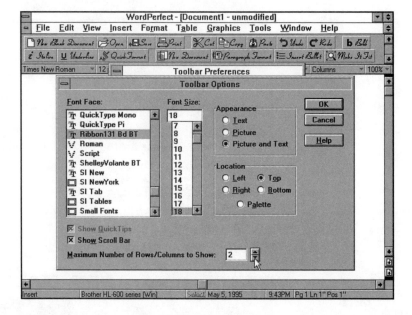

5 Park the Toolbar on the bottom or either side of the editing window by choosing a new Location, if you want to. P̲alette arranges the Toolbar buttons on a floating palette that you can drag around the screen.

6 Click OK in the Toolbar Options dialog box and C̲lose in the Toolbar Preferences dialog box when you're done.

The changes you make to the Toolbar's appearance are saved from one WordPerfect session to the next.

If you change your mind about your changes, select P̲icture in the Toolbar Options dialog box to return to the default Toolbar look, and select the 6.1 WordPerfect Toolbar.

You can also make a copy of an existing Toolbar and then modify it. From the Toolbar Preferences dialog box, click Copy, select the Toolbar you want to copy, click Copy again, provide a new name for the Toolbar, and choose OK. Then remove, add, and rearrange the buttons on the copied Toolbar however you like.

Power Bar remodeling is possible, too

For compulsive remodelers, you can change the Power Bar as well. Right-click the Power Bar for the QuickMenu and select Edit to add or remove buttons in the Toolbar Editor dialog box. Add buttons from the list of Features, or drag them off the Power Bar to get rid of them again.

While you're at it, change the way the Power Bar looks, too. Right-click the Power Bar and select Options from the Power Bar QuickMenu for the Power Bar Options dialog box. Select Picture for the Power Bar look shown in figure 20.12.

Fig. 20.12

For those who insist on icons and more icons, the Power Bar can be converted to pictures.

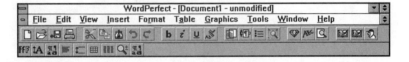

Click Default in the Power Bar Options dialog box to return to the default text buttons.

Short of buttons? Create your own

Redecorating WordPerfect's interior, while fun, may or may not be useful. It really depends on how strongly you feel about what you see on the screen every day.

Here's one custom feature that might come in handy: adding a Toolbar button that types text for you. Suppose you have to type your name and title in dozens of memos and letters every day. You can add a Toolbar button that automatically types that text for you.

Here's how to do it:

1 Right-click the Toolbar for the QuickMenu and select Edit to pop up the Toolbar Editor dialog box.

2 In the Toolbar Editor dialog box, select Play a Keyboard Script.

3 Click the Type the Script This Button Plays edit box to put the insertion point in the box; then type whatever text you want played back when you click the new button.

4 Click <u>A</u>dd Script. That saves your keyboard script, and adds a button to the Toolbar to play the script, as shown in figure 20.13.

Fig. 20.13
Keyboard scripts are handy for repetitive typing jobs, such as typing your name and title.

Click the new button, and the text you typed will be inserted at the insertion point.

Click the arrows to display hidden Toolbar buttons.

5 Click OK in the Toolbar Editor dialog box, and your new Toolbar button is ready to use. It even has its own QuickTip.

? *Q&A*

How come I don't see my new Toolbar button?

There's no room for the new addition on the first row of Toolbar buttons, so it's been placed in a second row. Click the scroll arrows at the right of the Toolbar to display the rows of buttons.

Can I change the way this button looks?

One thing you'll notice right away if you create several custom buttons to play keyboard scripts: all the new buttons look the same. You can fix that by drawing your own button.

To change the look of any Toolbar button:

1 Right-click the Toolbar for the QuickMenu and select Edit to pop up the Toolbar Editor dialog box.

2 Display the button whose appearance you want to change. If it's not already visible, click the scroll buttons at the right of the Toolbar.

3 Double-click the button you want to edit. That pops up the Customize Button dialog box (see fig. 20.14).

Fig. 20.14

Use the Customize Button dialog box to edit QuickTips and Help Prompts, and to change a button's appearance.

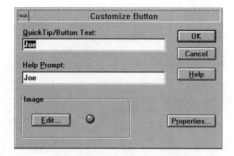

4 If you want, type new text for the QuickTip/Button Text, that little label that appears when you point at a button. The Help Prompt is the longer description that appears in the title bar when you point at a button, and you can add new text for that, too. You might want this to say something like "Types my name and title."

5 To change the way the button looks, click Edit to pop up the Image Editor dialog box shown in figure 20.15.

Fig. 20.15

The Image Editor displays an enlarged (and distorted) picture of the Toolbar icon.

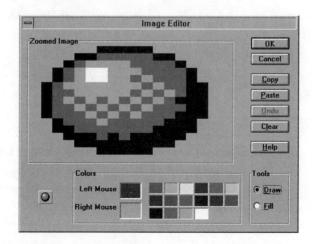

6 In the Image Editor dialog box, you have two choices: you can edit the existing image, or click C̲lear and start from scratch. In either case, click D̲raw to draw.

7 Click a color from the palette with the left mouse button. If you're adept at mousing, drag in the Zoomed Image area to draw your new image. Otherwise, click to add rectangles of color one at a time, and build your image that way. Figure 20.16 shows a Toolbar button image taking shape.

Fig. 20.16
I cleared the original image first; notice the normal-sized button in the lower-left corner of the dialog box.

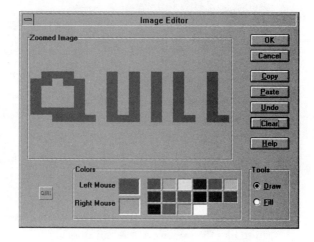

8 Click or drag with the right mouse button to erase mistakes.

(Tip)

> To erase, make sure the selected color in the Right Mouse box is the background color. It is by default; if you've changed the background, just click the background color on the palette with the right mouse button.

9 For background color, click F̲ill, click a color, then click in the Zoomed Image area.

10 When you've finished drawing, keep clicking OK in the various dialog boxes to return to the editing window. Figure 20.17 shows the finished button on the Toolbar, complete with custom Help P̲rompt and QuickTip.

Fig. 20.17
My custom buttons
give me a renewed
appreciation for the
artistry of Word-
Perfect's icon creators.

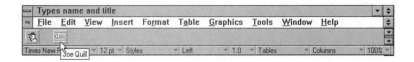

Custom math quizzes?
Use the Equation Editor

WordPerfect is a program so rich in features that some may be used rarely, if ever. The Equation Editor is one such feature. You may not need typeset-quality equations very often, but if you ever do, WordPerfect's Equation Editor can create them.

To use the Equation Editor, click Graphics, Equation. If the Drag to Create option is already selected, drag the little graphics hand to create a graphics box. When you release the mouse button, the Equation Editor pops up, as shown in figure 20.18.

Fig. 20.18
The Equation Editor
has all the tools you
need to create typeset-
quality equations in
your documents.

*Click the Com-
mands button to
access palettes
of mathematical
symbols, characters,
and functions.*

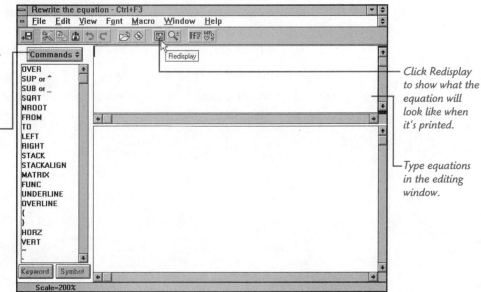

*Click Redisplay
to show what the
equation will
look like when
it's printed.*

*Type equations
in the editing
window.*

Create a simple equation with the Equation Editor

You can also use the Equation Editor to build simple equations:

1 Click <u>G</u>raphics, E<u>q</u>uation, drag the graphics box to size, and release the mouse button for the Equation Editor.

2 If, for example, you wanted the equation for the area of a circle, r^2, click the Commands button and select Greek.

3 Double-click the Greek character Pi to pop the word "pi" into the editing window.

As you become familiar with the commands used in equations, you can save time by simply typing them in the editing window.

4 Type **r^2** and click the Redisplay button on the Toolbar (refer to fig. 20.18) to display the equation in the display window, as shown in figure 20.19.

5 Click the Equation Font button to edit the font face, size, and attributes of the equation characters. When you're done creating your equation, click Close on the Toolbar. That puts the equation in a graphics box in the current document and pops up the Graphics Feature Bar.

6 Use the Graphics Feature Bar to add a border, fill, and to change the font size and attributes of the equation, and you might wind up with something like figure 20.20.

Fig. 20.19

Equations are typed into the editing window, then displayed in the display window when you click Redisplay.

Click the Close button to pop the equation into a document.

Click the Equation Font button to edit the equation characters.

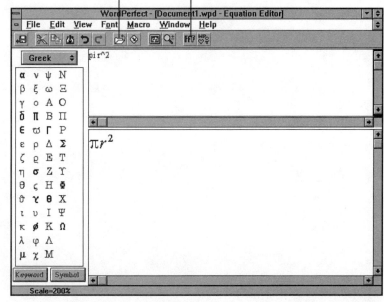

Fig. 20.20

Even if you're not a math whiz, you can use the Equation Editor for graphics effects.

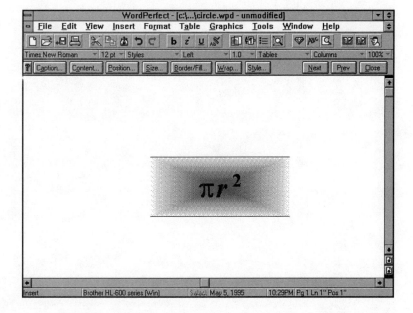

21

Import, Export, Convert: Sharing Files between Programs

If you manage a team of applications on your computer, you'll find WordPerfect's file importing and exporting features make it a terrific team player.

Anthony Trollope wrote dozens of fine novels, including those *Masterpiece Theater* regulars, the Palliser stories. A hundred and forty years ago, he also gave England its first mail boxes. Before Trollope, sending a letter meant a hike to the post office.

The mail box made exchanging documents a lot easier. Windows and WordPerfect do for file exchanges between applications what the mail box does for sending letters: they make the job simple, fast, and reasonably foolproof.

How can I turn this file into a WordPerfect 6.1 document?

Give a speech at the United Nations, and your non-English speaking audience will understand you. Your words are converted into Chinese, Spanish, Arabic and the other UN languages by simultaneous translators.

That's pretty much how WordPerfect file conversions work. If you open a file written in a different application, the program translates it to "WordPerfect" automatically. You don't have to do a thing.

Figure 21.1 shows a file in WordPerfect 5.0, an old DOS version of the program.

Fig. 21.1
Print preview, DOS style. This is about as close to WYSIWYG as you got in those days.

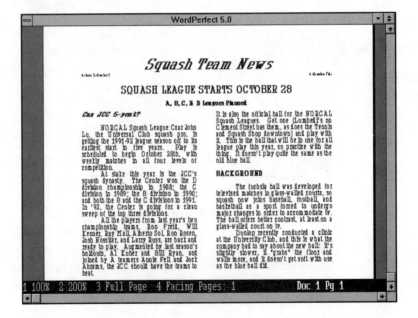

To convert a file from an older, DOS version of WordPerfect:

1 Click the Open File button on the Toolbar to pop up the Open File dialog box.

2 Select the directory where your old file is located in the Directories box, then double-click the file in the Filename list. WordPerfect's simultaneous translator goes to work, and the Conversion dialog box pops up. This is one dialog box that doesn't require any further input from you; just sit back and watch.

3 The file appears in the editing window in WordPerfect 6.1, more or less the same way it looked in WordPerfect 5.0, as shown in figure 21.2.

Fig. 21.2
WordPerfect's file conversion isn't perfect, but it's close.

Although WordPerfect does a pretty good job of converting files from older versions of itself, the conversion isn't perfect. The more heavily formatted the old document, the less faithful to the original the WordPerfect 6.1 version will be.

In the case of the file in figure 21.2, WordPerfect 6.1 got the basic layout right but the fonts weren't duplicated perfectly (not that they were anything to write home about in the first place).

Chances are, you'll have to tweak your converted files once you open them in WordPerfect 6.1. As we've seen in earlier chapters, changing fonts and formats is easily done, and all the WordPerfect formatting features are available for the job.

My file isn't being converted into WordPerfect 6.1 automatically

WordPerfect converts files created in older versions of the program without any prompting, but if you open a file from a non-WordPerfect application, you get the Convert File Format dialog box. WordPerfect guesses your file's format, and most likely that guess will be correct. Just click OK in the Convert File Format dialog box if the displayed file format is indeed the correct one.

If WordPerfect guesses wrong, you can correct it. Click the Convert File Format From drop-down arrow in the Convert File Format dialog box and select the correct format, as shown in figure 21.3.

Fig. 21.3
It's unlikely that you'll have to second–guess WordPerfect's file format choice, but you can if you have to.

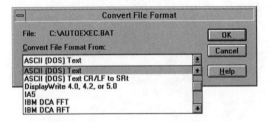

I need to save this WordPerfect document in another format

Once you import a file from another application into WordPerfect 6.1, tweak the formatting, and are satisfied with the results, you can save the file as a WordPerfect document. If you have to save the file in another format, you can do that too. Why would you want to?

You might, for example, want to edit your AUTOEXEC.BAT file in Word-Perfect. If you save the AUTOEXEC.BAT file as a WordPerfect document, DOS will ignore it. You have to save system files like AUTOEXEC.BAT as ASCII files for your editing changes to be recognized by DOS. Or maybe you're working with a partner on a document, and she uses Microsoft Word instead of WordPerfect. In order to share documents, you have to save the file in a format her program can understand.

To save a file in a format other than WordPerfect 6.1, click File, Save As for the Save As dialog box. Click the Save File as Type drop-down arrow and select the format you want (see fig. 21.4).

Fig. 21.4
DOS system files like AUTOEXEC.BAT and CONFIG.SYS have to be saved as ASCII files.

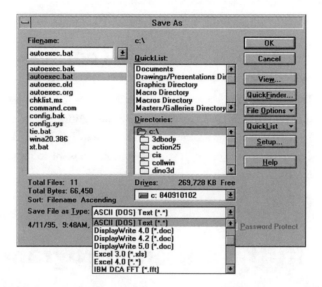

WordPerfect saves you from Save errors

Clicking the Save button on the Toolbar is a good habit to get into as you work on WordPerfect documents. Clicking Save regularly saves you from losing your work in the event of application or system hang-ups.

But what happens if you click the Save button when you're working on a non-WordPerfect 6.1 document, like a DOS system file? WordPerfect saves you from yourself. The Save Format dialog box pops up, as shown in figure 21.5. Just select the ASCII (DOS) Text choice in the Save Format dialog box and click OK.

Fig. 21.5
Don't worry if you
automatically reach for
the Save button;
WordPerfect lets you
pick your Save format.

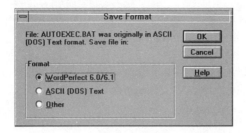

 Q&A

> **Help! I accidentally saved my DOS system file as a WordPerfect 6.1 document!**
>
> That's easy to do, especially if you're a click-before-you-look type like me. Just resave the file as ASCII text. Click File, Save As for the Save As dialog box. Select ASCII (DOS) Text from the Save File as Type drop-down list (refer to fig. 21.4), and click Yes when you're asked if you want to replace the WordPerfect 6.1 file you created by mistake.

Can I copy stuff from one program to another?

Wonderful as it is, WordPerfect can't do everything. You're likely to need to use a spreadsheet program instead of a WordPerfect table, or a database program instead of a simple WordPerfect data file. For example, if you use PerfectOffice, the Novell suite of applications that includes WordPerfect, you also have a powerful spreadsheet program called Quattro Pro.

Whatever your Windows application, you can copy, cut, and paste text and objects between programs to your heart's content. If the applications support OLE (all the PerfectOffice applications do), you can even edit pasted material without leaving WordPerfect. (See Chapter 19 for more information about editing OLE objects.)

X<Caution> Copying and pasting OLE objects is a nifty trick, but, at least on my computer, it leads to the occasional ugly Windows error message. Someday they'll work out the bugs so that these unpleasantries won't occur. In the meantime, though, save yourself some pain by saving your work before and after attempting OLE maneuvers.

* {Note} One of the more insidious things about Windows is that you start with a limited supply of system resources, and then deplete them every time you open and close an application. You get some forewarning when your system resources near a crisis level, because everything slows down. When that happens, save all your work, shut down all your applications, and exit Windows. Type **win** at the C: prompt, and you'll restart Windows with a fresh supply of system resources.

There's no need to be ANSI about ASCII

ASCII and ANSI are a couple of computer terms that get tossed around casually, as though normal (as in non-computer) people know instinctively what they mean. ASCII (pronounced *ASK-ee*) is an acronym for American Standard Code for Information Interchange. When you type characters on your keyboard, your computer translates them into combinations of 0s and 1s—binary digits. Exactly which combination of binary digits represents a particular keyboard character varies from one computer program to another.

ASCII standardizes keyboard character–binary digit equivalents. It's a standard set of binary digit combinations that represent a standard set of keyboard characters. Since all PC programs use ASCII, WordPerfect can read an ASCII file written in Microsoft Word with no problems.

ANSI (*AN-see*) stands for American National Standards Institute, an organization originally founded to establish standard ways of representing things like screw threads in engineers' drawings. In computer lingo, ANSI is a standard character set, like ASCII, but with the addition of graphical and formatting characters. Windows and Windows applications use the ANSI standard, so if you write a file in the Windows Notepad, you can open it in WordPerfect.

> To check the current level of your system resources, click <u>H</u>elp, <u>A</u>bout WordPerfect.

How do I put my Quattro Pro graph in my WordPerfect document?

Although WordPerfect has a pretty good charting feature (see Chapter 19), you'll probably use Quattro Pro for serious number crunching and graphing.

Here's the easiest way to insert a Quattro Pro graph into a WordPerfect document:

1 With both Quattro Pro and WordPerfect running, switch to your Quattro Pro graph.

> The fastest way to switch from application to application in Windows is to hold down the Alt key and press Tab repeatedly. Each time you press Tab, the title of an active Windows application is displayed in a box on the screen. When you get to the application you want to switch to, release the Alt key.

2 Click the graph background to select it. The handles will pop up around the graph, as shown in figure 21.6.

3 With the graph selected, click the Copy button on the Toolbar. That copies the graph to the Windows Clipboard.

4 Switch to your WordPerfect document and put the insertion point where you want the graph to appear.

5 Click the Paste button on the Toolbar. Take a stretch or get a cup of coffee—even on a 90MHz Pentium, pasting OLE objects can take a few minutes. When done, your graph pops into the WordPerfect document, as shown in figure 21.7.

Fig. 21.6

Working with graphic objects in Quattro Pro is just like working with those objects in Word-Perfect—click to select them, and right-click for the QuickMenus.

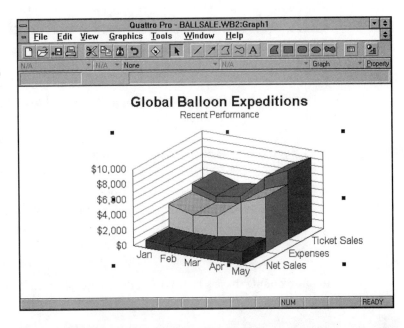

Fig. 21.7

Don't worry about where you place imported graphics in a WordPerfect document; you can easily move and resize them.

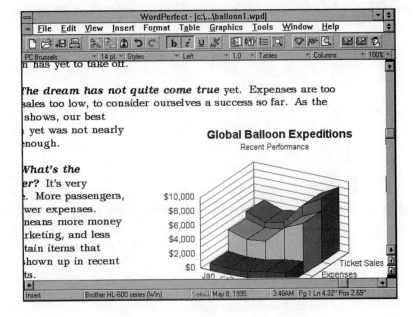

Edit embedded objects with the application that created them

Embedding an object, as we did earlier, creates a copy that can be edited using the same application that created it. It's as though the object takes a chunk of its original application with it.

{Note}

> If you copy a graph in Quattro Pro, shut down Quattro Pro, and then paste the graph in WordPerfect, it's pasted as an ordinary Windows graphic. It will probably look identical to an embedded graph, but you won't be able to use Quattro Pro to edit it. Instead, double-clicking the object pops up the WP Draw tools (or Presentations, which replaces WP Draw if you use PerfectOffice).

In our example, here's how you'd edit the graph from WordPerfect, but using Quattro Pro:

<Caution>

> Make sure you save whatever you're working on before you try this procedure, because it'll tax your system resources. If you experience a system crash, you won't lose your hard-earned work!

1 In WordPerfect, double-click the embedded Quattro Pro graph.

2 After a moment, a broken border appears around the graph, and the Quattro Pro Graphics Toolbar pops up right over your WordPerfect document, as shown in figure 21.8.

3 Use the Quattro Pro tools to edit the graph. When you're done, click anywhere outside the graphics box to close Quattro Pro and return to WordPerfect.

❝ *Plain English, please!*

In OLE jargon, the application that created an object is called the **server**, or the **source**. The application in which you embed the object is the **client**, or the **destination**. In the example, Quattro Pro is the server or source, and WordPerfect is the client or destination. ❞

Fig. 21.8

Opening an embedded Quattro Pro object opens Quattro Pro as well—without leaving WordPerfect.

Click outside the graphics box to shut down Quattro Pro and return to WordPerfect.

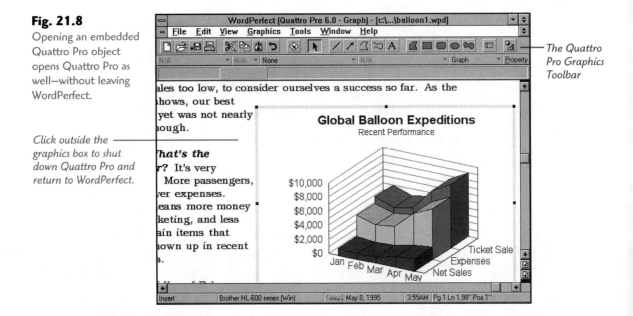

The Quattro Pro Graphics Toolbar

What's a link?

Providing both applications are running, copying and pasting from one OLE application to another creates an **embedded object**, as we saw in figure 21.8.

Copy an object and use the Edit, Paste Special command instead of the Paste button on the Toolbar, and you get some other pasting options:

- If you **link** OLE objects, any changes you make in the original object show up automatically in the linked copy. Use links when you plan on making changes to the original object that you want to appear in the copy. If the data that underlies your graph is going to change, use a link.

- Pasting an object as a **picture** inserts it as an ordinary Windows graphic image. You don't get the automatic updates of a link, and you can't use the server application to edit the object the way you can if you embed it. On the other hand, a pasted picture needs less memory than a linked or embedded object. Paste as a picture if you just want a static copy of the original object.

- Linked or embedded objects can be displayed as icons in your document.

In most cases, copied objects are identical to the originals, no matter what paste method you use. But if the copy doesn't faithfully reproduce the original, just try a different paste choice.

Link one application to another for fast updates

Linking a server object to the client copy is like setting off a controlled chain reaction in a lab experiment. Change the underlying data for a linked graph, and the original graph changes, then the copied graph changes, too.

To set up a link between a Quattro Pro graph and a WordPerfect copy:

1 Click the Quattro Pro graph to select it, then click the Copy button on the Toolbar.

2 Press Alt+Tab to flip to WordPerfect and move the insertion point to the spot in the document where you want the graph to appear.

3 Click Edit, Paste Special for the Paste Special dialog box shown in figure 21.9.

Fig. 21.9
Select an option from the list, and read the descriptions of what will happen next in the Result box.

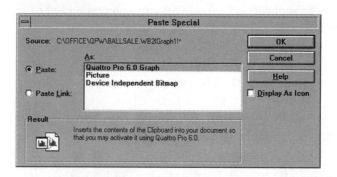

Select Paste As Picture and WordPerfect may try to confuse you by telling you about the Windows' Metafile format or the Device Independent Bitmap. This just means you're copying the object as a regular graphic image without links to any other program.

4 Click Paste Link, then click OK. The linked object is pasted into the document at the insertion point.

Once you've pasted your linked object, you can move it around or resize it, just as you would with an ordinary graphic image.

Double-click the object to edit it, and the server application (here, it's Quattro Pro) opens. The original object is displayed, as shown in figure 21.10.

Fig. 21.10

When you open a linked object, you actually make your edits in the original object.

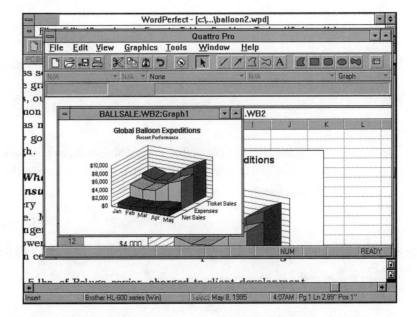

As you edit the object, or change the underlying data in the Quattro Pro table, the changes show up immediately in the linked copy in WordPerfect. When you're done editing, click File, Exit in Quattro Pro to return to WordPerfect.

Keep up your links, or break them

Once you've got linked objects in two OLE applications, the copied object is updated automatically when you make changes in the original. The underlying data can be changed only in the server (original) program; you can't make changes in WordPerfect, for example, and see those changes in Quattro Pro.

Suppose you try a few what-if scenarios with your Quattro Pro data, and you don't want those changes to show up in the WordPerfect copy of the your graph. If you don't want automatic updates, click Edit, Links for the Links dialog box shown in figure 21.11.

Fig. 21.11
Use the Links dialog box to control updates between linked objects.

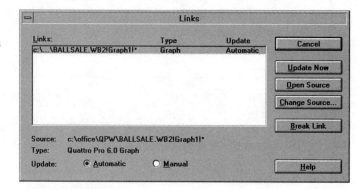

Click Manual in the Links dialog box, and changes you make in the original object won't be reflected in the copy until you return to the Links dialog box and click Update Now.

Can I stick my Presentations graphic in a WordPerfect document?

PerfectOffice users have a nifty program called Presentations that's used to create drawings, graphics of all kinds, and slide shows.

Inserting a Presentations graphic in a WordPerfect document is just like inserting a Quattro Pro graph. Presentations is another OLE application, so you can embed, link, or copy the graphic as a picture.

Unless you really need to link your Presentations graphic to the WordPerfect copy, pasting it as a WordPerfect graphic is probably the best choice. It'll use less memory, and you'll be editing it with Presentations tools from Word-Perfect anyway.

To paste a Presentations creation as a graphic in WordPerfect:

1 Click the Presentations graphic to select it, as shown in figure 21.12.

Fig. 21.12
For non-artists, Presentations comes with a gallery of ready-made images like this one.

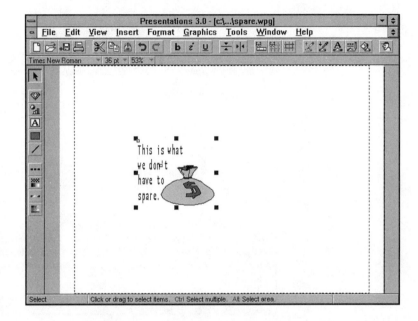

2 Click the Copy button on the Toolbar.

3 Press Alt+Tab to flip to WordPerfect and move the insertion point to the spot where you want the graphic.

4 Click Edit, Paste Special for the Paste Special dialog box shown in figure 21.13.

Fig. 21.13
Selecting the WPG20 format gives you the most faithful copy; choosing Presentations 3.0 Drawing embeds the graphic in WordPerfect.

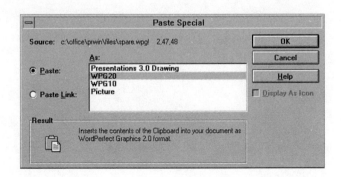

5 Select <u>P</u>aste <u>A</u>s WPG20 graphic and click OK.

6 The Presentations graphic pops into your WordPerfect document at the insertion point, as shown in figure 21.14.

Fig. 21.14

Like any other inserted graphic image, your pasted Presentations creation can be moved and resized by dragging with the mouse.

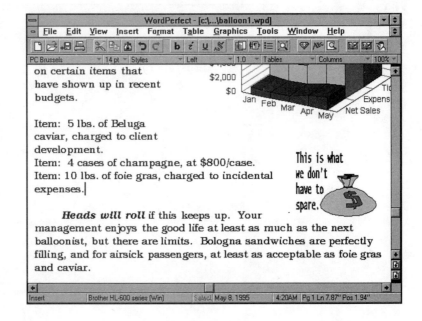

To edit a pasted Presentations graphic, just double-click it. That'll pop up all the Presentations tools and editing features.

Action Index

Edit documents

Format characters

Format documents

When you need to:	Turn to page
Add headers and footers	113
Add paragraph borders	179
Add paragraph fill	179
Adjust column widths	230
Adjust margins with the ruler bar	90
Center text	97
Change margin settings	88
Clear/change tab stops	91
Copy formatting with QuickFormat	176
Create a newsletter	170
Create custom page numbers	110
Indent paragraphs	92
Justify text	96
Turn on columns	226
Use bulleted or numbered lists	102

Cut down on typing chores

When you need to:	Turn to page
Create abbreviations	190
Edit a macro	202
Play a macro	199
Record a macro	196

Insert graphics

Print

Manage documents

continues

When you need to:	Turn to page
Outline a document	306
Preview documents	323
Save files	35

Help Index

Use this list of common troubles and errors to help you figure out what's going wrong or why something isn't working the way you think it should.

Menus and commands

Entering and editing text

Text formatting

If you have this problem...	Turn to...
I need to get rid of a paragraph style	185
I need to get the original one-inch margins back	91
The Manual Kerning menu command is grayed out	257
Only the first font shows up in a QuickStyle	183
Page numbers and footnotes still use the old font, even though I changed the document font	83
The Format Toolbar button makes the paragraph look weird	96

Document setup

If you have this problem...	Turn to...
I accidentally deleted the [Pg #] code in the Page Numbering Options dialog box	111
I can't see a preview of my page number text in the Sample Facing Pages windows	111
I can't see page numbers	108
The pages of my printout aren't numbered	146

Printing

If you have this problem...	Turn to...
I can't find the Insert Pre-Written Letter button	168
I need to print letters and envelopes separately from the same document	218

If you have this problem...	Turn to...
My envelope won't print	154
My labels won't print	158
My printed text is all scrunched up toward the top of the page, with lots of white space at the bottom	148
The abbreviation I created doesn't work	191

Tables, columns, and outlines

If you have this problem...	Turn to...
I can't find the subdocument icon	317
I can't see the outline level icons	306
I only get horizontal lines when selecting Column Between borders from the Paragraph Border dialog box	236
Multiple columns are set, but text only appears in the first column	227
Parallel columns are too difficult to work with	238
The editing handle won't change to a crosshair	337
The Tables button display keeps disappearing	285

{ Index }